Certified Professional Secretary® Examination Review Series

Betty L. Schroeder, *Series Editor*

Schroeder, Lauer, and Stricklin *Certified Professional Secretary® Review for Behavioral Science in Business, Module I, Second Edition*

Cherry *Self-Study Guide to CPS® Review for Behavioral Science, Module I*

Schroeder, Clark, and DiMarzio *Certified Professional Secretary® Review for Business Law, Module II, Second Edition*

Cherry *Self-Study Guide to CPS® Review for Business Law, Module II*

Schroeder, Lewis, and Stricklin *Certified Professional Secretary® Review for Economics and Management, Module III, Second Edition*

Cherry *Self-Study Guide to CPS® Review for Economics and Management, Module III*

Schroeder and Webber *Certified Professional Secretary® Review for Accounting, Module IV, Second Edition*

Cherry *Self-Study Guide to CPS® Review for Accounting, Module IV*

Schroeder and Graf *Certified Professional Secretary® Review for Office Administration and Communication, Module V, Second Edition*

Cherry *Self-Study Guide to CPS® Review for Office Administration and Communication, Module V*

Schroeder and Graf *Certified Professional Secretary® Review for Office Technology, Module VI, Second Edition*

Cherry *Self-Study Guide to CPS® Review for Office Technology, Module VI*

Certified Professional Secretary®
Examination Review Series

Accounting, Module IV

Second Edition

Betty L. Schroeder, Ph.D., Editor
Northern Illinois University

Sally A. Webber, M.S., CPA
University of Texas at Arlington

A joint publication of
PSI® Professional Secretary International and

REGENTS/PRENTICE HALL
Englewood Cliffs, New Jersey 07632

Library of Congress Cataloging-in-Publication Data
(Revised for volumes 3 and 4)

Certified professional secretary examination review
    series

    Contents: module 1. Behavioral science in business /
Wilma D. Stricklin, Deborah Lauer—   — module 3.
Review for Economics and management — module 4. Review
for accounting
    1. Office practice—Problems, exercises, etc.
I. Stricklin, Wilma D.   II. Lauer, Deborah.
III. Professional Secretaries International.
HF5547.5.C44   1992   651.3'74'076   87-100577
ISBN 0-13-188558-8

Acquisitions editor: *Elizabeth Kendall*
Production editor: *Jacqueline A. Martin*
Copy editor: *Patty Boyd*
Cover designer: *Marianne Frasco*
Prepress buyer: *Ilene Levy*
Manufacturing buyer: *Ed O'Dougherty*
Supplements editor: *Lisamarie Brassini*
Editorial assistant: *Jane Baumann*

© 1992, 1984 by Prentice-Hall, Inc.
A Simon & Schuster Company
Englewood Cliffs, New Jersey 07632

The following are registered marks owned by Professional Secretaries International:

Trademarks and Registered Service Marks

PSI®
Professional Secretaries International®
Since 1942 known as The National Secretaries Association (International)
10502 N.W. Ambassador Drive, Kansas City, MO 64153, 816-891-6600

A.I.S.P. (French equivalent of PSI®)
l'Association Internationale des Secretaires Professionalles

CPS®
Certified Professional Secretary®
Professional Secretaries Week®
Professional Secretaries Day
The Secretary®

FSA®
Future Secretaries Association®
International Secretary of the Year®
All rights reserved. No part of this book may be
reproduced, in any form or by any means,
without permission in writing from the publisher.

Printed in the United States of America
10 9 8 7 6 5 4 3 2

ISBN 0-13-188558-8

Prentice-Hall International (UK) Limited, *London*
Prentice-Hall of Australia Pty. Limited, *Sydney*
Prentice-Hall Canada Inc., *Toronto*
Prentice-Hall Hispanoamericana, S.A., *Mexico*
Prentice-Hall of India Private Limited, *New Delhi*
Prentice-Hall of Japan, Inc., *Tokyo*
Simon & Schuster Asia Pte. Ltd., *Singapore*
Editora Prentice-Hall do Brasil, Ltda., *Rio de Janeiro*

Contents

Preface	XIII
Acknowledgments	XVII

CHAPTER 1 Introduction To Accounting   1

Overview 1

Definition of Terms 1

- A. Accounting Process 2
    1. Accounting Entity 3
    2. Types of Business Entities 3
    3. Recording Financial Information 3
    4. Classifying Financial Information 4
    5. Summarizing Financial Information 4
    6. Using Accounting Information 4
- B. Reporting Accounting Information 5
    1. External Financial Statements 5
    2. Internal Financial Reports 6
- C. Basic Concepts and Principles 6
    1. Going Concern 6
    2. Relevance 6
    3. Periodicity 6
    4. Estimation 6
    5. Consistency 6
    6. Conservatism 7
    7. Full Disclosure 7
    8. Materiality 7

Review Questions 9

Solutions 13

CHAPTER 2 Theory and Classification of Accounts   15

Overview 15

Definition of Terms 15

    A.   Accounts 17
            1.   Recording Information in Accounts 17
            2.   Using T-Accounts 17
            3.   Recording Debits and Credits 18
            4.   Recording Entries 18
            5.   Calculating the Account Balances 18
            6.   The Ledger 18
    B.   Classification of Permanent Accounts 18
            1.   Assets 18
            2.   Liabilities 19
            3.   Owners' Equity (Stockholders' Equity) 20
            4.   Balance Sheet Accounts 21
    C.   The Accounting Equation 21
            1.   Equality Represented 21
            2.   Sources of Assets 21
            3.   Continual Changes in Composition 22
            4.   Residual Aspect of Owners' Equity 22
            5.   Debits and Credits 22
            6.   Double-Entry Accounting 22
    D.   Recording Accounting Transactions 22
            1.   Journalization 22
            2.   Posting to the Ledger 24
            3.   Typical Accounting Transactions 25
    E.   Classification of Temporary Accounts 27
            1.   Revenues 27
            2.   Expenses 28
            3.   Net Income 28
            4.   Investments by Owners 29
            5.   Withdrawals and Dividends 29
            6.   Typical Transactions including Revenues and Expenses 30

Review Questions 35

Solutions 43

CHAPTER 3 Basic Financial Statements   47

Overview 47
Definition of Terms 47
    A.   Balance Sheet 49
            1.   Accounting Equation 49
            2.   Heading 49
            3.   Classification of Assets on the Balance Sheet 50
            4.   Classification of Liabilities on the Balance Sheet 53
            5.   Classification of Owners' Equity on the Balance Sheet 54
            6.   Basic Forms of the Balance Sheet 55
    B.   Income Statement 56
            1.   Net Income Related to Revenues and Expenses 59
            2.   Gains and Losses 59
            3.   Net Income Related to Gains and Losses 59

Contents

        4.   Heading 59
        5.   Basic Forms of the Income Statement 60
  C. Statement of Retained Earnings 63
        1.   Increases in Retained Earnings 64
        2.   Decreases in Retained Earnings 64
  D. Statement of Changes in Capital 64
        1.   Increases in Capital 64
        2.   Decreases in Capital 64
  E. Statement of Cash Flows 64

Review Questions 65

Solutions 71

CHAPTER 4 The Accounting Cycle   75

Overview 75

Definition of Terms 75

  A. Analyzing Transactions and Recording 76
  B. Posting 76
  C. Trial Balance 76
        1.   Equality of Debits and Credits 76
        2.   Preparation of Trial Balance 76
  D. Worksheet 78
        1.   Columns on the Worksheet 78
        2.   End-of-Period Adjustments 78
        3.   Journalizing and Posting 78
  E. Preparing Financial Statements 78
  F. Adjusting Entries 78
        1.   Estimates 78
        2.   Prepaid/Unearned Accounts 79
        3.   Accruals 84
        4.   Use of the Worksheet 85
  G. Closing Entries 88
        1.   Closing Revenue and Gain Accounts 89
        2.   Closing Expense and Loss Accounts 89
        3.   Closing the Income Summary Account 90
        4.   Closing Withdrawal and Dividend Accounts 90
        5.   Journalizing and Posting 90
  H. Postclosing Trial Balance 92
  I.   The Next Accounting Cycle 92

Review Questions 93

Solutions 101

CHAPTER 5 Accounting For Cash   105

Overview 105

Definition of Terms 105

- A. Cash Receipts 106
  1. Cash 106
  2. Major Types of Cash Receipts 106
  3. Internal Controls 107
- B. Subsidiary Ledgers and Special Journals 108
  1. Control Account 108
  2. Subsidiary Account 108
  3. Special Journals 110
- C. Cash Disbursements 112
  1. Cash Disbursement Records 112
  2. Trade and Cash Discounts 113
  3. Imprest Petty Cash 115
  4. Checks and Check Registers 116
  5. The Voucher System and Recording of Accounts Payable 116
  6. Internal Control of Cash Disbursements 118
  7. Cash Over and Short 120
- D. Bank Statements and Cash Balance 120
  1. Reconciliation 120
  2. Detection and Correction of Errors 122
  3. Preparation of a Bank Reconciliation 122
  4. Journal Entries to Record Reconciling Items 123

Review Questions 125

Solutions 133

CHAPTER 6 Accounting For Investments 135

Overview 135

Definition of Terms 135

- A. Introduction to Investments 136
  1. Short-term Investments 136
  2. Long-term Investments 136
- B. Real Estate 136
- C. Bonds and Interest Income 137
  1. Issuance of Bonds 137
  2. Accounting for Bonds and Interest Income 137
  3. Amortization of Premium or Discount on Long-Term Bonds 139
  4. Accounting for Sale of Bond Investment 141
- D. Stocks and Dividend Income 141
  1. Recording Investment in Stock 141
  2. Recording Dividend Income 144
  3. Sale of Investments in Stock 145

Review Questions 147

Solutions 155

Contents

CHAPTER 7 Accounting for Inventories   159

    Overview   159

    Definition of Terms   159

        A.   Types of Inventory Systems   160
            1.   Perpetual Inventory Systems   160
            2.   Periodic Inventory Systems   161
        B.   Inventory Pricing   163
            1.   FIFO (First-In First-Out)   163
            2.   LIFO (Last-In First-Out)   163
            3.   Weighted Average   164
            4.   Specific Identification   165
        C.   Applying Lower of Cost or Market   165
            1.   Cost of Inventory   165
            2.   Market Value of Inventory   165
        D.   Determining Cost of Goods Sold   168
            1.   Periodic Inventory System   168
            2.   Perpetual Inventory System   169
            3.   Estimate as Percentage of Sales   169
            4.   Gross Profit Method   169
            5.   Retail Inventory Method   170
        E.   Evaluating Effect of Inventory on Net Income   170
            1.   Inventory Valuation   170
            2.   Method of Inventory Valuation Used   172

    Review Questions   173

    Solutions   181

CHAPTER 8 Property, Plant, and Equipment Records   185

    Overview   185

    Definition of Terms   185

        A.   Acquisition Cost   186
            1.   Cost of Fixed Assets   186
            2.   Cost of Acquiring Land   186
        B.   Allocation of Costs: Depreciation and Depletion   187
            1.   Depreciation   187
            2.   Depletion   191
        C.   Repairs   192
            1.   Extraordinary Repairs   192
            2.   Effect on Depreciation   192
        D.   Disposition of Property Items   193
            1.   Sale of a Property Item   193
            2.   Exchange of Property Items   194
            3.   Abandonment of Property Items   196
        E.   Depreciation for Income Tax Purposes   196
        F.   Price-Level Indexing   196

1. Construction of a Price Index 197
2. Using a Price Index 197

Review Questions 199

Solutions 209

CHAPTER 9 Other Assets   213

Overview 213

Definition of Terms 213

A. Notes Receivable 214
1. Interest-Bearing Note Receivable 214
2. Noninterest-Bearing Note Receivable 215
3. Recording Accrued Interest Receivable 217
4. Discounting of Notes Receivable 217
B. Accounts Receivable and Bad Debts 219
1. Aging of Accounts Receivable 219
2. Percentage of Accounts Receivable 221
3. Percentage of Credit Sales 221
4. Writing Off an Uncollectible Account 222
5. Collection of Uncollectible Account 222
6. Direct Write-Off 222
C. Prepaid Expenses 223
1. Insurance 223
2. Supplies 224
D. Intangible Assets and Amortization 225
1. Value of Intangible Assets 225
2. Capitalization of Intangible Assets 225
3. Amortization of Intangible Assets 225

Review Questions 227

Solutions 237

CHAPTER 10 Debit Equities or Liabilities   241

Overview 241

Definition of Terms 241

A. Short-Term Obligations 242
1. Notes Payable 242
2. Accounts Payable 246
3. Accruals 246
B. Long-Term Obligations 246
1. Notes Payable 246
2. Mortgages 248
3. Bonds Payable 249

Review Questions 255

Solutions 263

CHAPTER 11 Owners' Equity 267

Overview 267

Definition of Terms 267

A. Sole Proprietorships and Partnerships 268
   1. Advantages of Sole Proprietorships and Partnerships 269
   2. Disadvantages of Sole Proprietorships and Partnerships 269
   3. Accounting for Owners' Equity 269
B. Corporations 271
   1. Advantages of the Corporate Form of Ownership 271
   2. Disadvantages of the Corporate Form 272
C. Accounting for Stockholders' Equity of a Corporation 272
   1. Contributed Capital 272
   2. Retained Earnings 280

Review Questions 283

Solutions 291

CHAPTER 12 Income Statement Accounts 295

Overview 295

Definition of Terms 295

A. Revenues 296
B. Expenses 296
   1. Operating Expenses 296
   2. Federal Individual Income Taxes 300

Review Questions 305

Solutions 311

CHAPTER 13 Analysis and Interpretation of Financial Statements 313

Overview 313

Definition of Terms 313

A. Statement of Changes in Financial Position 314
   1. Working Capital 314
B. Statement of Cash Flows 317
   1. Operating Activities 317

                2. Investing Activities **319**
                3. Financing Activities **319**
                4. Noncash Investing and Financing Activities **320**
                5. Presentation of a Statement of Cash Flows **320**
        C. Comparative Statements **322**
        D. Ratio Analysis **322**
                1. Liquidity Ratios **323**
                2. Debt Ratios **323**
                3. Profitability Ratios **324**

    Review Questions **331**

    Solutions **337**

CHAPTER 14 Managerial Accounting — **341**

    Overview **341**

    Definition of Terms **341**

        A. Cost Analysis **342**
                1. Determining Unit Costs **343**
                2. Variable and Fixed Costs **343**
                3. Cost-Volume Profit Analysis **344**
                4. Reporting for a Manufacturing Concern **346**
                5. Cost Accounting **349**
        B. Budgets **345**
                1. Types of Budgets **356**
                2. Factors Considered in Budget Preparation **358**
                3. Budget Variation and Analysis **359**
        C. Standard Costing and Variance Analysis **362**
                1. Management by Exception **362**
                2. Variance **362**
        D. Forecasting **364**
                1. Types of Forecasts **364**
                2. Factors Considered in Preparation of Forecasts **364**
                3. Proforma Statements **365**

    Review Questions **367**

    Solutions **377**

Glossary — **383**

Preface

The PRENTICE HALL CERTIFIED PROFESSIONAL SECRETARY® EXAMINATION REVIEW SERIES consists of six review manuals, jointly published by Prentice Hall and Professional Secretaries International® (PSI®), designed as review materials for the Certified Professional Secretary® (CPS®) Examination. The content of each module is based on the current CPS® Study Outline published in *CAPSTONE,* the publication of the Institute for Certifying Secretaries publicizing application and requirements for the CPS® Examination.

Module IV—Accounting is meant to be a *review* for those secretaries who already have completed one or more courses in accounting or an *introduction* to accounting for those secretaries who have never before enrolled in an accounting course. A thorough study of this module, of course, does not guarantee passage of Part IV of the CPS® Examination. Using this review manual, however, should provide valuable assistance for self-study or group review sessions. In addition to using this review manual for study, it will probably be necessary for secretaries to enroll in at least one accounting course for a more thorough review.

The format used for each of the six modules in the series is identical. The current CPS® Study Outline and Bibliography were used initially to define exactly what the content of the module should be and the types of references that the Institute was recommending for study. Then, this outline was expanded so that more comprehensive coverage of the topics could be planned and included in the manual. Each chapter includes:

- an **Overview** introducing the reader to the chapter and its content.
- the **Definition of Terms** to be found within the chapter.
- a complete **sentence/paragraph outline**, with examples highlighted in italic type to enhance the sentence outline.
- **Review Questions** at the end of the chapter, developed in similar format to those found on the CPS® Examination.
- **Solutions** to the review questions, with the identification of the correct answer, any necessary explanation of that answer, and reference to the sentence/paragraph outline.

Module IV—Accounting emphasizes basic content in accounting, as outlined in the current CPS® Study Outline. The question formats used for the review questions at the end of each chapter include multiple-choice questions, matching sets, and problem situations with multiple-choice questions pertaining to them. The current CPS® Examination presents questions primarily as multiple-choice questions, alone or in problem situations. For review of technical terms as well as developing an understanding of basic concepts and principles, the author believes that other question formats can also be helpful tools. Therefore, some matching sets are included with each set of review questions to provide adequate practice in studying terms, definitions, and other basic principles included in the chapter. Past CPS® Examinations have sometimes included questions in this format as well.

The solutions to the review questions are presented in a format that should be particularly helpful for review. These solutions include the correct answer, a reference to the section of the chapter content that has a more complete explanation, and any additional explanation that the author believes may be necessary in understanding the correct response to the question. Here is an example:

Answer   Refer to Chapter Section

4. (a)   [B-5-a(2)]   Interest is considered to be a financing item . . .

The content reference [B-5-a(2)] refers to:
Section B, Point 5, Subpoint a(2) of the chapter.

When a solution seems unclear, it is an excellent idea to return to the sentence/paragraph outline and review the material included under that topic. Review questions have been included to give candidates further review and practice with questions similar to those found on the exam before going on to the next chapter.

The accounting portion of the CPS Examination (Part IV) does require the candidate to be able to perform appropriate accounting computations. A small hand-held calculator may be used during the examination to perform these computations. A review suggestion is to practice the computations included within the chapter as well as those required in the review questions in order to prepare well for the examination.

At the end of this module, a complete Glossary of terms and definitions included in each chapter of *Module IV—Accounting* is presented as a quick guide to terms. A reference is included to the chapter where the term may be found in context.

The question arises as to why this review manual and the other review manuals in the series are organized in this particular way. The response is simple: we want you to have a thorough, but rather quick, review of the content that may appear on the CPS® Examination this year. You should still refer to other accounting references, especially those referred to in the CPS® Study Outline and Bibliography, for more detailed explanations and/or a variety of learning materials to test your knowledge and competence in these topical areas.

The INSTRUCTOR'S MANUAL is a separate publication, correlated to accompany *Module IV—Accounting* of THE CERTIFIED PROFESSIONAL SECRETARY® EXAMINATION REVIEW SERIES. This manual is available to instructors of CPS review courses in accounting and includes the following helpful materials:

- **Teaching Suggestions**: Suggested teaching ideas for accounting review sessions; learning activities to incorporate into classroom or seminar instruction.
- **Test Bank**: A sample test for accounting; solutions for the test, with outline/page references correlated with the review manual.

- **Reading References**: Bibliography of books, periodicals, and special references that may be helpful to secretaries as well as instructors of CPS® review courses for accounting.

We hope that the contents of this INSTRUCTOR'S MANUAL will help instructors provide a successful CPS® review program in accounting.

Betty L. Schroeder, Ph.D.
Series Editor

Acknowledgments

The development of the second edition of *Module IV—Accounting* of the PRENTICE HALL CERTIFIED PROFESSIONAL SECRETARY® EXAMINATION REVIEW SERIES was possible only because of the sincere and dedicated efforts of a number of individuals who are committed to helping secretaries, office administration students, and business educators become Certified Professional Secretaries. Like the other review manuals in the series, *Module IV—Accounting* has become a successful review tool because of the contributions of a number of people who have given of their time and expertise to ensure that the content is appropriate for this particular examination.

We gratefully acknowledge the contributions of Ms. Joan Bedell, CPS, Ms. Linda M. Gronert, CPS, Ms. Adella C. LaRue, CPS, and Dr. Kenton Ross, for their extremely helpful reviews and critiques of the manuscript.

Professional Secretaries International, through the Institute for Certifying Secretaries, has provided not only the incentive for the development of the Second Edition of this review manual but also valuable input during the review process. We sincerely thank the following individuals for their continued interest in and enthusiasm for the development and revision of the series:

Mrs. Jean Mills, Dean, Institute for Certifying Secretaries

Jerome Heitman, Executive Director, Professional Secretaries International

Dr. Susan Fenner, Education/Professional Development Manager, Professional Secretaries International

Mrs. Janet Head, Operations/CPS/Membership Manager, Professional Secretaries International

A very special thank you is given to the members of the Illinois Division of Professional Secretaries International, and in particular, those members of Kishwaukee Chapter, DeKalb, Illinois, who have pursued or have received their professional certification over the past several years. They have continued to be extremely supportive and positive about the use of these review manuals, and their friendship is very much appreciated.

Lastly, we are most appreciative of the leadership and assistance given by Harry Moon and Liz Kendall of Prentice Hall, Inc., for their continued strong support of this series. It is a joy to work with individuals so professional in their judgment of what secretaries need in preparation for the CPS Examination.

And, of course, thank you to anyone else who helped along the way!

We hope that all of the input provided by professionals throughout the revision process will continue to make this review manual and the other five in the series the leaders in providing an excellent review for the CPS® Examination in the future.

Sally A. Webber, M.S., CPA
Betty L. Schroeder, Ph.D.

CHAPTER 1
Introduction to Accounting

OVERVIEW

This section is designed to introduce the candidate to the study of accounting. Understanding the functions of accounting and the basic concepts and principles should aid the candidate in further study within the accounting module. Knowledge attained from this chapter should help the candidate in answering questions throughout the exam.

DEFINITION OF TERMS

ACCOUNTING. The process of recording, measuring, summarizing, analyzing, and interpreting financial information and communicating this information to various users.

ACCOUNTING ENTITY. Any business, individual, or not-for-profit organization whose financial affairs can be viewed as being distinct from those of any other entity or unit.

ASSETS. Economic resources from which an entity can expect to receive benefits now or in the future, a thing of value owned.

AUDIT (INDEPENDENT EXTERNAL). An examination of the financial statements of an entity by an independent accountant in order to determine the fairness of the financial statements. The accounting records are referred to in assessing the fairness of the financial statements.

BOOKKEEPING. The record-keeping phase of accounting.

CONSERVATISM. The principle that requires that the accounting method which is least likely to overstate income and financial position be used.

CONSISTENCY. The principle which requires that once an accounting or reporting method is selected it should be used from one period to another.

CORPORATION. A business entity which is created by state or federal law and has a separate legal existence from that of its owners.

ESTIMATION. Much of what is included in financial reports is the result of an estimate.

EXTERNAL FINANCIAL REPORTS. The standard financial reports issued by entities primarily for the use of decision makers other than the management of the entity (the Balance Sheet, the Income Statement, and the Statement of Cash Flows).

EXTERNAL USERS. Users of accounting information who are not part of the management of the company (examples: bankers, creditors, investors).

FULL DISCLOSURE. The accounting principle that requires all information which may be relevant to decision makers be included in the financial statements.

GENERALLY ACCEPTED ACCOUNTING PRINCIPLES (GAAP). The standards governing the recording and reporting of information published in external financial statements.

GOING CONCERN. The assumption that an entity will exist for an indefinite period of time.

HISTORICAL COST. The concept that assets should be recorded at their original purchase cost.

INTERNAL FINANCIAL REPORTS. Reports issued for use by managers of an entity that are usually more detailed than external reports. These reports are also called managerial accounting reports.

INTERNAL USERS. The managers of an entity who use accounting information.

MATERIALITY. The accounting principle which states that insignificant items need not be accounted for in the same manner as more relevant or significant items.

MONEY MEASUREMENT. A common unit of measure (money) used to record all information in the accounting records.

OBJECTIVITY. The accounting principle which requires that financial information be factual, verifiable, and unbiased.

PARTNERSHIP. A business with two or more owners who have agreed to operate the business as co-owners.

PERIODICITY. The concept in accounting which requires that the life of a business be broken down into specific time periods for periodic reporting purposes. The normal accounting period is one year.

A. **Accounting Process**

Accounting is the process of recording, measuring, summarizing, analyzing, and interpreting financial information and communicating this information to various users for decision-making purposes.

1. *Accounting Entity:* Accounting information is recorded separately for each accounting entity. An accounting entity is any business, individual, or not-for-profit organization whose financial affairs can be viewed as being distinct from those of any other entity or unit.

    EXAMPLE: John Jones owns and operates a small grocery store. John Jones is one accounting entity, and his grocery store is an entirely separate business entity. Separate accounting records should be kept for John and his store. If John Jones mixes the recording of his personal and business expenses, he will be unable to make valid decisions about the profitability of his business.

2. *Types of Business Entities:* Accountants are concerned primarily with three basic types of business entities: the sole proprietorship, the partnership, and the corporation.

    a. *Sole proprietorship:* A business owned by one individual. A sole proprietorship is not a separate legal entity from its owner; however, it is a separate accounting entity.

    b. *Partnership:* A business with two or more owners who have agreed to operate as co-owners and who share the profits and losses of the business in an agreed-upon proportion. For most purposes, a partnership is not a separate legal entity from its owners; however, it is a separate accounting entity.

    c. *Corporation:* A separate legal entity created by state or federal law. Corporations usually have the same legal rights and obligations as individuals. In order to form a corporation, a corporate charter must be obtained from the state where the business is formed. A corporation issues shares of capital stock in exchange for money, assets, or services. Owners of the capital stock are called *stockholders* or *shareholders* of the company; stockholders are the owners of the corporation.

    Corporations are both separate legal entities and separate accounting entities. Characteristics of corporations as well as the advantages and disadvantages of the three types of business entities are discussed further in Chapter 11 of this module.

3. *Recording Financial Information:* Financial information is normally recorded when an economic transaction takes place.

    a. *Money measurement:* There must be a common unit of measure for recording economic events. In accounting, money is that unit of measure. This is known as the *money measurement principle.*

    EXAMPLE: A business has $500 in the bank and owns a building. If the business wishes to determine the total value of its assets, a monetary value must first be assigned to the building.

b. *Historical cost:* If accountants are to record the building in the previous example as a monetary value, it is necessary to make an assumption in determining that value. There are a number of possible alternatives for valuation. For example, cost of replacing the building, potential selling price of the building, the owner's estimation of the fair market value, or original purchase cost might be used to value the building. In accounting, it has been decided that the original purchase (historical) cost should be used to value assets.

(1) Historical cost was chosen because it can be determined with objectivity. The term *objective* in accounting refers to valuations which can be factually substantiated and can be verified by an independent party. Historical cost is determined in a market transaction, and it is easily verifiable. At the time an asset is acquired, the cost represents the fair market value of the asset. The other valuation methods suggested result in subjective estimates of value which are changing constantly.

(2) As time passes, historical cost may not represent the current fair market value of the asset. Because operational assets are not intended for resale, however, current market value may not be relevant to accounting purposes.

c. *Stable dollar:* By recording assets at their historical costs in terms of money, accountants are implying that the dollar is a stable unit of measure. This is another assumption of accounting termed the *stable dollar concept*. The stable dollar concept assumes that a dollar today is worth the same amount as a dollar used to buy an asset in the past.

4. *Classifying Financial Information:* After financial information is recorded, it must be classified according to the areas which are affected. This is done by recording information in different accounts.

5. *Summarizing Financial Information:* Due to the large number of economic transactions which are recorded, the information must be summarized into reports in order for decision makers to be able to use it effectively.

EXAMPLE: Ajax Company recorded 5,000 transactions in June. These transactions related to purchases of materials; sales of goods to customers; payments for utilities, rent, and services; salaries paid to employees; and various other business activities. If decision makers were provided with information about all of these 5,000 transactions individually, they would find it difficult to make a decision. They would first have to summarize the data into a meaningful format. Accountants, therefore, summarize the material into reports before providing the information to decision makers.

Introduction to Accounting

6. *Using Accounting Information:* A number of different groups use accounting information. Such users may be *internal* or *external* users of accounting information.

   a. *Internal users:* The managers of a business represent one important group of users of accounting information. Managers are generally referred to as internal users of accounting data.

   b. *External users:* There are a number of users of accounting data external to the company's management. A business would be unable to issue one set of financial statements which meets the specific needs of all groups of external users. General purpose financial statements are prepared and issued for use by external users of accounting data.

   EXAMPLES OF EXTERNAL USERS: Bankers, creditors, investors, stockholders, employees, customers, and governmental agencies.

B. **Reporting Accounting Information**

   1. *External Financial Statements:* The standard general purpose reports (financial statements) which are issued are the Balance Sheet (the Statement of Financial Position), the Income Statement, the Statement of Retained Earnings, and the Statement of Cash Flows.

      a. *Generally accepted accounting principles:* The format of these statements and the methods of recording the data summarized within them are governed by a set of rules called *generally accepted accounting principles.* These rules are considered necessary because external users do not normally have access to financial information other than that provided by management of the company. Generally accepted accounting principles (GAAP) consist of pronouncements issued by the accounting profession, industry-wide practices, and other methods developed over the history of accounting which have authoritative support. GAAP are currently set by a private sector organization called the Financial Accounting Standards Board (FASB). The rules comprising generally accepted accounting principles will be discussed throughout the rest of this module.

      b. *Audits:* In order that external users may have more confidence in external financial reports, they may be audited by an independent Certified Public Accountant (CPA). This type of audit consists of an independent auditor (CPA) reviewing the financial statements in order to determine their conformity with generally accepted accounting principles. The auditor then issues an opinion regarding the fairness of the financial statements. A CPA might also perform a number of accounting services for a business such as management advising or tax return preparation.

The major function of a CPA is to perform an audit of the financial statements.

2. *Internal Financial Reports:* Internal reports generated for use by managers within the particular accounting entity do not need to follow generally accepted accounting principles. Internal users have access to the entity's accounting information system and are able to request reports in any form they desire. Internal financial reports are generally more detailed than external reports. There are certain accounting reports and techniques frequently used by managerial accountants. These will be discussed in more detail in Chapter 14. Managers of the business also use the financial statements generated for external users in making decisions about the operations of the company.

C. **Basic Concepts and Principles**

Some of the basic concepts, principles, and methods used in accounting will be introduced here. Many of them will be elaborated on later in this module.

1. *Going Concern:* In accounting, the going concern assumption states that the accountant assumes that the entity is going to exist for an indefinite period of time. The going concern assumption is often used to justify the historical cost concept. Since we assume that the business entity will continue in existence for an indefinite period of time, the fixed assets of the entity will be needed to continue its operations. The fixed assets cannot be sold without disrupting the operations of the business. Thus, historical cost is a relevant measure of the value of the fixed assets being used by the business.

2. *Relevance:* Accounting information must be relevant or pertain to the specific decisions which are to be made from the information.

3. *Periodicity:* The life of an entity is divided into time intervals for reporting purposes. The only time an *exact* accounting of the financial affairs of an entity can be made is at the end of the life of the entity. If an entity is a going concern, decision makers need accounting information about the entity prior to its termination in order to make decisions. The accountant must make periodic reports about the economic affairs of the entity. The traditional time period for financial reporting is one year. An accounting period which consists of 12 consecutive months is called a *fiscal year*. When a fiscal year ends on December 31, it is called a *calendar year-end*. A fiscal period may also follow the natural business year and end when inventories are at their lowest point and business activities are at their lowest level.

4. *Estimation:* The student of accounting needs to realize that much of what is included in financial reports is an estimate. Since accountants divide the life of an entity into arbitrary periodic time intervals, it is necessary to estimate many of the amounts included in the periodic financial reports.

5. *Consistency:* Consistency is the accounting principle which requires that, once an accounting or reporting method is selected, it should be used from one period to another. This ensures that financial reports of an entity will be comparable from period to period. If a change in accounting method is made, the consistency principle requires that the change be disclosed in the financial statements.

6. *Conservatism:* The principle of conservatism requires that, when doubt exists about the valuation of an asset or the recording of an accounting transaction, the accounting method which is the least likely to overstate income and financial position should be chosen.

7. *Full Disclosure:* The full disclosure principle requires that all information which may be relevant to decision makers be communicated to them through the financial statements.

8. *Materiality:* Materiality refers to the relative importance of an item or event to the decisions which users will be making. If an item is very insignificant when compared to other items, it is not necessary to follow accounting theory precisely. In determining materiality, the important consideration is whether knowledge of the item would influence the decisions of users. Materiality is a relative concept.

    EXAMPLE: For a company with sales of $100,000, $10,000 would be material; whereas $10,000 would be immaterial for a company with $10,000,000 in sales.

Introduction to Accounting

Chapter 1: Review Questions

PART A: Multiple-Choice Questions

DIRECTIONS: Select the best answer from the four alternatives. Write your answer in the blank to the left of the number.

____d____ 1. The process which involves identifying, recording, measuring, and communicating financial information is

  a. bookkeeping.
  b. relevance.
  c. generally accepted accounting principles.
  d. accounting.

____c____ 2. The principle which requires that the accounting method used be the one least likely to overstate income and financial position is called

  a. the consistency principle.
  b. the objectivity principle.
  c. the conservatism principle.
  d. the periodicity concept.

____b____ 3. The accounting concept that states that accounting information should pertain to the problem at hand and provide useful information about the problem is

  a. objectivity.
  b. relevancy.
  c. full disclosure.
  d. materiality.

____a____ 4. The accounting principle which requires that once an accounting or reporting method is selected it should be used from one period to another is

  a. consistency.
  b. periodicity.
  c. estimation.
  d. comparability.

____d____ 5. Accounting reports issued solely for use by the management of a company are called

  a. external reports.
  b. periodic reports.
  c. balance sheets.
  d. internal reports.

___a___ 6. The going concern assumption

   a. states that the accountant assumes the entity will exist for an indefinite period of time.
   b. requires that assets be written up to market value when market value is higher than the cost of the asset.
   c. requires that the accounting method least likely to overstate income and financial position be chosen.
   d. states that the life of an entity is limited.

___a___ 7. Generally accepted accounting principles

   a. are currently set by the Financial Accounting Standards Board.
   b. must be followed when reporting to internal financial statement users.
   c. consist only of pronouncements issued by the accounting profession.
   d. state that assets should be reported at replacement cost.

___d___ 8. A corporation

   a. is a separate legal entity.
   b. normally has the same rights and obligations as an individual.
   c. requires obtaining a corporate charter.
   d. all of the above.

___c___ 9. The principal function of an independent CPA is to

   a. prepare tax returns.
   b. conduct an audit the purpose of which is to guarantee that the financial statements are free of fraud.
   c. conduct an audit to determine whether the company's financial statements are presented fairly in accordance with GAAP.
   d. provide advisory services to management.

Introduction to Accounting 11

PART B: Matching Sets

MATCHING SET 1

Select the accounting principle (A-D) that is illustrated by each statement (10-14). Write the letter of your answer in the blank to the left of each statement.

ACCOUNTING PRINCIPLES

A. Accounting Entity Principle
B. Full Disclosure Principle
C. Historical Cost Principle
D. Materiality Principle

STATEMENTS

_____A_____ 10. Sue Smith carefully separates her personal accounting records from those of her business.

_____B_____ 11. A potential liability resulting from a product deficiency is described in a footnote to the financial statements.

_____D_____ 12. John Jones treats an item which cost $50 as an expense rather than as an asset even though the item is expected to last five years.

_____C_____ 13. Allison Arnold records the purchase of a building at $120,000 which is the amount she paid for the building. Her realtor told her that the building is easily worth $140,000.

_____A_____ 14. Paul Cedar owns a garage operated as a sole proprietorship, and he is also a partner in the P & J Used Car Lot. Paul's Garage and the P & J Used Car Lot keep separate accounting records.

MATCHING SET 2

Classify each of the individuals listed (15-20) into the appropriate user group (A-B). Each individual is interested in information about ABC Company.

USER GROUPS

A. Internal Users of Accounting Information
B. External Users of Accounting Information

INDIVIDUALS

____A____ 15. Vice-President of Manufacturing for ABC Company.

____B____ 16. Loan officer at XYZ Bank.

____B____ 17. Jerry May, owner of 10 shares of ABC Company stock.

____A____ 18. Controller of ABC Company.

____B____ 19. George Sully, a union employee in the ABC Company factory.

____B____ 20. Linda Sims who owns a company which supplies ABC Company with raw materials.

PART C: Problem Situations

DIRECTIONS: Select the best answer from the four alternatives. Write your answer in the blank to the left of the number.

Problem 1

Lew Co. purchased a plot of land for $100,000 five years ago. The appraised value of the land at that time was $105,000. Land in this area is generally worth about 50 percent more today than it was five years ago.

_____ 21. The value of the land on Lew Co.'s current records should be

    a. $105,000.
    b. $100,000.
    c. $150,000.
    d. $152,000.

Introduction to Accounting

Chapter 1: Solutions

PART A: Multiple-Choice Questions

	Answer	Refer to Chapter Section
1.	(d)	[A]
2.	(c)	[C-6]
3.	(b)	[C-2]
4.	(a)	[C-5]
5.	(d)	[B-2]
6.	(a)	[C-1]
7.	(a)	[B-1-a]
8.	(d)	[A-2-c]
9.	(c)	[B-1-b] There is a common misconception among external users that audits provide a guarantee against fraudulent reporting. Auditors must be aware of the possibility of fraud and design their audits to provide reasonable assurance of detecting fraud. They cannot guarantee that fraud does not exist.

PART B: Matching Sets

MATCHING SET 1

10.	(A)	[A-1]
11.	(B)	[C-7]
12.	(D)	[C-8]
13.	(C)	[A-3-b]
14.	(A)	[A-1]

MATCHING SET 2

15.	(A)	[A-6-a]
16.	(B)	[A-6-b]

17. (B) [A-6-b]

18. (A) [A-6-a]

19. (B) [A-6-b] Factory laborers are not part of the management of a company and do not normally have access to the internal reports generated for managers.

20. (B) [A-6-b]

PART C: Problem Situations

21. (b) [A-3-b] The land should be valued at historical cost.

CHAPTER 2
Theory and Classification of Accounts

OVERVIEW

The theory and classification of accounts is the most fundamental area in accounting. The candidate must thoroughly understand the recording of debits and credits in asset, liability, owners' equity, revenue, and expense accounts in order to understand the discipline of accounting.

The candidate should understand the definitions of asset, liability, owners' equity, revenue, and expense accounts; how to record transactions in the accounts; the accounting equation and its relationship to debits and credits in the accounts.

DEFINITION OF TERMS

ACCOUNT. A device used to collect and summarize information.

ACCOUNT BALANCE. The difference between the total debits and total credits recorded in an account.

ACCOUNTING EQUATION. Assets = Liabilities + Owners' Equity or, stated another way, Assets − Liabilities = Owners' Equity.

ACCOUNTS PAYABLE. The account used for recording the liabilities a company has incurred for goods or services purchased on open account.

ACCOUNTS RECEIVABLE. The account used to record the right a company has to receive payment for sales made on open account.

ACCRUAL. The concept which states that revenues should be reported when earned rather than when received and expenses should be reported when incurred rather than when paid.

ASSETS. Economic resources from which an entity can expect to receive benefits now or in the future.

CAPITAL STOCK. Ownership of a corporation is evidenced by shares of capital stock. Capital stock is also the title of the account used to record the total investment in shares of stock of a corporation.

CREDIT. An entry recorded on the right-hand side of an account.

DEBIT. An entry recorded on the left-hand side of an account.

DIVIDEND. A distribution of assets by a corporation to its owners.

DOUBLE ENTRY ACCOUNTING. In double entry accounting, an equal dollar amount of debits and credits must be recorded in the accounts whenever an accounting transaction is recorded. This is also called the duality principle.

EXPENSES. The costs of goods and services consumed (used up) by an entity in order to earn revenues.

INVENTORY. An asset account which is comprised of goods or merchandise held for future sale.

JOURNAL. An accounting record where business transactions are recorded in chronological order. The journal is also known as the book of original entry.

LEDGER. A collection of all of the accounts of a business. Information contained in the journal(s) is posted to the ledger.

LIABILITY. An obligation or debt of an entity owed to another party.

MATCHING. The principle which states that expenses incurred in earning revenues should be matched with those revenues in order to determine net income.

NET INCOME. Revenues - Expenses = Net Income [or Net Loss if Revenues < Expenses].

OWNERS' EQUITY. The resources invested in the business by owners plus profits from successful operations which have been retained in the business. Owners' equity may also be called capital, net worth, or proprietorship.

PERMANENT ACCOUNTS. Asset, liability, and owners' equity accounts (balance sheet accounts). These may also be called real accounts.

POSTING. The process of transferring the information contained in the journal to the ledger accounts.

RETAINED EARNINGS. The portion of the stockholders' equity consisting of earnings of the corporation which have been retained in the corporation rather than paid out as dividends.

REVENUE. Earnings resulting from the receipt of cash or other assets in exchange for goods sold by the entity or services performed by the entity.

REVENUE REALIZATION. The principle which states that revenue is usually recognized only after an exchange has taken place or a service has been performed.

SOURCE DOCUMENT. The document which is normally prepared when an accounting transaction occurs. Source documents serve as the source of information for making journal entries.

STOCKHOLDERS' EQUITY. The term used for the owners' equity of a corporation.

Theory and Classification of Accounts 17

T-ACCOUNT. A representation of an account which is used for instructional or problem-solving purposes.

TEMPORARY ACCOUNTS. Revenue, expense, and drawing accounts; temporary accounts are reduced to zero at the end of the accounting period through the closing process (see Chapter 4, Section G).

A. **Accounts**

Accounts are used for the collection and summarization of data resulting from economic transactions. An account is a device used to collect and summarize information. Accounts are sometimes called ledger accounts.

1. *Recording Information in Accounts:* The data comprising an account may be recorded in a number of forms.

    a. *Computerized systems:* Many companies keep their accounting records on a computer; their accounts are recorded in the form of magnetic tape or discs.

    b. *Manual systems:* A company using a manual accounting system might use a three-column account format. (See Figure 2-1.)

Figure 2-1
Three-Column Account Cash Account

DATE	EXPLANATION	REF	RECEIPTS (dr)	PAYMENTS (cr)	BALANCE
1/1	Beginning Balance	✓			100.00
1/5	Purchased Materials	CD #1		50.00	
1/10	Sold Materials	CR #2	25.00		75.00

2. *Using T-Accounts:* The easiest way to represent an account for instructional or problem-solving purposes is to use a T-account. A T-account resembles a capital *T*. T-accounts are *teaching tools* and are not used in the actual recording of data by businesses.

    EXAMPLE:

    Name of the Account

debit side	credit side
(abbreviated *dr*)	(abbreviated *cr*)

3. *Recording Debits and Credits:* A debit is an entry recorded on the left-hand side of a T-account. A credit is an entry recorded on the right-hand side of a T-account. It is important that the candidate understand that debit and credit simply mean left-hand and right-hand sides of an account respectively. Some individuals become confused because they attribute more than this to the meaning of debits and credits.

4. *Recording Entries:* Entries for individual transactions are recorded in the various accounts. Each account serves as a summary of a particular type of transaction during a period of time.

5. *Calculating the Account Balances:* The difference between the total debits and total credits recorded in an account is called the *account balance*. (Note that the T-account in Figure 2-2 is a record of the same information as Figure 2-1.)

Figure 2-2
Cash Account

CASH

	dr	cr	
Balance 1/1	100.00		
1/10 Sold Merchandise	25.00	50.00	1/5 Purchased Merchandise
Balance 1/10	75.00		

6. *The Ledger:* The group of all the accounts maintained by an entity is called the ledger.

B. **Classification of Permanent Accounts**

1. *Assets:* Assets are economic resources from which an owner can expect to receive benefits now or in the future. Here is another way of defining the term *assets:* things of value which are owned by the entity.

   EXAMPLE: Accounts receivable constitute one of the assets of a business. When a customer charges an item at a store, the store records an account receivable from the customer for the amount of the sale. This account represents the right of the business to receive cash from the customer in the future.

   EXAMPLE: Inventory is another common asset account. When a business purchases goods for resale, those goods are classified as inventory. Inventory is an asset since it has the potential to be sold in the future.

Theory and Classification of Accounts 19

a. *Asset accounts:* Some asset accounts are cash, accounts receivable, notes receivable, inventory, prepaid expenses, land, buildings, equipment, supplies, investments, patents, copyrights, and goodwill. The term *receivable* refers to an asset which is an amount the business has the right to collect in the future from another party.

b. *Debits and credits:* Increases in assets are recorded as *debits*. Decreases in assets are recorded as *credits*. Asset accounts normally have debit balances. The normal balance of any account falls on the increase side of the account.

EXAMPLE:

Asset Account

dr	cr
Normal Balance	
Increases are recorded as debits	Decreases are recorded as credits

c. *Recording of assets:* As discussed earlier, assets are recorded at cost following the money measurement, stable dollar, and historical cost conventions of accounting. This is done because costs can be objectively determined and verified.

2. *Liabilities:* Liabilities are obligations or debts of an entity which are owed to other parties. Liabilities come about from purchasing goods or services on credit; borrowing cash in order to finance the operations of the business; receipt of payment in advance of providing a product or service; and the adjustment process discussed in Chapter 4, Section F. Accounts payable constitute one of the liabilities of a business. Accounts payable arise when a company purchases merchandise on credit for use in its business.

EXAMPLE: *John Jones, who owns a small grocery store, went to a wholesaler and purchased 100 boxes of cereal on credit. He intends to sell this cereal in his store. John Jones would record an account payable to the wholesaler for the amount of the purchase. John has an obligation to pay the wholesaler (creditor) for the goods purchased, and the wholesaler has a claim on the assets of John's store equal to the amount of the account payable.*

a. *Liability accounts:* Some liability accounts are accounts payable, notes payable, mortgages payable, bonds payable, wages payable, and unearned income. The term *payable* refers to an obligation the entity owes another party.

b. *Debits and credits:* Increases in liabilities are recorded as *credits*. Decreases in liabilities are recorded as *debits*. Liability accounts normally have credit balances.

EXAMPLE:

Liability Account

dr	cr
	Normal Balance
Decreases are recorded as debits	Increases are recorded as credits

3. *Owners' Equity (Stockholders' Equity)*: Owners' equity represents the resources invested in the business by owners. Owners' equity is a residual claim. This means that, legally, the claims of creditors (liabilities) come first and owners are entitled to whatever remains after creditors are paid.

   Owners' Equity = Total Assets − Total Liabilities

   EXAMPLE: The ABC Company has total assets equaling $5,000. The firm owes suppliers $1,000 for goods purchased on credit (accounts payable) and has a $2,000 note owed to the bank. Therefore, total liabilities at this time are $3,000. Owners' equity is the residual amount of $2,000 ($5,000 total assets minus $3,000 total liabilities).

   a. *Sole proprietorship:* In a sole proprietorship, owner's equity is recorded in the owner's capital account.

      EXAMPLE: John Jones owns a sole proprietorship. His owners' equity account is called John Jones, Capital.

   b. *Partnership:* In a partnership, each owner has a separate capital account.

   c. *Corporation:* In a corporation, owners' equity is divided into two categories. Investment by owners of the corporation is classified as contributed capital, and earnings of the company which have been retained in the business are classified as retained earnings.

   d. *Increases in owners' equity:* Owners' equity may be increased in two ways:

      (1) from investment by owners, or

      (2) from retention of earnings generated by the business.

   e. *Decreases in owners' equity:* Owners' equity may be decreased in two ways:

(1) through distribution of cash or other assets of the business to its owners, or

(2) through losses incurred in the operation of the business.

    f. *Debits and credits to owners' equity:* Increases in owners' equity are recorded as *credits*. Decreases in owners' equity are recorded as *debits*. The normal balance of owners' equity is a credit.

EXAMPLE:

Owners' Equity Account

dr	cr
	Normal Balance
Decreases are recorded as debits	Increases are recorded as credits

4. *Balance Sheet Accounts:* Asset, liability, and owners' equity accounts are included on the *balance sheet* of an entity. They are called balance sheet, permanent, or real accounts. These accounts remain on the books of the business permanently. The balance sheet is also known as the *statement of financial position.* (The balance sheet will be discussed in Chapter 3.)

C. The Accounting Equation

The accounting equation is a representation of the relationship: "Assets are equal to liabilities plus owners' equity."

$$\text{Assets} = \text{Liabilities} + \text{Owners' Equity}$$

1. *Equality Represented:* This equality must always hold true in accounting since assets must always be equal to the rights or claims associated with the assets.

2. *Sources of Assets:* Another way of looking at the liabilities and owners' equity side of the equation is to view liabilities and owners' equity as sources of the assets. All of the resources used to obtain assets are provided either through creditors' holdings (liabilities) or through owners' investments (owners' equity).

EXAMPLE: Sara Stone has started a business which sells bicycles. She has named the business Stone's Bicycles. She purchased 20 bicycles for $2,000 on June 1, 19XA. She used $1,000 of her own money to buy the bicycles and borrowed $1,000 from the bank. She gave the bank a six-month note payable in exchange for the $1,000. Stone's Bicycles has $2,000 worth of assets represented by the bicycles. Sara has ownership rights or owners' equity in the amount of $1,000 which she *contributed toward the purchase of the bicycles. Since Sara used $1,000 of borrowed money to purchase the bicycles, she does not have owners' equity equal to the total amount of the cost of the bicycles. The bank owns some of the equity in the bicycles in the form of a claim against the assets (a liability). The bank's claim is the right to be repaid $1,000 six months from now. The accounting equation for Stone's Bicycles would appear as follows:*

$$\text{Assets} = \text{Liabilities} + \text{Owner's Equity}$$
$$\$2,000 = \$1,000 + \$1,000$$

3. *Continual Changes in Composition:* The composition of the assets, liabilities, and owners' equity of a business changes continually. However, the equality of the basic equation must always be maintained.

4. *Residual Aspect of Owners' Equity:* The accounting equation may be written as Assets - Liabilities = Owners' Equity. When written in this way, it emphasizes the residual aspect of owners' equity.

5. *Debits and Credits:* As stated earlier, increases in assets are recorded as debits and decreases in assets are recorded as credits. Assets normally have debit balances. Increases in liabilities and owners' equity are recorded as credits, and decreases are recorded as debits. Liabilities and owners' equity normally have credit balances. Amounts are recorded in the accounts in this fashion in order to maintain the equality of the accounting equation.

6. *Double-Entry Accounting:* Whenever an accounting transaction is recorded, the total dollar amount of the debits recorded must equal the total dollar amount of the credits recorded. If a larger amount of debits were recorded than credits, or vice versa, the accounting equation would be out of balance. This recording of an equal amount of debits and credits is called *double-entry accounting*. It is also sometimes referred to as the duality concept. By recording data in this fashion, a periodic check of the equality of the total debit and credit balances in the accounts can be made and used to help in discovering errors made in recording transactions.

D. **Recording Accounting Transactions**

1. *Journalization:* Accounting transactions are first recorded in *journals* or books of original entry. This is called journalization. Transactions are recorded in a journal in chronological order.

    a. *Source document:* When accounting transactions occur, some sort of document is usually prepared. This document is called a *source document*. Source documents serve as the source of information for recording transactions in the journal. Examples of source documents: checks, sales invoices, purchase orders, receipts. Source documents are often called business papers.

Theory and Classification of Accounts

b. *General journal:* This is the most common type of journal. When a business keeps only a general journal, all types of transactions are recorded in the general journal. (Some businesses may keep special journals as well as a general journal. Special journals are discussed in Chapter 5.)

(1) The general journal serves as a complete record of each accounting transaction since both sides of the transaction are recorded in one place.

(2) The general journal entry contains the following elements:

(a) Date of the transaction.

(b) Ledger account to be debited and the amount.

(c) Ledger account to be credited and the amount.

(d) An explanation of the transaction including an identification of the source document.

EXAMPLE: ABC Company purchased a machine for $2,000 cash on August 8. This transaction would be recorded in the general journal as shown in Figure 2-3. The account (or accounts) to be debited is listed first, and the amount is recorded in the debit column. The account (or accounts) to be credited is listed next, and the amount is recorded in the credit column. Note that the account to be credited is indented. This indentation is used to indicate that the account is credited. Following the debit and credit entries is an explanation of the transaction. The reference column is provided so that the journal entry may be cross-indexed to the ledger account.

Figure 2-3
General Journal

Page 10

Date	Explanation	Ref	Debit	Credit
Aug. 8	Machinery		2,000	
	Cash			2,000
	Purchased Stamping Machine, Check Number 112			

In order to conserve space the journal entries throughout the rest of the book will be presented in the following format:

		dr	cr
Aug. 8	Machinery	2,000	
	Cash		2,000
	Purchased Stamping Machine		
	Check Number 112		

Note that the position of the accounts indicates which account is to be debited and which is to be credited. The explanation may be omitted from journal entries when the transaction is routine and the entry is clear without the explanation.

2. *Posting to the Ledger:* Information which is recorded in the journal is periodically transferred to the ledger accounts. The transfer of information from the journal to the ledger is called *posting*.

Figure 2-4

Cash/Machinery Accounts

ACCT. #01 CASH

Date	Explanation	Ref	Debit	Credit	Balance
Aug. 8		10		2,000	10,000 8,000

ACCT. #10 MACHINERY

Date	Explanation	Ref	Debit	Credit	Balance
Aug. 8		10	2,000		100,000 102,000

Figure 2-4 shows the posting of the transaction journalized in Figure 2-3 to the ledger. The debit side of the journal entry is posted first. The machinery ledger account is located, the debit amount from the journal entry is recorded in the debit column, the date of the transaction is recorded, and the journal page number from which the entry was taken is recorded in the reference column. The ledger account number is then recorded in the reference column of the journal. This is done in order to cross reference the entry and to record that the transaction has been posted. The referencing procedure may be somewhat different depending upon the business involved. Some sort of referencing is necessary in order to provide an audit trail. The *audit trail* is the information which makes it possible for the accountant to trace each transaction back to its source document in order to determine that it was recorded properly. The same procedure would be followed for transferring the credit entry to the cash account.

Theory and Classification of Accounts

3. *Typical Accounting Transactions:* In the following examples, journal entries are shown, and the amounts are posted to T-accounts. The T-accounts represent the general ledger. The explanations will be omitted from the journal entries although in reality they would be included.

Figure 2-5
Cash/Equipment Accounts

	dr	CASH		cr
A. Aug. 1	1,000			
B. Aug. 3	2,000	C. Aug. 8		1,500
		D. Aug. 10		500
		E. Aug. 20		250
Bal. Aug. 20	750			

	EQUIPMENT & TOOLS		
C. Aug. 8	1,500		
Bal. Aug 20	1,500		

	NOTES PAYABLE		
		B. Aug. 3	2,000
		Bal. Aug. 20	2,000

	INVENTORY OF PARTS		
D. Aug. 10	750		
Bal. Aug. 20	750		

	ACCOUNTS PAYABLE		
E. Aug. 20	250	D. Aug. 10	250
		Bal. Aug. 20	-0-

	OWNERS' EQUITY		
		A. Aug. 1	1,000
		Bal. Aug. 20	1,000

a. Henry Smith starts a small business repairing television sets. On August 1, he invests $1,000 of his own money in the business. This transaction results in an increase in the asset Cash of $1,000 and an increase in Owners' Equity of $1,000. The journal entry would be:

		dr	cr
Aug. 1	Cash	1,000	
	Owners' Equity		
	(Henry Smith Capital)		1,000

This is posted as transaction A in the T-accounts in Figure 2-5.

b. Henry borrowed $2,000 from the bank on August 3. He gave the bank a note payable. As a result of this transaction, the asset Cash is increased by $2,000 and the liability Notes Payable is increased by $2,000. The journal entry would be:

		dr	cr
Aug. 3	Cash	2,000	
	Notes Payable		2,000

See transaction B in the T-accounts in Figure 2-5.

c. Henry purchased $1,500 of testing equipment and tools for use in his business on August 8. He paid for the equipment in cash. This transaction resulted in an increase in the asset Equipment and Tools of $1,500 and a decrease in the asset Cash of $1,500. The journal entry would be:

		dr	cr
Aug. 8	Equipment and Tools	1,500	
	Cash		1,500

See transaction C in the T-accounts in Figure 2-5.

d. Henry purchased $750 worth of parts to use in repairing television sets on August 10. He paid for the parts by using $500 cash and charging the other $250 on open account. This transaction resulted in an increase of $750 in the asset Inventory of Parts, a decrease of $500 in the asset Cash, and an increase of $250 in the liability Accounts Payable. The journal entry would be:

		dr	cr
Aug. 10	Inventory of Parts	750	
	Cash		500
	Accounts Payable		250

This journal entry is called a *compound journal entry* because more than two accounts are affected by the transaction. This transaction is posted as transaction D in Figure 2-5.

e. Henry paid the $250 account payable on August 20 using cash. As a result of this transaction, the asset Cash decreased by $250 and the liability Accounts Payable decreased by $250. The journal entry would be:

		dr	cr
Aug. 20	Accounts Payable	250	
	Cash		250

See transaction E in the T-accounts in Figure 2-5.

f. After recording transactions A through E, the T-accounts have been totaled in order to determine the account balances. When the

Theory and Classification of Accounts

increases and decreases recorded in an account are separately added and the sum of the decreases is subtracted from the sum of the increases, the procedure is called *determining the account balance*. Note that the asset accounts Cash, Inventory of Parts, and Equipment and Tools all have debit balances. The liability Accounts Payable has a zero balance, and the liability Notes Payable has a credit balance. The Owner's Equity account also has a credit balance.

TOTAL ASSETS		TOTAL LIABILITIES AND OWNER'S EQUITY	
Cash	750	Notes Payable	2,000
Inventory of Parts	750	Owner's Equity	1,000
Equipment and Tools	1,500		
Total	3,000	Total	3,000
Total Assets =		Total Liabilities and Owner's Equity	
Total Debits =		Total Credits	

E. **Classification of Temporary Accounts**

1. *Revenues:* Revenues are earnings resulting from the receipt of cash or other assets (or the reduction of a liability) in exchange for goods sold by an entity or services performed by an entity. Income is another term for revenues.

    a. *Revenue realization principle:* Revenue is usually recognized only after exchange has taken place or a service has been rendered.

    EXAMPLE: *Henry Smith repaired his neighbor's television set and received $85 for his services. The $85 represents revenue earned by Henry in exchange for his services. The account used to record revenue from services is called Service Fees or Service Revenue.*

    EXAMPLE: *Stone's Bicycles sold two bicycles for a total of $250. The person who purchased the bicycles promised to pay for them within 30 days. The $250 represents revenue earned from the sale of goods. The fact that the $250 has not yet been received in cash does not affect the recording of revenue since an exchange has taken place. The account used to record revenue from the sale of goods is called Sales.*

    b. *Increases and decreases in revenues:* Increases in revenues are recorded as credits. Decreases in revenues are recorded as debits. Revenue accounts normally have a credit balance.

EXAMPLE:

Revenue Account

dr	cr
	Normal Balance
Decreases are recorded as debits	Increases are recorded as credits

2. *Expenses:* Expenses are the costs of goods and services consumed (used up) by the entity as a result of earning revenue.

   a. *Incurring expenses:* In order to earn revenue, it is necessary to incur expenses.

   EXAMPLE: The cost of the parts Henry Smith used in repairing his neighbor's television set represents an expense or cost used up in earning revenue.

   EXAMPLE: The rent for the building where Sara Stone stores her bicycles represents an expense. It is a cost incurred in order to produce revenue.

   b. *Increases and decreases in expenses:* Increases in expenses are recorded as debits. Decreases in expenses are recorded as credits. Expense accounts normally have a debit balance.

   EXAMPLE:

   Expense Account

dr	cr
Normal Balance	
Increases are recorded as debits (+)	Decreases are recorded as credits (−)

3. *Net Income:*

   REVENUES − EXPENSES = NET INCOME

   The excess of total revenues over total expenses of an entity represents the net income of the entity. Net income is measured over a specific period of time. If total expenses exceed total revenues, a net loss is incurred.

   a. *Reporting net income:* Net income is reported periodically on the Income Statement.

Theory and Classification of Accounts

b. *Accrual concept:* Revenues should be reported when earned rather than when the cash is received, and expenses should be reported when incurred rather than when paid.

EXAMPLE: The previous example, where Stone's Bicycles sold two bicycles in exchange for an account receivable, illustrates the accrual concept. The revenue was reported when earned (at the time of the sale) rather than when the cash was received.

c. *Matching principle:* The matching principle states that expenses incurred in earning revenues should be matched with those revenues in order to determine net income. Expenses should be reported in the same period as the revenues to which they correspond.

EXAMPLE: Arnold is a salesman for the ABC Company. During July, he sold merchandise totaling $100,000. His sales commission will be included as part of his August paycheck. The sales commission should be reported as an expense on ABC's records in July. In this way, the sales revenue and sales commission expense are matched.

d. *Increases in owners' equity:* Net income represents an increase in owners' equity. A net loss represents a decrease in owners' equity.

e. *Income summary account:* At the end of an accounting period, revenues and expenses are closed to an income summary account which is then closed to owners' equity. Revenue, expenses, income summary, and drawing accounts are called temporary accounts since they are periodically closed to owners' equity. The closing process will be discussed in Chapter 4.

4. *Investments by Owners:*

   a. *Increases in assets and owners' equity:* Additional investments by owners of a business are not revenue. They are recorded as increases in assets and increases in owners' equity.

   b. *Sale of stock:* If a corporation sells shares of stock, the resulting cash obtained is not revenue but an additional investment by owners. The sale of stock is recorded as an increase in the asset Cash and an increase in the owners' equity account Capital Stock.

5. *Withdrawals and Dividends:*

   a. *Withdrawal of assets:* Withdrawals of assets from a business by the owners are not expenses. They are a decrease in the owners' equity in the business. A withdrawal is recorded as a decrease in cash and a decrease in owners' equity.

b. *Dividends:* Dividends represent distributions of assets by a corporation to its owners (stockholders).

   (1) Dividends are paid to stockholders when declared by the corporation's board of directors.

   (2) Payment of a dividend is not an expense. It is a distribution of assets similar to a withdrawal of assets by owners in a sole proprietorship.

6. *Typical Transactions Including Revenues and Expenses:* In the following examples, journal entries are shown, as well as postings to T-accounts. The T-accounts are shown in Figure 2-6. Waldorf Corporation sells widgets. The following are some of the transactions for Waldorf Corporation for the month of January.

   a. Waldorf Corporation sold 10,000 widgets during January. Two thousand widgets were sold for cash, and 8,000 widgets were sold on account. Widgets sell for $10 each. As a result of this transaction, sales revenue was increased by $100,000 (10,000 units sold x $10 per unit); cash was increased by $20,000 (2,000 units sold for cash x $10 per unit) and accounts receivable was increased by $80,000 (8,000 units sold on open account x $10 per unit). The journal entry to record this transaction would be:

	dr	cr
Cash	20,000	
Accounts Receivable	80,000	
Sales Revenue		100,000

   This transaction was recorded as transaction A in the T-accounts in Figure 2-6.

   b. The cost of the widgets sold during January was $50,000. This cost represents an expense in the period the widgets were sold. When the widgets were purchased, the asset account Inventory was debited. *Expensing* of the cost of the widgets in the same period they are sold results in proper matching of revenues and expenses. As a result of this transaction, the asset Inventory of Widgets decreased by $50,000 and the expense Cost of Goods Sold increased by $50,000. The journal entry for this transaction would be:

	dr	cr
Cost of Goods Sold	50,000	
Inventory		50,000

   Note: This is the entry which would be prepared using the perpetual inventory method. Another method of recording inventory transactions is called the periodic method. Both the perpetual and periodic methods will be discussed in Chapter 7. This transaction was recorded as transaction B in Figure 2-6.

Figure 2-6
T-Accounts for Waldorf Corporation

	dr CASH		cr
Bal. Jan. 1/9-	$30,000	D.	$20,000
A.	20,000	F.	7,000
C.	50,000	H.	40,000
		I.	5,000

	ACCOUNTS RECEIVABLE		
Bal. Jan. 1/9-	$50,000		
A.	80,000	C.	$50,000

	INVENTORY OF WIDGETS		
Bal. Jan. 1/9-	$50,000		
G.	90,000	B.	$50,000

	ACCOUNTS PAYABLE		
		45,000 Bal.	Jan. 1/9-
H.	$40,000	G.	$90,000

	SALES COMMISSIONS PAYABLE		
		7,000 Bal.	Jan. 1/9-
F.	$7,000	E.	$8,000

	SALES REVENUE		
		A.	$100,000

	SALARIES EXPENSE		
D.	$20,000		

	SALES COMMISSION EXPENSE		
E.	$8,000		

	COST OF GOODS SOLD		
B.	$50,000		

	RENT EXPENSE		
I.	$5,000		

c. Waldorf Corporation collected $50,000 for widgets sold on account in December. The revenue from the sales of these widgets was recorded in December when the sale took place (revenue realization). At that time, an account receivable was set up for the

$50,000. Now Waldorf Corporation will record the collection of that account receivable. As a result of this transaction, cash was increased by $50,000 and accounts receivable was decreased by $50,000. The journal entry to record this transaction would be:

	dr	cr
Cash	50,000	
Accounts Receivable		50,000

See transaction C in the T-accounts in Figure 2-6.

d. Waldorf Corporation paid the sales representatives $20,000 in salaries for the month of January. This payment represents an expense incurred in generating the revenue from sales of widgets. As a result of this transaction, Salaries Expense was increased by $20,000 and Cash was decreased by $20,000. The journal entry to record this transaction would be:

	dr	cr
Salaries Expense	20,000	
Cash		20,000

This transaction was recorded as transaction D in the T-accounts in Figure 2-6.

e. The sales representatives earned $8,000 in selling commissions related to the January sales. These selling commissions will be paid in February. The selling commissions relate to January revenue and should be expensed in January according to the matching principle. In order to record the expense in January, a liability account (Sales Commissions Payable) must be set up. As a result of this transaction, Sales Commissions Expense was increased by $8,000 and Sales Commissions Payable was increased by $8,000. The journal entry to record this transaction would be:

	dr	cr
Sales Commissions Expense	8,000	
Sales Commissions Payable		8,000

This transaction was recorded as transaction E in Figure 2-6.

f. Sales commissions incurred in December were $7,000. These commissions were paid to the sales representatives in January. The Sales Commissions Expense related to this transaction was recorded in December according to the matching principle. When the expense was recorded in December, Sales Commissions Payable was increased by $7,000. This transaction represents payment of that $7,000 liability. As a result of this transaction, Sales Commissions Payable was decreased by $7,000 and Cash was decreased by $7,000. The journal entry to record this transaction would be:

Theory and Classification of Accounts

	dr	cr
Sales Commissions Payable	7,000	
Cash		7,000

This transaction was recorded as transaction F in the T-accounts in Figure 2-6.

g. During the month of January, Waldorf Corporation purchased $90,000 worth of widgets from its suppliers on account. As a result of this transaction, the asset Inventory of Widgets was increased by $90,000 and the liability Accounts Payable was increased by $90,000. The journal entry to record this transaction would be:

	dr	cr
Inventory of Widgets	90,000	
Accounts Payable		90,000

This transaction was recorded as transaction G in the T-accounts in Figure 2-6.

h. During January, Waldorf Corporation paid for $40,000 worth of widgets which had been purchased on open account previously. As a result of this transaction, the liability Accounts Payable decreased by $40,000 and the asset Cash decreased by $40,000. The journal entry for this transaction would be:

	dr	cr
Accounts Payable	40,000	
Cash		40,000

This transaction was recorded as transaction H in the T-accounts in Figure 2-6.

i. During January, Waldorf Corporation paid $5,000 rent on the building used for operations. The rent on the building represents an expense of doing business. It is necessary to have a building to operate from, in order to earn revenue. The rental expense cannot be matched with any specific revenues. Therefore, the rent expense is matched with the revenues earned in the same accounting period that the expense is incurred. As a result of this transaction, the Rent Expense account increased by $5,000 and the Cash account decreased by $5,000. The journal entry to record this transaction would be:

	dr	cr
Rent Expense	5,000	
Cash		5,000

This transaction was recorded as transaction I in the T-accounts in Figure 2-6.

Theory and Classification of Accounts 35

Chapter 2: Review Questions

PART A: Multiple-Choice Questions

DIRECTIONS: Select the best answer from the four alternatives. Write your answer in the blank to the left of the number.

_____c_____ 1. An account is

   a. always kept in computerized form.
   b. used to ensure that debits equal credits.
   c. used to collect and summarize information.
   d. a record where business transactions are recorded in chronological order.

_____a_____ 2. In accounting the term credit means

   a. an entry made on the right-hand side of an account.
   b. increases in accounts.
   c. decreases in accounts.
   d. an increase in an asset.

_____d_____ 3. The left-hand side of an account is called

   a. the journal.
   b. the balance.
   c. the increase side.
   d. the debit side.

_____b_____ 4. The difference between total debits and total credits recorded in an account is called

   a. the accounting equation.
   b. the balance.
   c. the inventory.
   d. owner's equity.

_____a_____ 5. The normal balance of an account may be described as follows

   a. The normal balance is indicated by the increase side.
   b. The normal balance is indicated by the decrease side.
   c. The normal balance is indicated by the debit side.
   d. The normal balance is indicated by the credit side.

__c___ 6. An obligation or debt of an entity owed to one of its creditors is called

   a. an asset.
   b. an expense.
   c. a liability.
   d. owner's equity.

__d___ 7. Which of the following accounts would be classified as a temporary account?

   a. Cash
   b. Buildings
   c. Accounts payable
   d. Service fees

__b___ 8. Economic resources from which future benefits can be received are called

   a. debits.
   b. assets.
   c. capital.
   d. dividends.

__a___ 9. Which of the following is a correct form of the accounting equation?

   a. Assets = Liabilities + Owners' Equity
   b. Assets + Liabilities = Owners' Equity
   c. Assets + Owners' Equity = Liabilities
   d. Assets = Liabilities + Contributed Capital

__b___ 10. A net loss results in

   a. no change in owners' equity.
   b. a decrease in owners' equity.
   c. an increase in owners' equity.
   d. a credit to the capital account.

__b___ 11. Accounting transactions are first recorded in

   a. the general ledger.
   b. the journal.
   c. a T-account.
   d. alphabetical order.

__c___ 12. The stock of goods which an entity holds for future sale is called

   a. accounts receivable.
   b. cost of goods sold.
   c. inventory.
   d. accounts payable.

Theory and Classification of Accounts

___d___ 13. The periodic transfer of information from the journal to the ledger is called

    a. journalizing.
    b. matching.
    c. crediting.
    d. posting.

___d___ 14. Liabilities

    a. can arise from purchasing goods on credit.
    b. can arise from borrowing cash in order to finance the operations of the business.
    c. are decreased by recording a debit.
    d. All of the above statements pertain to liabilities.

___a___ 15. Owners' equity

    a. is a residual claim which is equal to Total Assets - Total Liabilities.
    b. represents the resources invested in the business by creditors.
    c. is increased by debiting an owners' equity account.
    d. is usually called capital in a corporation.

___d___ 16. Owners' equity can be decreased through

    a. investment by owners.
    b. payment of a note payable.
    c. retention of earnings generated by the business.
    d. withdrawals made by owners.

___b___ 17. In double-entry bookkeeping

    a. total increases in the accounts must always equal total decreases in the accounts.
    b. total debits must always equal total credits.
    c. the accounting equation may be temporarily out of balance after certain types of transactions occur.
    d. whenever an asset account is debited, a liability account or owners' equity account must be credited.

___d___ 18. Expenses

    a. should always be reported in the period during which they are paid.
    b. normally have a credit balance.
    c. are recorded according to the realization principle.
    d. should be matched with the revenues to which they correspond.

___a___ 19. Which of the following statements about revenues is false?

   a. Revenue should be realized when cash is received.
   b. Revenues are increased by recording a credit and decreased by recording a debit.
   c. Revenue is usually recognized only after an exchange has taken place or a service has been performed.
   d. Revenues are the earnings of a business normally resulting from the sale of goods or the performance of services.

___c___ 20. Net income

   a. is reported periodically on the Statement of Cash Flows.
   b. is equal to Revenues − Liabilities.
   c. is reported periodically on the Income Statement.
   d. represents a decrease in owners' equity.

___b___ 21. Investments made in the entity by owners

   a. represent revenue to the entity.
   b. are recorded in the capital account in a sole proprietorship.
   c. are recorded in the retained earnings account of a corporation.
   d. all of the above.

___d___ 22. Dividends

   a. should be reported on the income statement.
   b. are paid upon the request of stockholders.
   c. are an expense incurred by a corporation.
   d. result in a reduction of stockholder's equity.

___d___ 23. A journal entry contains

   a. the date of the transaction.
   b. an explanation of the transaction.
   c. the ledger accounts and amounts to be debited or credited.
   d. all of the above.

Theory and Classification of Accounts

PART B: Matching Sets

MATCHING SET 1

Select the appropriate accounting classification (A-E) for each of the following accounts (24-32). Write the letter of your answer in the blank to the left of each number.

ACCOUNTING CLASSIFICATIONS

A. Asset
B. Liability
C. Owners' Equity
D. Revenue
E. Expense

ACCOUNTS

__B__ 24. Accounts Payable

__E__ 25. Salary Expense

__D__ 26. Sales

__A__ 27. Office Supplies

__E__ 28. Rent Expense

__A__ 29. Accounts Receivable

__C__ 30. S. Webber, Capital

__A__ 31. Land

__B__ 32. Wages Payable

MATCHING SET 2

Determine whether each of the following items (33-42) should be recorded as a debit (A) or a credit (B). Write the letter of your answer in the blank to the left of each number.

RECORDING

A. Record as a Debit
B. Record as a Credit

ITEMS

_____A_____ 33. An increase in cash.

_____B_____ 34. An increase in accounts payable.

_____A_____ 35. A decrease in wages payable.

_____A_____ 36. An increase in accounts receivable.

_____B_____ 37. A decrease in equipment.

_____A_____ 38. An increase in wages expense.

___B_ A___ 39. An increase in service fees.

_____B_____ 40. A decrease in cash.

_____B_____ 41. A decrease in prepaid insurance.

_____A_____ 42. A decrease in A. Arnold, capital.

Theory and Classification of Accounts

PART C: Problem Situations

> DIRECTIONS: For each of the following problem situations, select the best answer from the four alternatives. Write the letter of your answer in the blank to the left of the number.

Problem 1

Accounting transactions need to be recorded correctly. The following three questions pertain to accurate handling of specific transactions.

_____C_____ 43. When an account receivable is collected

    a. total assets increase.
    b. total assets decrease.
    c. total assets remain unchanged.
    d. total owners' equity increases.

_____d_____ 44. Which of the following items could not result from the correct recording of a transaction?

    a. An increase in assets and an increase in owners' equity.
    b. A decrease in an asset and a decrease in a liability.
    c. A decrease in an asset and a decrease in owners' equity.
    d. An increase in an asset and a decrease in a liability.

_____c_____ 45. The journal entry to record the purchase of office supplies on account would be

    a. debit office supplies; credit cash.
    b. debit accounts payable; credit supplies expense.
    c. debit office supplies; credit accounts payable.
    d. debit supplies expense; credit office supplies.

Problem 2

A typewriter having a list price of $1,200 was purchased by Jones Co. for $1,100 cash.

_____c_____ 46. Which of the following entries represents the correct recording of the transaction?

a.	Office Equipment	1,100	
	Jones Capital		1,100
b.	Cash	1,100	
	Office Equipment		1,100
c.	Office Equipment	1,100	
	Cash		1,100
d.	Office Equipment	1,200	
	Cash		1,200

Problem 3

Arnold Co. purchased a building in exchange for $20,000 cash and an $80,000 note payable which will come due in four years.

_____c_____ 47. Which of the following journal entries correctly records the transaction?

a. Building	80,000	
Note Payable		80,000
b. Building	80,000	
Cash	20,000	
Note Payable		100,000
c. Building	100,000	
Cash		20,000
Note Payable		80,000
d. Building	20,000	
Cash		20,000

Theory and Classification of Accounts 43

Chapter 2: Solutions

PART A: Multiple-Choice Questions

	Answer	Refer to Chapter Section
1.	(c)	[A]
2.	(a)	[A-3]
3.	(d)	[A-3]
4.	(b)	[A-5]
5.	(a)	[B-1-b and B-2-b] The increase side of an account is the side where the balance would normally occur.
6.	(c)	[B-2]
7.	(d)	[E-3-e] Revenue, expense, income summary, and drawing accounts are temporary accounts. Service fees is a revenue account. All the other accounts listed are balance sheet or permanent accounts.
8.	(b)	[B-1]
9.	(a)	[C]
10.	(b)	[B-3-e] A net loss represents a loss incurred in the operation of the business which decreases owners' equity.
11.	(b)	[D-1]
12.	(c)	[B-1]
13.	(d)	[D-2] When information is transferred from the journal to the ledger, it is called posting.
14.	(d)	[B-2]
15.	(a)	[B-3]
16.	(d)	[B-3-e]
17.	(b)	[C-6] In double entry bookkeeping, debits must always equal credits and assets must always equal liabilities plus owners' equity.
18.	(d)	[E-2 and E-3-c]

44 Theory and Classification of Accounts

19. (a)   [E-1]

20. (c)   [E-3-a]

21. (b)   [B-3-a and E-4-a]

22. (d)   [E-5]

23. (d)   [D-1-b (2)]

PART B: Matching Sets

MATCHING SET 1

24. (B)   [B-2-a]

25. (E)   [E-2]

26. (D)   [E-1]

27. (A)   [B-1]

28. (E)   [E-2]

29. (A)   [B-1]

30. (C)   [B-3-a]

31. (A)   [B-1]

32. (B)   [B-2]

MATCHING SET 2

33. (A)   [B-1-b] Cash is an asset which is increased with a debit.

34. (B)   [B-2-b] Accounts payable is a liability which is increased with a credit.

35. (A)   [B-2-b] Wages payable is a liability which is decreased with a debit.

36. (A)   [B-1-b] Accounts receivable is an asset which is increased with a debit.

37. (B)   [B-1-b] Equipment is an asset which is decreased with a credit.

38. (A)   [E-2-b] Wages expense is an expense account which is increased with a debit.

39. (B)   [E-1-b] Service fees is a revenue account which is increased with a credit.

Theory and Classification of Accounts 45

    40. (B)   [B-1-b] Cash is an asset account which is decreased with a credit.

    41. (B)   [B-1-b] Prepaid insurance is an asset account which is decreased with a credit.

    42. (A)   [B-3-f] A. Arnold, Capital is an owners' equity account which is decreased with a debit.

PART C: Problem Situations

    43. (c)   [E-6-c] The entry to record collection of an account receivable includes a debit to cash and a credit to accounts receivable. The asset cash increases while the asset accounts receivable decreases, therefore, total assets remain unchanged.

    44. (d)   [C] The accounting equation is: Assets = Liabilities + Owners' Equity. Answer (d) is impossible since any entry which only increased an asset and decreased a liability would cause the accounting equation to be out of balance.

    45. (c)   [D-3-d]

    46. (c)   [D-3-c and A-3-b]

    47. (c)   [D-3-d]

CHAPTER 3

Basic Financial Statements

OVERVIEW

This section is designed to introduce the candidate to the basic financial statements of accounting. These statements are the final product of financial accounting.

The candidate should know the format and classification of the balance sheet and what is included in the various asset, liability, and owners' equity accounts. The candidate should know the classified forms of the income statement and the nature of revenue, expense, gain, and loss accounts. The candidate should also know how the statement of retained earnings shows the changes in the retained earnings account from one period to the next.

DEFINITION OF TERMS

ALLOWANCE FOR UNCOLLECTIBLE ACCOUNTS. Contra-accou[nt] accounts receivable account used for reporting accounts receivable at t[he] which is expected to be received.

BALANCE SHEET. A financial statement which shows the fina[ncial] an entity as of a specific time. Although *balance sheet* is the this financial statement, the formal title is the *statement of f[inancial]*

BONDS PAYABLE. Long-term liabilities consisting of s[ecurities] in stated denominations with a stated interest rate an[d] numerous types of bonds.

BOOK VALUE OR CARRYING VALUE. The carrying value of an asset on the books, which is the original cost less any accumulated depreciation related to that asset.

COMMON STOCK. A classification of capital stock which has no preferences relative to the corporation's other classes of stock. Common stockholders have the right to all residual assets left after the claims of creditors and preferred stockholders have been met.

CONTRA-ASSET ACCOUNT. An account which is related to a specific asset account and has a credit balance. Contra-assets are reported as deductions from the related asset on the balance sheet. Allowance for uncollectible accounts and accumulated depreciation are examples of contra-asset accounts.

COST OF GOODS SOLD. The cost of merchandise sold to customers, which is shown as a deduction from sales on the income statement to arrive at gross margin (gross profit).

CURRENT ASSETS. Those assets which are expected to be used in operations of the business within the operating cycle of the business or one year, whichever is longer.

CURRENT LIABILITIES. Obligations of a business that are to be repaid during the next operating cycle or one year, whichever is longer.

DEPRECIATION. A systematic and rational allocation of the cost of an asset over its useful life.

EARNINGS PER SHARE. The amount of net income earned per share of common stock during an accounting period.

FIXED ASSETS. Long-lived assets used in the operation of the business.

GAINS. Revenues generated from an activity that is not part of the normal operations of the business.

GROSS MARGIN (or GROSS PROFIT). The amount that remains after deducting the cost of goods sold from net sales.

INCOME STATEMENT. A financial statement which summarizes the operations of a business showing revenues, expenses, gains, and losses over an accounting period.

INTANGIBLE ASSETS. Long-lived assets that do not have any tangible existence. Examples are patents, copyrights, goodwill, and trademarks.

INVESTMENTS. Long-term assets held by the company for investment purposes in the operations of the business.

asily an asset can be converted to cash, the higher is its

TIES. Obligations of an entity that will not come due operating cycle.

decreases in owners' equity which do not result from e business.

erm obligation which is normally secured by real estate and istallments.

oligations of an entity consisting of signed documents which c amounts of money plus interest on specific future dates.

LE. Signed documents given to an entity by a customer

Basic Financial Statements

promising to pay a specific amount of money plus interest on a specific future date.

OPERATING CYCLE. The period of time it takes for a firm to buy merchandise, sell the merchandise, collect the accounts receivable resulting from the sale of the merchandise, and pay the accounts payable of the firm.

OTHER ASSETS. The balance sheet classification used for assets which do not fit under the normal balance sheet classifications of current assets, investments, fixed assets, or intangible assets.

OTHER LIABILITIES. The balance sheet classification used for liabilities which do not fit under the normal balance sheet classifications of current liabilities or long-term liabilities.

PREFERRED STOCK. A form of capital stock of a corporation which entitles its owners to certain preferences, such as receipt of a guaranteed amount of annual dividends before common shareholders may receive dividends.

PREPAID EXPENSES. Expenses that consist of the cost of goods or services bought for use in the business which are not used up at the end of the accounting period.

STATEMENT OF CASH FLOWS. The financial statement that shows the operating, investing, and financing cash flows of a company.

STATEMENT OF CHANGES IN CAPITAL. The financial statement that explains the changes in the capital (owners' equity) account for the period.

STATEMENT OF RETAINED EARNINGS. The financial statement that shows the changes in retained earnings from one period to the next.

TEMPORARY INVESTMENTS. Investments in marketable securities which are expected to be held for a short period of time; may also be referred to as marketable securities.

A. Balance Sheet

The balance sheet is a financial statement which shows the financial position of an entity as of a specific time. The balance sheet lists all of the assets, liabilities, and owners' equity of an entity. The balance sheet is formally called the statement of financial position.

1. *Accounting Equation:* The balance sheet is a formal statement which shows the accounting equation (Assets = Liabilities + Owner's Equity) at a specific time.

2. *Heading:* Every balance sheet should have a proper heading. The heading includes the following information:

    a. The name of the company.

    b. The title of the statement.

    c. The date of the statement (the balance sheet is dated as of a specific day).

EXAMPLE:

Stone's Bicycles
Statement of Financial Position
December 31, 19XA

3. *Classification of Assets on the Balance Sheet:* Assets are typically classified as current assets, investments, fixed assets, intangible assets, and other assets.

   a. *Current assets:* The first category of assets shown on the balance sheet is current assets. Current assets are those assets expected to be used in the operations of an entity within its operating cycle or one year, whichever is longer. The operating cycle is defined as the period of time it takes a firm to buy merchandise (or produce it), sell the merchandise, collect the customers' accounts receivable resulting from sale of the merchandise, and pay the accounts payable of the firm. This cycle will vary depending upon the nature of the business. Most businesses have an operating cycle which is shorter than one year, and they use a period of one year for the purpose of classifying current assets.

   Within the category of current assets, the individual asset accounts are listed according to their degree of liquidity. *Liquidity* is a measure of the speed with which an asset can be converted into cash. The more easily an asset can be converted into cash, the more liquid it is considered to be. The normal order in which current assets are listed is:

   (1) *Cash:* Cash includes coins, paper money, checks, money orders, and money on deposit in banks.

   (2) *Temporary investments:* Temporary investments consist of government bonds, corporate securities, or other securities which can be converted into cash very quickly. These may also be called short-term marketable securities. Temporary investments are expected to be held for less than one year or one operating cycle.

   EXAMPLE: Investments in U.S. Treasury bills would usually be considered a temporary investment.

   (3) *Notes receivable:* Notes receivable are promissory notes given to a business by its customers. These notes normally indicate the amount of the future payment, the interest rate, and the time at which payment is to be made by the customers. Notes receivable are signed documents which are transferable.

   (4) *Accounts receivable:* Accounts receivable are amounts owed to a business by customers for sales made on open account.

Basic Financial Statements

(a) *Uncollectible accounts receivable:* It is usually not realistic to assume that the total amount of the accounts receivable will be collected. Some portion of the accounts receivable will normally prove to be uncollectible.

(b) *Allowance for uncollectible accounts:* The amount of the accounts receivable which is estimated to be uncollectible is recorded in the allowance for uncollectible (or doubtful) accounts.

(c) *Contra-assets:* The allowance for uncollectible accounts is a contra-asset account. Contra-asset accounts have credit balances and are shown as deductions from their related asset accounts on the balance sheet. The allowance account is shown as a deduction from the total accounts receivable balance on the balance sheet, showing the *net* amount which is expected to be collected. (See disclosure in Figures 3-2 and 3-3.)

EXAMPLE: *ABC Company has accounts receivable totaling $100,000. Of this amount it is estimated that $10,000 will be uncollectible. The balance in the allowance for uncollectible accounts before recording the $10,000 uncollectible estimate is zero. The entry to record the estimate of the uncollectible accounts would be made as follows:*

	dr	cr
Bad Debt Expense	10,000	
Allowance for Uncollectible Accounts		10,000

(5) *Inventory:* Inventory is an asset which consists of goods on hand held by a business for future sale.

(a) Merchandising firms normally have one inventory control account.

(b) Manufacturing firms normally have three types of inventory control accounts.

Raw materials: Raw materials inventory is made up of the store of raw materials a company holds for use in producing goods.

Work in process: Work in process inventory consists of goods on hand which are still in the process of being completed.

Finished goods: Finished goods inventory consists of products completed and on hand awaiting sale to customers.

(6) *Prepaid expenses:* Prepaid expenses consist of the cost of goods or services bought for use in the business which are not used up by the end of the accounting period. Prepaid expenses are assets for as long as future benefits may be obtained from them. Examples of prepaid expense accounts are supplies, prepaid rent, and prepaid insurance.

EXAMPLE 1: A company pays rent one year in advance on a building used in operating the business. The payment of the rent in advance results in an asset called prepaid rent expense. The prepaid rent is an asset because the company has the right to use the building for 12 months without paying rent.

EXAMPLE 2: Full payment is made in advance on a fire insurance policy which covers two years. The insurance coverage to which the firm is entitled in the future is an asset called prepaid insurance expense.

The amounts in the prepaid expense accounts are written off to expense as their potential for future benefit is consumed.

b. *Investments:* The second category of assets listed on the balance sheet is investments. Investments are assets held by the company for investment purposes, not for use in the operations of the business. The investments category is used for assets which are expected to be held for longer than one year.

EXAMPLES OF INVESTMENTS: Stocks of other corporations, cash surrender value of life insurance, savings accounts kept for a specific purpose (debt retirement, construction of a new building), and bonds of other corporations.

c. *Fixed assets:* The third category of assets listed on the balance sheet is fixed assets. Fixed assets are often called plant and equipment. Fixed assets are long-lived assets used in the operations of the business and not held for sale to customers.

(1) *Tangible nature of fixed assets:* Fixed assets are *tangible property* such as land, machinery, equipment, buildings, furniture, and fixtures.

(2) *Depreciation:* Depreciation is the systematic and rational allocation of the original cost of an asset over its expected useful life. Depreciation takes place even though an asset is not in use—such as during a strike. Depreciation is the process of allocating the cost of an asset to the periods in which it is used. Fixed assets normally wear out or deteriorate with time and use. Land is an example of a fixed asset which does not deteriorate. However, machinery, equipment, buildings, furniture, and fixtures do deteriorate. These types of assets are subject to depreciation. The depreciation of an

Basic Financial Statements

asset is recorded in an account called *accumulated depreciation.*

EXAMPLE: ABC Company purchased a machine for $12,000. The machine is expected to last for six years. The decision has been made to depreciate the asset an equal amount during each year of its life. After the first year of use, the following entry is made to record depreciation:

	dr	cr
Depreciation Expense	2,000	
Accumulated Depreciation		2,000
To record depreciation on machine		
($12,000/6 yrs. = $2,000 per year)		

There are a number of different methods of computing depreciation expense. These methods will be discussed in Chapter 8, Section B-1.

(3) *Accumulated depreciation account:* The accumulated depreciation account is a contra-asset account. Accumulated depreciation is shown as a deduction from the related fixed asset account on the balance sheet. The fixed asset account contains the original cost of the asset. (See Figures 3-2 and 3-3 for disclosure.)

(4) *Book value:* The original cost of an operational asset less the accumulated depreciation related to that asset is equal to the book value or carrying value of the asset.

d. *Intangible assets:* The fourth category of assets listed on the balance sheet is intangible assets. Intangible assets are long-lived assets that do not have any tangible existence. Intangible assets represent rights that the company owns.

EXAMPLES: Patents, copyrights, trademarks, franchises, leaseholds, and goodwill.

e. *Other assets:* The last category of assets listed on the balance sheet is other assets. Other assets include long-lived assets which do not fit the criteria for classification in another area.

4. *Classification of Liabilities on the Balance Sheet:* Liabilities are typically classified as current liabilities, long-term liabilities, and other liabilities.

a. *Current liabilities:* Current liabilities are obligations of a business that are due to be paid within the next operating cycle or one year, whichever is longer.

EXAMPLES OF CURRENT LIABILITIES: accounts payable, short-term notes payable, wages payable, taxes payable, unearned revenue, interest payable, current interest due on long-term debt.

b. *Long-term liabilities:* Long-term liabilities are obligations of a business that will not come due during the next operating cycle.

EXAMPLES OF LONG-TERM LIABILITIES: mortgages payable, bonds payable, and long-term notes payable.

(1) *Mortgage:* A mortgage is a long-term obligation which is usually secured by real estate and is usually repaid in installments which are made up partially of interest and partially of a repayment of the principal of the loan.

(2) *Bond:* A bond is a security issued by an entity wishing to borrow a large sum of money. Bonds are issued in stated denominations, and they pay a stated rate of interest.

(3) *Long-term notes payable:* A note payable is an obligation of an entity consisting of a signed document which promises to pay a specific amount of money plus interest at a specific time in the future. Ordinarily a long-term note payable does not come due within the next operating cycle.

The current portion of long-term liabilities should be classified as a current liability.

EXAMPLE: ABC Company has a $200,000 note on one of their buildings. They make yearly payments of $20,000 on this note. They would have to reclassify $20,000 of this long-term liability as a current liability on the balance sheet since the $20,000 comes due within the next year.

c. *Other liabilities:* Other liabilities is the category used in some balance sheets to classify long-term liabilities which do not fit the criteria for classification in another area.

5. *Classification of Owners' Equity on the Balance Sheet:* Owners' equity is classified in the accounts differently depending upon the form of the ownership of the business.

a. *Sole proprietorship:* In a sole proprietorship, there is one owner's equity account called *Capital*. This account reflects all increases and decreases in the owner's equity.

b. *Partnership:* In a partnership, there is a separate owner's equity (capital) account for each partner. This account shows an individual partner's contributions of capital to the business, any distribution of assets to the partner from the business, and the partner's share of any profits or losses incurred by the business. The sum of all of the individual partners' equity accounts would equal the total owners' equity of the partnership.

c. *Corporation:* The stockholders' equity of a corporation is disclosed in two amounts: the amount invested by stockholders of

Basic Financial Statements

the corporation and the amount generated by retention of earnings from the business.

(1) *Capital stock:* Investments in the business by stockholders are shown in the contributed capital section. When stockholders invest in a corporation, they receive capital stock. There may be two classes of capital stock: common stock and preferred stock.

    (a) *Common stock:* All corporations *must* issue common stock. Common stock is sold to owners who receive no assurance of income from ownership of their stock. They have the rights to all residual assets left after creditors' and preferred stockholders' claims have been met. Common stockholders have the right to vote.

    (b) *Preferred stock:* Preferred stock is issued mostly by large corporations. Preferred stock has a preference over common stock. Preferred stockholders often have the right to receive a specified but limited amount of dividends before any distribution of dividends may be made to common shareholders. Preferred stockholders usually do not have the right to vote. (Preferred and common stock will be discussed further in Chapter 11.)

(2) *Retained earnings:* The amount generated by retention of earnings is called retained earnings. Retained earnings consist of the cumulative income and losses of a corporation less any dividends paid out to shareholders.

EXAMPLE: DEF Corporation had retained earnings of $100,000 on December 31, 19XA. During 19XB DEF Corporation earned $50,000 net income and paid $35,000 dividends to its shareholders. On December 31, 19XB, the retained earnings of DEF Corporation would be $115,000.

Retained Earnings 12/31/XA	$100,000
+ Net Income for 19XB	50,000
− Dividends	(35,000)
Retained Earnings 12/31/XB	$115,000

Figure 3-1 shows the balance sheet presentation of owners' equity for a sole proprietorship, a partnership, and a corporation.

6. *Basic Forms of the Balance Sheet:* The balance sheet may appear in account form or report form. The account form is usually used for internal managerial purposes whereas the report form is usually used in presenting information such as an annual report to stockholders.

Figure 3-1
Balance Sheet Presentations
of Owners' Equity

Sole Proprietor:	*Owner's Equity*		
	John Jones, Capital		20,000
Partnership:	*Partners' Equity*		
	Alice Smith, Capital	10,000	
	Robert Adams, Capital	8,000	
	Total Partners' Equity		18,000
Corporation:	*Stockholders' Equity*		
	Capital Stock	1,000,000	
	Retained Earnings	523,000	
	Total Stockholders' Equity		1,523,000

    a. *Account form:* The form of the balance sheet which shows assets on the left side and liabilities and owners' equity on the right side is called the *account form*. Figure 3-2 shows a balance sheet for a corporation in account form.

    b. *Report form:* The form of the balance sheet which shows assets on the top and liabilities and owners' equity below assets is called the *report form*. Figure 3-3 shows a balance sheet for a partnership in report form.

B. Income Statement

The income statement is a financial report which summarizes the operations of the business resulting in revenues, expenses, gains, and losses. The income statement shows the increase or decrease in owners' equity, resulting from the operation of the business over a period of time (the accounting period).

    1. *Net Income Related to Revenues and Expenses:* This equation defines net income from normal operations of a business as revenues minus expenses:

$$\text{Net Income} = \text{Revenues} - \text{Expenses}$$

Figure 3-2
Statement of Financial Position
Account Form

ABC COMPANY
STATEMENT OF FINANCIAL POSITION
DECEMBER 31, 19XB

Assets			Liabilities and Owners' Equity		
Current Assets			**Current Liabilities**		
Cash		25,000	Notes Payable		5,000
Temporary Investments		20,000	Accounts Payable		70,000
Notes Receivable		10,000	Salaries Payable		10,000
Accounts Receivable	100,000		Taxes Payable		2,000
Less: Allowance for Uncollectible Accounts	10,000	90,000	Current Portion of Mortgage		36,000
Inventory		100,000	Total Current Liabilities		123,000
Prepaid Insurance		2,000	**Long-Term Liabilities**		
Total Current Assets		247,000	Mortgage Payable	200,000	
Investments			Less: Current portion	36,000	164,000
Investment in Securities		80,000	Notes Payable		50,000
Cash Surrender Value of Life Insurance		20,000	Bonds Payable 10% due 2000		150,000
Total Investments		100,000	Total Long-Term Liabilities		364,000
Fixed Assets			**Other Liabilities**		
Land		60,000	Estimated Warranty Liability		56,000
Buildings	900,000		Deferred Income Taxes		23,000
Less: Accumulated Depreciation	200,000	700,000	Total Other Liabilities		79,000
Machinery and Equipment	1,000,000		Total Liabilities		566,000
Less: Accumulated Depreciation	450,000	550,000	**Owners' Equity**		
Total Fixed Assets		1,310,000	Contributed Capital		
Intangible Assets			Preferred Stock 7%, $100 per 500 shares outstanding		50,000
Patents		25,000	Common Stock 100,000 Shares outstanding		616,000
			Total Contributed Capital		666,000
			Retained Earnings		450,000
			Total Stockholders' Equity		1,116,000
Total Assets		1,682,000	Total Liabilities and Stockholders' Equity		1,682,000

Figure 3-3
Statement of Financial Position
Report Form

XYZ COMPANY
STATEMENT OF FINANCIAL POSITION
DECEMBER 31, 19XB

Assets

Current Assets

Cash		10,000	
Accounts Receivable	50,000		
Less: Allowance for			
Uncollectible Accounts	2,000	48,000	
Supplies		2,000	
Prepaid Expense		1,500	
Total Current Assets			61,500

Investments

Land held for future development	10,000	
Total Investments		10,000

Fixed Assets

Equipment	10,000		
Less: Accumulated Depreciation	5,000	5,000	
Furniture and Fixtures	6,000		
Less: Accumulated Depreciation	2,000	4,000	
Total Fixed Assets			9,000

Total Assets	80,500

Liabilities and Owners' Equity

Liabilities

Current Liabilities		
Accounts Payable	35,000	
Interest Payable	800	
Total Current Liabilities		35,800

Long-term Liabilities

Notes Payable 16%	10,000	
Total Long-Term Debt		10,000

Partners' Equity

Capital, Xavier	10,000	
Capital, Yancy	10,000	
Capital, Zonly	14,000	
Total Capital		34,700

Total Liabilities and Partners' Equity	80,500

Basic Financial Statements

2. *Gains and Losses:* A business may earn revenues which are not part of the normal operations of the business (gains) or incur expenses which do not result from normal operations of the business (losses). Gains and losses result in increases and decreases in owners' equity and are a part of the net income of a company. Since gains and losses do not result from the normal operations of a business, they are usually reported separately on the income statement.

    a. *Gain:* One example of a gain might be the sale of a fixed asset for more than its book value. Assume the DEF Corporation owns land which cost $20,000 and is currently being used as a parking lot. DEF Corporation is in the business of selling lawnmowers. DEF sells this land for $30,000. The land did not constitute goods held for sale in the normal course of the business; therefore, the sale results in a gain.

    Gains and losses are measured on a net basis. Rather than report revenue of $30,000 from the sale of the land and an expense of $20,000 for the cost of the land, accountants report only a gain of $10,000 (the net amount).

Revenue from Sale of Land	$30,000
− Cost of Land	−20,000
Net Gain on Sale of Land	$10,000

    b. *Loss:* Assume that DEF Corporation sold the parking lot land for $18,000 instead of $30,000. In this case a net loss of $2,000 would be incurred.

Revenue from Sale of Land	$18,000
− Cost of Land	−20,000
Net Loss on Sale of Land	$ 2,000

    Gains and losses may also occur as a result of uncontrollable events such as fires, floods, or tornadoes. If the damages received from an insurance company exceed the book value of the property destroyed, a gain would result. If the damages received were less than the book value of the property lost, a loss would result.

3. *Net Income Related to Gains and Losses:* This equation describes the net income from normal operations of a business as well as revenues or expenses which are not a part of the business's normal operations:

Net Income = Revenues − Expenses + Gains − Losses

4. *Heading:* Every income statement should have a proper heading. The heading includes the following information:

    a. The name of the company.

    b. The title of the statement.

c. The period of time which the statement covers.
(Note: The income statement is dated over a period of time while the balance sheet is as of a *specific* date.)

EXAMPLE:

Stone's Bicycles
Income Statement
For the Year Ending December 31, 19XA

5. *Basic Forms of the Income Statement:* An income statement may be reported in a classified form or an unclassified form. Figure 3-4 shows a classified income statement, and Figure 3-5 shows an unclassified income statement.

   a. *Format of a classified income statement:*

   (1) *Operating income:* Operating income consists of the revenues and expenses which result from the normal operations of the business. The expenses incurred in the normal operations of the business are subtracted from the revenues generated in the normal operations of the business to arrive at operating income. Operating income is the first section of a classified income statement.

   (a) *Revenue:* Revenue from sales of goods or services is reported first in the operating income section.

   (b) *Cost of goods sold:* Next, the cost of goods sold is reported in the classified income statement of a merchandising firm. Cost of goods sold is the cost of merchandise sold to customers. Sales of goods minus cost of goods sold is called margin (or gross profit) on sales. In a firm that only provides services rather than selling a product, there is no cost of goods sold.

   (c) *Operating expenses:* Operating expenses are divided into at least two categories: selling expenses and general and administrative expenses. Selling expenses are expenses that are directly related to the selling of a product. General and administrative expenses are expenses related to the office and administrative costs.

   Gross Profit – Total Operating Expenses
   = Operating Income

   (2) *Other income and expenses:* Other income and expenses are reported after operating income. Other income and expenses consist of revenues and expenses which are not connected with the primary operations of the business. This category would include gains and losses, investment

Basic Financial Statements

income (dividends received or interest earned on investments), interest expense, and incidental rental revenue. Interest expense is considered to be a financing expense rather than an operating expense and as such is included in the *other income and expense* category.

Figure 3-4
Income Statement for a Corporation

ABC COMPANY
INCOME STATEMENT
FOR THE YEAR ENDING DECEMBER 31, 19XB

Sales		5,000,000	
Less: Cost of goods sold		2,450,000	
Gross margin			2,550,000
Selling expenses			
Sales salaries	300,000		
Sales commissions	210,000		
Advertising	175,000		
Travel	25,000		
Total selling expense		710,000	
General and administrative expenses			
Salaries	458,000		
State and local taxes	47,600		
Telephone	8,400		
Legal and professional fees	9,200		
Insurance	12,450		
Depreciation	198,550		
Bad debt expense	10,000		
Total general and administrative expenses		744,200	
Total operating expenses			1,454,200
Operating income			1,095,800
Other income and expenses			
Investment revenue	98,000		
Gain on sale of land	12,000	110,000	
Interest expense	(85,000)		
Loss on equipment due to fire	(8,500)	(93,500)	
Total other income			16,500
Net income before income taxes			1,112,300
Less: Applicable income taxes			444,920
Net income after income taxes			667,380
Earnings per share (on 100,000 shares)			6.67

Figure 3-5
Income Statement for a Partnership

XYZ COMPANY
INCOME STATEMENT
FOR THE YEAR ENDING DECEMBER 31, 19XB

Revenues and gains:		
Service fees		225,000
Gain on sale of equipment		7,500
Total revenues and gains		232,500
Less expenses and losses:		
Salaries	120,000	
Rent for office building	30,000	
Supplies	2,500	
Depreciation	2,000	
Bad debts	1,800	
Interest	1,600	
Maintenance	500	
Total expenses and losses		158,400
Net income		74,100

NOTE: XYZ is a partnership. Therefore, there is no income tax expense shown on the income statement. On an unclassified income statement of a corporation, income taxes would be included under expenses and losses.

(3) *Net income before income taxes:* Operating income plus other income or minus other expenses results in net income before income taxes (corporate use only).

(4) *Net income after income taxes:* Income tax expense is deducted from "net income before income taxes" to arrive at "net income after income taxes."

  (a) *Corporations:* As separate legal entities, corporations pay taxes on their net income. The steps for reporting income taxes on the income statement refer only to corporations.

  (b) *Sole proprietorships:* Because sole proprietorships are not separate legal entities, the business is not responsible for the payment of income taxes. The *owner* must include the income of the business on his or her personal tax return and pay the taxes individually. Hence, income tax expense is not reported on the income statement of a sole proprietorship. Operating income plus other income or minus other expenses would result in the net income of the business, and the income statement would be complete.

  (c) *Partnerships:* The individual partners are responsible for paying the taxes on their share of the income of the partnership. They report this income on their personal

Basic Financial Statements

tax returns. The partnership pays no income taxes; thus, no income taxes are reported on the income statement of a partnership. As with a sole proprietorship, operating income plus/minus other income/expenses would result in the net income of the business, and the income statement would be complete.

(5) *Earnings per share:* A corporation also reports earnings per share on the income statement. Earnings per share is determined by dividing net income after taxes by the average number of shares of common stock held by owners during the period. Earnings per share is abbreviated EPS. The detailed calculation of earnings per share will not be discussed in this module. (See the presentation of simple EPS in Figure 3-4.)

Note: Partnerships and sole proprietorships do not issue common stock and, therefore, do not report earnings per share.

b. *Format of an unclassified income statement:*

(1) *Revenues and gains:* In an unclassified or single-step income statement all revenues and gains are grouped together first.

(2) *Expenses and losses:* Next, all expenses and losses are deducted from total revenues and gains to arrive at net income.

C. Statement of Retained Earnings

A corporation may present a statement of retained earnings. The statement of retained earnings shows the changes in retained earnings from one period to another. Figure 3-6 shows an example of a statement of retained earnings.

Figure 3-6
Statement of Retained Earnings

ABC COMPANY
STATEMENT OF RETAINED EARNINGS
FOR THE YEAR ENDING DECEMBER 31, 19XB

Retained earnings, December 31, 19XA	282,620
Add: Net income	667,380
Total	950,000
Less: Dividends	500,000
Retained Earnings, December 31, 19XB	450,000

1. *Increases in Retained Earnings:* Net income results in an increase in retained earnings.

2. *Decreases in Retained Earnings:* Net loss results in a decrease in retained earnings. Dividends decrease retained earnings.

D. **Statement of Changes in Capital**

If the business is a sole proprietorship or a partnership, the company may present a statement of changes in capital. This statement shows the changes in the capital account from one period to another.

1. *Increases in Capital:* Increases in capital result from total net income and additional contributions.

2. *Decreases in Capital:* Decreases in capital result from total net losses and withdrawals.

E. **Statement of Cash Flows**

The final basic financial statement is the statement of cash flows. This statement shows the cash flows provided or used by the operating, investing, and financing activities of the business. This statement will be discussed further in Chapter 13.

Basic Financial Statements

Chapter 3: Review Questions

PART A: Multiple-Choice Questions

DIRECTIONS: Select the best answer from the four alternatives. Write your answer in the blank to the left of the number.

_____ 1. Which of the following headings would be correct for the income statement of Morrison Company?

    a. Morrison Company
       Income Statement
       December 31, 19XA

    b. Morrison Company
       Income Statement

    c. Income Statement
       For the year ending December 31, 19XA

    d. Morrison Company
       Income Statement
       For the year ending December 31, 19XA

_____ 2. Current assets are listed on the balance sheet according to

    a. size of dollar amount.
    b. importance to the owner.
    c. liquidity.
    d. order of acquisition.

_____ 3. The financial statement that shows cash provided and used by operating, financing, and investing activities is called the

    a. statement of financial position.
    b. statement of changes in financial position.
    c. retained earnings statement.
    d. statement of cash flows.

_____ 4. In a classified (multiple-step) income statement, interest revenue would be reported

    a. as another income or expense item.
    b. along with sales.
    c. as part of operating expenses.
    d. after income tax expense.

5. Obligations of a business that will not come due within one year or the current operating cycle are called

   a. other equities.
   b. current liabilities.
   c. long-term liabilities.
   d. prepaid expenses.

6. Revenues which are generated from operations not a part of the normal operations of the business are called

   a. gains.
   b. operating revenues.
   c. losses.
   d. intangible revenue.

7. Which of the following transactions would result in the recording of a prepaid expense account?

   a. Payment of a two-year insurance policy on January 1, 19XA. The policy expires on December 31, 19XB.
   b. Payment of an account payable which resulted from the purchase of office supplies.
   c. Payment of rent for June on June 30.
   d. Purchase of stock in another corporation.

8. Income tax expense would be shown on the income statement for

   a. corporations, sole proprietorships, and partnerships.
   b. corporations and partnerships.
   c. partnerships.
   d. corporations.

9. Current liabilities

   a. will normally require the use of current assets for repayment.
   b. include trademarks, franchises, and goodwill.
   c. should include the current portion of long-term liabilities.
   d. Both (a) and (c) are correct answers.

10. Which of the following statements is true of owners' equity?

    a. In a partnership, there is a separate capital account for each partner.
    b. The owner's equity of a sole proprietorship is divided into two categories for balance sheet disclosure purposes: the amount invested by the owner and the retained earnings.
    c. Retained earnings consists of the cumulative income and losses of a corporation.
    d. Total stockholders' equity in a corporation includes only the contributed capital accounts.

Basic Financial Statements

_____ 11. Within the statement of retained earnings

  a. decreases in retained earnings result from dividends and net losses.
  b. net income is shown as an increase in retained earnings.
  c. the change in the retained earnings balance during the period is explained.
  d. All of the above statements are true.

_____ 12. In a classified (multiple-step) income statement

  a. operating expenses typically include selling and general and administrative expenses.
  b. other income and expense items are included with operating expenses.
  c. earnings per share are shown on all classified income statements.
  d. All of the above statements are true.

_____ 13. Contra asset accounts

  a. are related to asset accounts.
  b. have debit balances.
  c. are shown as a deduction from their related accounts on the income statement.
  d. include the allowance for uncollectible accounts and the depreciation expense accounts.

PART B: Matching Sets

MATCHING SET 1

Indicate which of the two financial statements (A-B) would include the following accounts (14-25). Write the letter of your answer in the blank to the left of each number.

FINANCIAL STATEMENTS

A. Balance Sheet (Statement of Financial Position)
B. Income Statement

ACCOUNTS

_____ 14. Accounts Receivable

_____ 15. Rent Expense

_____ 16. Accumulated Depreciation

_____ 17. Common Stock

_____ 18. Service Fees

_____ 19. Depreciation Expense

_____ 20. Sales

_____ 21. Notes Payable

_____ 22. Cash

_____ 23. Gain on Sale of Equipment

_____ 24. Interest Earned

_____ 25. Allowance for Doubtful Accounts

Basic Financial Statements

MATCHING SET 2

For each account (26-35), decide which classification (A-G) would be appropriate. Write the letter of your answer in the blank to the left of each number.

CLASSIFICATIONS

A. Current Assets
B. Investments
C. Fixed Assets (or Property, Plant, and Equipment)
D. Intangible Assets
E. Current Liabilities
F. Long-term Liabilities
G. Stockholders' Equity

ACCOUNTS

_____ 26. Patents

_____ 27. Marketable Securities (short-term)

_____ 28. Allowance for Uncollectible Accounts

_____ 29. Delivery Equipment

_____ 30. Accounts Payable

_____ 31. Common Stock

_____ 32. Bonds Payable

_____ 33. Inventory

_____ 34. Wages Payable

_____ 35. Cash Surrender Value of Life Insurance

Basic Financial Statements

PART C: Problem Situations

DIRECTIONS: For each of the questions relating to the following problem situations, select the best answer from the four alternatives. Write the letter of your answer in the blank to the left of the number.

Problem 1

Rohas Corporation purchased a machine for $50,000. The post-closing balance in the accumulated depreciation account which relates to the machine was $20,000 on December 31, 19XA. The machine could be sold currently for $24,000. Depreciation expense for 19XA was $5,000.

_____ 36. What is the book value of the machine?

    a. $30,000
    b. $25,000
    c. $24,000
    d. $50,000

Problem 2

During 19XC, Steve's Grocery, a sole proprietorship, had revenues of $500,000 and expenses of $300,000. Owner's equity was $150,000 on January 1, 19XC. Steve withdrew $50,000 cash from the business during 19XC.

_____ 37. What was the balance in Steve's capital account on December 31, 19XC?

    a. $350,000
    b. $300,000
    c. $100,000
    d. $200,000

Problem 3

Miller Corporation had sales of $1,000,000 during 19XB. Cost of goods sold was $500,000; selling expenses were $100,000; general and administrative expenses were $50,000; other expenses were $10,000; and income taxes were $20,000.

_____ 38. What was Miller Corporation's gross profit for 19XB?

    a. $400,000
    b. $350,000
    c. $340,000
    d. $500,000

_____ 39. What was Miller Corporation's net income before tax for 19XB?

    a. $340,000
    b. $320,000
    c. $400,000
    d. $500,000

Basic Financial Statements 71

Chapter 3: Solutions

PART A: Multiple-Choice Questions

	Answer	**Refer to Chapter Section**
1.	(d)	[B-4]
2.	(c)	[A-3-a]
3.	(d)	[E]
4.	(a)	[B-5-a(2)] Interest is considered to be a financing item rather than an operating item and should be classified as other income.
5.	(c)	[A-4-b]
6.	(a)	[B-2]
7.	(a)	[A-3-a(6)] The insurance policy will provide benefits to the company for two years following its purchase. It should be classified as a prepaid expense (prepaid insurance).
8.	(d)	[B-5-a(4)] Sole proprietorships and partnerships are not separate legal entities and do not pay income taxes. The income is reported on the owner's personal tax return.
9.	(d)	[A-4-a and A-4-b(3)]
10.	(a)	[A-5]
11.	(d)	[C]
12.	(a)	[B-5-a]
13.	(a)	[A-3-a(4)(c) and A-3-c(3)]

PART B: Matching Sets

MATCHING SET 1

14.	(A)	[A-3-a(4)]
15.	(B)	[B]
16.	(A)	[A-3-c(2)]
17.	(A)	[A-5-c(1)(a)]

18. (B) [B-5-a(1) and B-5-b(1)]

19. (B) [B-5-a(1)(c)]

20. (B) [B-5-a(1)]

21. (A) [A-4]

22. (A) [A-3-a(1)]

23. (B) [B-2]

24. (B) [B-5-a(2)]

25. (A) [A-3-a(4)]

MATCHING SET 2

26. (D) [A-3-d]

27. (A) [A-3-a(2)]

28. (A) [A-3-a(4)]

29. (C) [A-3-c]

30. (E) [A-4-a]

31. (G) [A-5-c(1)(a)]

32. (F) [A-4-b(2)]

33. (A) [A-3-a(5)]

34. (E) [A-4-a]

35. (B) [A-3-b]

Basic Financial Statements

PART C: Problem Situations

36. (a)   [A-3-c(4)]

Cost	$50,000
− Accumulated Depreciation	− 20,000
Book Value	$30,000

37. (b)   [D]

Capital 1/1/XC	$150,000
+ Net income (Revenues − Expenses)	+ 200,000
− Withdrawals	− 50,000
Capital 12/31/XC	$300,000

38. (d)   [B-5-a(1)(b)]

Sales	$1,000,000
− Cost of goods sold	− 500,000
Gross profit	$ 500,000

39. (a)   [B-5-a]

Sales		$1,000,000
− Cost of goods sold		− 500,000
Gross profit		$ 500,000
− Operating expenses:		
Selling expenses	$100,000	
General/adm. exp.	50,000	− 150,000
Net operating income		$ 350,000
− Other expenses		10,000
Net income before income tax		$ 340,000

CHAPTER 4

The Accounting Cycle

OVERVIEW

This section is intended to introduce the candidate to the steps involved in the accounting cycle. An understanding of the accounting cycle is necessary in understanding how transactions are recorded in the accounts and how financial statements are prepared.

The candidate should know the basic steps involved in the accounting cycle and how to complete each one of the steps. Journalizing and posting of transactions were discussed in Chapter 2, and financial statement format was discussed in Chapter 3. The candidate should review these topics if necessary.

DEFINITION OF TERMS

ACCOUNTING CYCLE. All of the procedures performed during an accounting period, including analyzing and journalizing of transactions, posting, taking a trial balance, preparing a worksheet, preparing financial statements, journalizing and posting adjusting entries, closing the temporary accounts, and taking a postclosing trial balance.

ADJUSTING ENTRIES. A journal entry made at the end of an accounting period to bring an account balance to the correct amount.

CLOSING ENTRY. A journal entry made at the end of an accounting period, which transfers the balance of a temporary account to the owners' equity or retained earnings account.

TRIAL BALANCE. A listing of all the account balances in the general ledger which is used to verify that the total dollar amount of debits is equal to the total dollar amount of credits.

WORKSHEET. An accounting tool used to make the end-of-period accounting procedures easier.

The accounting cycle consists of all of the accounting procedures performed during each accounting period. The accounting period for most businesses is one year. The following are the steps in the accounting cycle:

A. Analyzing Transactions and Recording

Accounting transactions occur, and source documents are prepared. The transactions are recorded in the journal(s) as they occur.

EXAMPLE: Stone's Bicycles sold a bicycle for $90 cash. A sales invoice (source document) was prepared when the transaction occurred. From the sales invoice, the transaction was recorded in a journal.

B. Posting

The debits and credits recorded in the journal entries are posted to the appropriate ledger accounts.

C. Trial Balance

A trial balance is a listing of all of the ledger account balances. Taking a trial balance is a process of summarizing all of the ledger accounts.

1. *Equality of Debits and Credits:* The trial balance proves the equality of total debits and total credits in the accounts.

    a. If total debits do not equal total credits in the trial balance, an error has been made in recording and/or posting the transactions.

    b. If total debits do equal total credits in the trial balance, this does *not* insure that no errors have been made in recording and posting transactions. An entry could have been posted twice, posted to an incorrect account, or for an incorrect amount; yet the trial balance could still balance.

2. *Preparation of Trial Balance:* A trial balance can be prepared at any time. Many companies prepare trial balances on a regular basis in order to provide a check on the equality of total debits and total credits in the accounts.

    a. The first step in the end-of-period accounting processes is to prepare an unadjusted trial balance from the ledger accounts.

The Accounting Cycle

b. This unadjusted trial balance can be included as a portion of the worksheet and might not be prepared as a separate step in the accounting cycle.

The accounts of PALS Partnership are presented below:

Cash		Accounts Receivable	
Bal 1,000		Bal 5,000	

Office Supplies		Accounts Payable	
Bal 400			Bal 3,000

Notes Payable		P.A., Capital	
	Bal 1,000		Bal 1,400

L.S., Capital	
	Bal 1,000

The trial balance of PALS Partnership is shown in Figure 4-1.

Figure 4-1
Trial Balance of PALS Partnership
PALS PARTNERSHIP
Trial Balance
December 31, 19XB

	Debits	Credits
Cash	1,000	
Accounts Receivable	5,000	
Office Supplies	400	
Accounts Payable		3,000
Notes Payable		1,000
P.A. Capital		1,400
L.S. Capital		1,000
Totals	6,400	6,400

D. Worksheet

The worksheet is an accounting tool which makes the end-of-period processes of adjusting the accounts, closing the accounts, and preparing the financial statements easier. (See Figure 4-4.)

1. *Columns on the Worksheet:* A worksheet has columns for the unadjusted trial balance, the adjusting entries, the adjusted trial balance, the income statement, and the balance sheet.

2. *End-of-Period Adjustments:* The worksheet provides a place for recording all of the end-of-period adjustments where errors may be detected and corrected easily.

3. *Journalizing and Posting:* After the worksheet has been completed, financial statements are prepared and the adjusting and closing entries are journalized and posted.

It is possible to complete the end-of-period processes without the use of a worksheet. Using a worksheet helps to minimize the errors made in adjusting and closing the accounts and preparing the financial statements.

E. Preparing Financial Statements

The basic financial statements are prepared using the worksheet information. The financial statements are prepared following the formats discussed in Chapter 3.

F. Adjusting Entries

Adjusting entry information is taken from the worksheet, recorded in the journal, and posted to the ledger. Adjusting entries are necessary to bring accounts up to date which have incorrect balances as of the end of the accounting period. In preparing financial statements, it is necessary to follow the accounting principles of revenue realization, accrual accounting, and matching. Since we prepare financial statements at periodic intervals, there are some accounts which have incorrect balances at year end. This occurs because an event which should be reported in accounting has occurred, but no formal transaction has occurred which resulted in preparation of a source document and recording of the transaction in the accounts. The following are basic types of adjusting entries:

1. *Estimates:*

    a. *Depreciation expense:* Depreciation expense recorded for a machine is an example of one of these types of adjustments. The cost of the machine is capitalized, and this cost is systematically apportioned to each period of the asset's useful life. There is no source document to initiate the recording of depreciation expense.

Therefore, an adjusting entry must be made to properly reflect the asset valuation and the depreciation expense at the end of each accounting period. See Chapter 8 for an example of the recording of depreciation expense.

b. *Allowance for uncollectible accounts:* The recording of the correct amount in the allowance for uncollectible accounts is also done through an adjusting entry at the end of the period. See Chapter 9 for an example of the recording of bad debt expense and the allowance for uncollectible accounts.

2. *Prepaid/Unearned Accounts:*

a. *Expenses:*

(1) *Expenses recorded initially as an asset:* Goods or services purchased for future use and paid for in advance may be recorded initially as assets. The adjustment process for expenses paid for in advance and recorded as assets is illustrated by some typical examples in (a) and (b) which follow.

(a) *Insurance expense:* Prepaid insurance, which has been recorded as an asset when paid, is an example where an adjusting entry is needed. Suppose Company A purchased a fire insurance policy on March 1, 19XB, for $2,000. The policy had a two-year life. When the policy was purchased, Company A made the following journal entry:

	dr	cr
Prepaid Insurance	2,000	
Cash		2,000

The end of Company A's fiscal year is August 31. On August 31, 19XB, the asset account Prepaid Insurance still has a $2,000 balance. An adjusting entry must be made to reflect the expiration of six months of insurance coverage benefits. Company A would make the following adjusting journal entry on August 31:

	dr	cr
Insurance Expense	500	
Prepaid Insurance		500

To record insurance expense for the period March 1 through August 31 ($2,000 x 6/24 months).

If this adjusting entry was not made, the asset Prepaid Insurance would be overstated and the amount of Insurance Expense would be understated in the financial statements.

(b) *Supplies expense:* Another type of adjusting entry is the entry to record use of supplies when the original purchases of supplies were recorded in an asset account. Assume that GEF Company purchased $500 of office supplies on April 12. The following journal entry was made on that date:

	dr	cr
Office Supplies Inventory	500	
Cash		500

GEF Company wishes to prepare financial statements on June 30. No entries were made between April 12 and June 30 to record the usage of office supplies. A physical count on June 30 reveals that there are $232 worth of office supplies left on hand. From this count, GEF Company can determine that $268 ($500 - $232) of office supplies were used. An adjusting entry must be made to record the expense and reduce the asset account Office Supplies. GEF Company would make the following adjusting entry on June 30:

	dr	cr
Office Supplies Expense	268	
Office Supplies Inventory		268

Figure 4-2
Office Supplies Inventory/Expense Accounts

Office Supplies Inventory			
April 12	500		
		June 30	268
June 30	Bal 232		

Office Supplies Expense			
June 30	268		
June 30	Bal 268		

(2) *Recorded initially as an expense:* Goods or services purchased for future use and paid for in advance might be recorded initially in an expense account rather than an asset account as discussed in Section F-2-a(1) of this chapter.

    (a) *Supplies expense:* If GEF Company had originally recorded the purchase of the office supplies on April 12 as an expense, it would be necessary to record an adjusting entry to reflect that some of the office supplies are still on hand. Assume that GEF Company made the following journal entry on April 12.

	dr	cr
Office Supplies Expense	500	
Cash		500

Assume that the physical count still indicated that $232 of office supplies were on hand on June 30. If no adjusting entry were made, Office Supplies Expense would be overstated and assets would be understated. GEF Company would make the following adjusting entry on June 30:

	dr	cr
Office Supplies Inventory	232	
Office Supplies Expense		232

To record office supplies on hand on June 30.

Figure 4-3

Office Supplies Expense/Inventory Accounts

Office Supplies Expense			
April 12	500		
		June 30	232
June 30	Bal 268		

Office Supplies Inventory			
June 30	232		
June 30	Bal 232		

Figures 4-2 and 4-3 show two different methods of recording the same transaction. Whether a company originally records the purchase of office supplies as an asset or as an expense is up to the managers of the company. Regardless of whether office supplies are originally recorded as an asset or as an expense, the final end-of-period amounts recorded in Office Supplies Inventory and Office Supplies Expense accounts should be the same.

(b) *Insurance expense:* When the purchase of an insurance policy is originally recorded as insurance expense and the life of the policy covers more than one accounting period, an adjusting entry must be made to reduce the amount of expense recorded and to set up the asset Prepaid (or unexpired) Insurance. Assume that Company A made the following entry when they purchased the fire insurance policy for $2,000 on March 1.

	dr	cr
Insurance Expense	2,000	
Cash		2,000

When their fiscal year ends on August 31, it would be necessary to record the following adjusting entry:

	dr	cr
Prepaid Insurance	1,500	
Insurance Expense		1,500

To record the portion of the fire insurance policy which is unexpired as of August 31, 19XB ($2,000 x 18/24 months).

b. *Revenues:*

(1) *Revenue recorded initially as a liability:* Revenue received in advance may be recorded initially in an unearned revenue (liability) account. The adjustment process for revenue received in advance and recorded as liabilities is illustrated by some typical examples in (a) and (b) which follow.

(a) *Unearned rental revenue:* Z Company received payment in advance for rental of a building for 12 months. The payment of $1,200 was received on June, 1 19XB, and the end of the company's accounting year is December 31, 19XB. Assume Z Company made the following journal entry on June 1:

	dr	cr
Cash	1,200	
Unearned Rental Revenue		1,200

As of December 31, the amount of seven months of the total rental revenue has been earned. If no adjusting entry were made, Rental Revenue would be understated and Unearned Rental Revenue would be overstated. Z Company would make the following adjusting entry on December 31:

	dr	cr
Unearned Rental Revenue	700	
Rental Revenue		700

To record the portion of rent received in advance which has been earned through December 31.

Examples b(1)(a) and b(2)(a) show two different ways of recording the same transactions. The end-of-period balances in the accounts are the same regardless of the method used.

(b) *Unearned subscription revenue:* Another example of the apportionment of a liability between periods would be the treatment of magazine subscriptions. Subscribers normally pay for magazines in advance. Assume that Dog Lovers Magazine receives $5,000 in cash on April 1, 19XB, for payment of two-year subscriptions to its monthly magazine. The year end is December 31. On April 1, Dog Lovers would have made the following entry:

	dr	cr
Cash	5,000	
Unearned Subscription Revenue		5,000

As of December 31, nine months of the 24-month payment would have been earned. If no adjusting entry were made, the liability Unearned Subscriptions Revenue would be overstated and Subscription Revenue would be understated. Dog Lovers would make the following adjusting entry on December 31:

	dr	cr
Unearned Subscription Revenue	1,875	
Subscription Revenue		1,875

To record the portion of subscriptions received in advance which has been earned as of December 31 ($5,000 x 9/24 months).

(2) *Revenue recorded initially as a revenue:* Revenue received in advance might be initially recorded in a revenue account rather than an unearned revenue account as discussed in Section F-2-b(1) of this chapter.

(a) *Rental revenue:* Z Company received payment in advance for rental of a building for 12 months. The payment of $1,200 was made on June 1 and the end of the company's accounting year is December 31, 19XB. Assume Z Company made the following entry to record the transaction on June 1:

	dr	cr
Cash	1,200	
Rental Revenue		1,200

(b) *Adjusting entry:* As of December 31, all of the rental revenue was not earned. If no adjusting entry were made on December 31, Rental Revenue would be overstated and the liability Unearned Rental Revenue would be understated. Z Company would make the following adjusting entry on December 31:

	dr	cr
Rental Revenue	500	
Unearned Rental Revenue		500

To record the portion of rent received which has not yet been earned ($1,200 x 5/12 months).

3. Accruals:

    a. *Accrued expenses:* Accrued expenses should be recorded when expenses have been incurred but have not yet been recorded as of the end of the accounting period. When an adjusting entry of this type is made, it results in the recording of an accrued liability.

       (1) *Accrued salaries:* Salaries have been earned by employees but have not yet been paid. Assume that Y Company's year end is November 30, 19XB, which is a Thursday. The employees of Y Company are paid weekly on Friday. As of November 30, the employees have earned salaries for four days' work which have not been paid or recorded. Assume that the amount earned by the employees from Monday through Thursday was $9,820. If no adjusting entry were made, Salaries Expense would be understated for the period and the liability Salaries Payable would be understated. Y Company would make the following adjusting entry on November 30:

	dr	cr
Salaries Expense	9,820	
Accrued Salaries Payable		9,820

To record salaries earned for the period ending November 30 which have not yet been paid.

       (2) *Accrued interest expense:* Interest expense on borrowed money accumulates on a day-to-day basis, but it is not normally recorded until it is paid. At the end of an accounting period, it is necessary to make an adjusting entry to record any interest expense incurred since the last payment date and to record the liability for payment of that interest at a future time. Assume that Z Company borrowed $5,000 from the bank on September 1, 19XB. Z Company signed a promissory note which stated that the note would be repaid on February 28, 19XC, with 15 percent interest. Z Company's year end is December 31. On September 1, Z Company made the following entry:

	dr	cr
Cash	5,000	
Note Payable to Bank		5,000

To record six-month 15% loan obtained from bank.

The Accounting Cycle

It is necessary for Z Company to make the following adjusting entry on December 31 to record the interest expense accrued from September 1 through December 31:

	dr	cr
Interest Expense	250	
Accrued Interest Payable		250

To record interest expense from September 1 through December 31 ($5,000 × .15 × 4/12 months).

Note: Interest rates are always quoted on an annual basis. In this example, interest had accrued for four months so it was necessary to multiply by 4/12 in order to determine the interest expense for the fraction of the year which had passed.

b. *Accrued revenues:* Accrued revenues should be recorded when revenues have been earned but have not yet been recorded as of the end of the accounting period. When an adjusting entry of this type is made, an accrued asset (receivable) and revenue are recorded.

(1) *Interest revenue:* Interest revenue is earned with the passage of time on notes receivable held by a company, but interest revenue is not normally recorded until it is received. At the end of an accounting period, it is necessary to make an adjusting entry to record any interest revenue earned which has not been received. Assume that Z Company accepted a four-month, 16 percent note receivable for $3,000 from a customer on November 1, 19XB. Z Company's year-end is December 31. As of December 31, Z Company has earned two months of interest revenue which has not been recorded. It would be necessary for Z Company to make the following adjusting entry on December 31:

	dr	cr
Accrued Interest Receivable	80	
Interest Revenue		80

To record interest earned on note receivable from November 1 through December 31 ($3,000 × .16 × 2/12 months).

4. *Use of the Worksheet:* Figure 4-4 shows a typical worksheet which includes a column for the unadjusted trial balance, the adjustments, the adjusted trial balance, the income statement, and the balance sheet.

Columns 1 and 2 show the unadjusted trial balance of Handy Corporation. This trial balance was taken from Handy Corporation's general ledger.

Columns 3 and 4 show the adjustments necessary to bring the accounts in the unadjusted trial balance to the proper year-end amounts.

Figure 4-4

HANDY CORPORATION
Worksheet
Year Ending 12/31/

	Unadjusted Trial Balance dr	Unadjusted Trial Balance cr	Adjustments dr	Adjustments cr	Adjusted Trial Balance dr	Adjusted Trial Balance cr	Income Statement dr	Income Statement cr	Balance Sheet dr	Balance Sheet cr
Cash	2230				2230				2230	
Accounts receivable	10000				10000				10000	
Allowance for uncollectible accounts		40		a. 760		800				800
Office supplies	550			b. 400	150				150	
Prepaid insurance	200			c. 80	120				120	
Furniture and fixtures	12000				12000				12000	
Accumulated depreciation		2200		d. 1000		3200				3200
Accounts payable		5400				5400				5400
Notes payable		2000				2000				2000
Capital stock		5000				5000				5000
Retained earnings 12/31/		5920				5920				5920
Service revenue		65700				65700		65700		
Loss of sales of equipment	2420				2420		2420			
Salaries expense	57860		e. 540		58400		58400			
Dividends	1000				1000				1000	
Totals	86260	86260								
Bad debt expense			a. 760		760		760			
Supplies expense			b. 400		400		400			
Insurance expense			c. 80		80		80			
Depreciation expense			d. 1000		1000		1000			
Salaries payable				e. 540		540				540
Interest expense			f. 50		50		50			
Interest payable				f. 50		50				50
Totals			2830	2830	88610	88610	63110	65700	25500	22910
Net income							2590			2590
							65700	65700	25500	25500

The Accounting Cycle

Adjustment a records the bad debt expense for the period and adjusts the allowance for uncollectible accounts balance. On December 31, 19XB, Handy Corporation estimated that $800 of the $10,000 accounts receivable balance would prove to be uncollectible. Since the allowance account had a credit balance of $40, it was necessary to make an adjusting entry crediting the allowance for uncollectible accounts for $760. The following adjusting entry was made on the worksheet:

		dr	cr
a.	Bad Debt Expense	760	
	Allowance for Uncollectible Accounts		760

Adjustment b records the amount of supplies used during the period. Handy Corporation records purchases of office supplies in the asset account Office Supplies. On December 31, 19XB, a physical count of the office supplies on hand was taken and $150 of supplies were on hand. The following adjusting entry was made to record the use of $400 ($550 - $150) of the supplies recorded in the office supplies account.

		dr	cr
b.	Supplies Expense	400	
	Office Supplies		400

Adjustment c records the portion of the asset Prepaid Insurance which has expired during the current period. Handy Corporation purchased a 20-month insurance policy on May 1 and made full payment for the policy at that time. The payment on May 1 of $200 was recorded as follows:

	dr	cr
Prepaid Insurance	200	
Cash		200

As of December 31, eight months of the life of the policy have expired. Handy Corporation made the adjusting entry to record the insurance expense and the reduction in the value of the insurance policy:

		dr	cr
c.	Insurance Expense	80	
	Prepaid Insurance		80
	($200 x 8/20 months)		

Adjustment d records depreciation expense for the period. Handy Corporation estimated that the $12,000 of furniture and fixtures had a useful life of 12 years when purchased. The straight-line depreciation method is used. Depreciation expense for the year would be $1,000, calculated as follows:

$$\$12,000/12 \text{ years} = \$1,000 \text{ per year}$$

The following adjusting entry was made to record depreciation expense:

		dr	cr
d.	Depreciation Expense	1,000	
	Accumulated Depreciation		1,000

Adjustment e records the salaries earned by employees in the final week of December, 19XB, which have not yet been paid or recorded. Handy Corporation employees earned $540 which had not been paid. The following adjusting entry was made to reflect the year-end liability for salaries earned and not paid.

		dr	cr
e.	Salaries Expense	540	
	Salaries Payable		540

Adjustment f records the interest which has accrued on the note payable through December 31. Handy Corporation borrowed $2,000 from the bank on November 1, 19XB. They agreed to pay the balance of the note plus 15% interest in 12 months. As of December 31, interest expense for two months has been incurred. The calculation of the interest expense was made as follows:

$$\$2,000 \times .15 \times 2 \text{ months}/12 \text{ months} = \$50$$

Handy Corporation made the following adjusting entry to record the accrued interest expense:

		dr	cr
f.	Interest Expense	50	
	Interest Payable		50

Columns 5 and 6 show the adjusted trial balance with the account balances after adjustment. Column 5 or 6 is the sum of the account balance shown in column 1 or 2 plus or minus any adjustments made in column 3 or 4. Note that debits = credits in columns 1 and 2, 3 and 4, and 5 and 6.

Columns 7 and 8 show the accounts taken from the adjusted trial balance (columns 5 and 6) which make up the income statement. The amount needed to make debits equal credits in the income statement column is the amount of net income or loss. Note that in Figure 4-4 the net income is $2,590. This amount of net income is carried over to the balance sheet credit column (column 10) because it is a portion of the ending retained earnings balance.

Columns 9 and 10 show the accounts taken from the adjusted trial balance (columns 5 and 6) that make up the balance sheet. The new retained earnings balance as of December 31, 19XB, consists of the sum of the December 31, 19XA, retained earnings balance ($5,920 credit), the dividends balance ($1,000 debit) and the net income balance ($2,590 debit) carried over from the income statement.

Figure 4-5 shows the adjusted trial balance after the adjusting entries have been journalized and posted.

G. Closing Entries

It is necessary to prepare entries to close the temporary accounts at the end of the accounting period. Revenue, expense, gain, and loss accounts are

The Accounting Cycle

summarized in the income statement and net income is added to the owners' equity or retained earnings account. Thus, the revenue, expense, gain, and loss accounts are actually subdivisions of the owners' equity account which are used to accumulate information during the accounting period. At the end of the accounting period, they have served their purpose and should be closed or "zeroed out." The Income Summary account is used in the closing procedures to summarize the amounts of revenues and expenses. The following are the procedures used in closing the temporary accounts:

Figure 4-5
Adjusted Trial Balance

HANDY CORPORATION
ADJUSTED TRIAL BALANCE
DECEMBER 31, 19XB

	Debits	Credits
Cash	2,230	
Accounts Receivable	10,000	
Allowance for Uncollectible Accounts		800
Office Supplies	150	
Prepaid Insurance	120	
Furniture and Fixtures	12,000	
Accumulated Depreciation		3,200
Accounts Payable		5,400
Notes Payable		2,000
Capital Stock		5,000
Retained Earnings 12/31/XB		5,920
Service Revenue		65,700
Loss on Sale of Equipment	2,420	
Salaries Expense	58,400	
Dividends	1,000	
Bad Debt Expense	760	
Supplies Expense	400	
Insurance Expense	80	
Depreciation Expense	1,000	
Salaries Payable		540
Interest Expense	50	
Interest Payable		50
Totals	88,610	88,610

1. *Closing Revenue and Gain Accounts:* Revenue and gain accounts are closed by debiting the individual revenue/gain accounts and crediting the Income Summary account.

2. *Closing Expense and Loss Accounts:* Expense and loss accounts are closed by debiting the Income Summary account and crediting the individual expense/loss accounts.

3. *Closing the Income Summary Account:* The Income Summary account is closed to Owners' Equity in a partnership or sole proprietorship or to Retained Earnings in a corporation. If a profit was earned during the period, the Income Summary account is closed by debiting Income Summary and crediting Owner's Capital or Retained Earnings. If a loss was incurred during the period, the Income Summary account is closed by debiting Owner's Capital or Retained Earnings and crediting the Income Summary account.

4. *Closing Withdrawal and Dividend Accounts:* Withdrawal (or drawing) accounts and dividends declared accounts are also closed at the end of the period. They are temporary accounts. However, they are not income statement accounts. The withdrawal account is closed by debiting Owner's Capital and crediting Withdrawals (drawings). The Dividends Declared account is closed by debiting Retained Earnings and crediting Dividends Declared.

5. *Journalizing and Posting:* The closing entries are first journalized and then posted to the ledger. See Figure 4-6 for an illustration of the closing journal entries and the T-account posting of the closing entries.

Figure 4-6
Closing Journal Entries and
T-Account Posting of Closing Entries

Closing Journal Entries for Handy Corporation

1. Service Revenue	65,700	
Income summary		65,700
2. Income Summary	63,110	
Salaries expense		58,400
Bad debt expense		760
Supplies expense		400
Insurance expense		80
Depreciation expense		1,000
Interest expense		50
Loss on sale of equipment		2,420
3. Income Summary	2,590	
Retained earnings		2,590
4. Retained Earnings	1,000	
Dividends Declared		1,000

T-Account Posting of Closing Entries
(Handy Corporation)

Service Revenue			Interest Expense	
	65,700 Bal.		Bal. 50	
65,700				(2.) 50
	-0- Balance		Balance -0-	

Salaries Expense			Loss on Sale of Equipment	
Bal. 58,400			Bal. 2,420	
	(2.) 58,400			(2.) 2,420
Bal. -0-			Bal. -0-	

Bad Debt Expense			Income Summary	
Bal. 760				(1.) 65,700
	(2.) 760		(2.) 63,110	
Bal. -0-			(3.) 2,590	
			Bal. -0-	

Supplies Expense				
Bal. 400				
	(2.) 400			
Bal. -0-			Retained Earnings	
				5,920 Bal.
				(3.) 2,590
Insurance Expense			(4.) 1,000	
Bal. 80				7,510 Bal.
	(2.) 80			
Bal. -0-			Dividends Declared	
			Bal. 1,000	
Depreciation Expense				(4.) 1,000
Bal. 1,000			Bal. -0-	
	(2.) 1,000			
Bal. -0-				

H. Postclosing Trial Balance

The final step of the accounting cycle is to take a postclosing trial balance. This ensures that debits still equal credits in the accounts after the adjusting and closing entries have been journalized and posted. The postclosing trial balance of Handy Corporation is shown in Figure 4-7. The postclosing trial balance includes only permanent accounts.

Figure 4-7
Postclosing Trial Balance

HANDY CORPORATION
POST-CLOSING TRIAL BALANCE
DECEMBER 31, 19XB

	Debits	Credits
Cash	2,230	
Accounts Receivable	10,000	
Allowance for Uncollectible Accounts		800
Office Supplies	150	
Prepaid Insurance	120	
Furniture and Fixtures	12,000	
Accumulated Depreciation		3,200
Accounts Payable		5,400
Salaries Payable		540
Interest Payable		50
Notes Payable		2,000
Capital Stock		5,000
Retained Earnings		7,510
Totals	24,500	24,500

I. The Next Accounting Cycle

The accounting cycle begins again on the first day of the next accounting period.

Note: The Certified Professional Secretary Examination Study Outline combines Steps G and H into one step. Because of this, the CPS Study Outline includes seven, rather than eight, steps in the accounting cycle.

Chapter 4: Review Questions

PART A: Multiple-Choice Questions

DIRECTIONS: Select the best answer from the four alternatives. Write your answer in the blank to the left of the number.

_____ 1. A trial balance which is prepared after all adjusting and closing entries have been posted is called the

   a. unadjusted trial balance.
   b. postclosing trial balance.
   c. adjusted trial balance.
   d. balance sheet.

_____ 2. The Withdrawals account would normally be closed to

   a. the Income Summary account.
   b. the Retained Earnings account.
   c. the Owner's Capital account.
   d. the Common Stock account.

_____ 3. The financial statements are normally prepared

   a. after the worksheet is completed.
   b. before beginning the worksheet.
   c. using the postclosing trial balance.
   d. from information taken from the unadjusted trial balance.

_____ 4. Taking a trial balance means

   a. making a listing of the account balances in the general journal.
   b. adjusting the books of the company.
   c. transferring the debits and credits from the journal to the ledger.
   d. making a listing of the general ledger accounts and their balances.

_____ 5. Which of the following accounts would not be included on a postclosing trial balance?

   a. Accounts Receivable
   b. Unearned Revenue
   c. Buildings
   d. Interest Revenue

6. Accounts that are closed at the end of each accounting period are called

    a. permanent accounts.
    b. temporary accounts.
    c. closing accounts.
    d. real accounts.

7. Which of the following is the first step in the accounting cycle?

    a. Posting transactions.
    b. Adjusting the accounts.
    c. Taking a trial balance.
    d. Analyzing and recording transactions in the journal.

8. On a worksheet, the net income amount is recorded

    a. only in the income statement credit column.
    b. only in the income statement debit column.
    c. in both the income statement debit column and the balance sheet credit column.
    d. in both the income statement credit column and the balance sheet debit column.

9. Failing to make an adjusting entry to record accrued wages payable would result in

    a. an overstatement of assets and an understatement of net income.
    b. an understatement of liabilities and an understatement of net income.
    c. an understatement of liabilities and an overstatement of net income.
    d. an understatement of liabilities but would have no effect on net income.

10. Little Company purchased an insurance policy which covers 18 months. At the time the policy was purchased, the payment was recorded as a debit in the prepaid insurance account. The adjusting entry at the end of the accounting period would require

    a. a debit to Insurance Expense and a credit to the Prepaid Insurance account.
    b. a debit to Prepaid Insurance and a credit to the Cash account.
    c. a debit to Prepaid Insurance and a credit to the Insurance Expense account.
    d. no adjusting entry at the end of the period.

11. Green Company originally recorded the purchase of office supplies in an expense account. At year end, Green Company counted the office supplies and found that $100 of supplies were still on hand. As a result of this

    a. no adjusting entry would be needed.
    b. an adjusting entry debiting Office Supplies Expense and crediting the asset Office Supplies should be made for $100.
    c. an adjusting entry debiting the asset Office Supplies and crediting Office Supplies Expense should be made for $100.
    d. an adjusting entry debiting Cash and crediting the asset Office Supplies should be made for $100.

The Accounting Cycle

12. Miller Company failed to record accrued rent receivable as of the end of the accounting period. As a result

   a. total assets would be understated and total net income would be understated.
   b. total assets would be understated and total net income would be overstated.
   c. total assets would be understated and total liabilities would be understated.
   d. total assets would be understated and net income would be unaffected.

13. Which of the following statements regarding trial balances is true?

   a. A trial balance may be taken any time.
   b. The last step of the accounting cycle is to prepare an adjusted trial balance.
   c. If total debits are equal to total credits in the trial balance, no errors have been made in the recording and posting of transactions.
   d. All of the above statements are true.

14. The worksheet

   a. is a tool which makes the end-of-period accounting processes easier.
   b. makes it unnecessary to record the adjusting entries in the journal and the ledger.
   c. ensures that no errors were made in the adjusting process if all column sets balance when it is completed.
   d. is required to complete the end-of-period accounting process.

15. Adjusting entries are needed to

   a. correct errors in the accounts.
   b. bring accounts which have incorrect balances as of the end of the accounting period up to date.
   c. bring the trial balance into balance.
   d. All of the above statements pertain to adjusting entries.

16. Which of the following entries would be considered to be an adjusting entry?

   a. The recording of accrued interest payable on a note payable held by Company Z.
   b. The recording by Company Z of the portion of unearned revenue which has been earned.
   c. The recording by Company Z of the expiration of a portion of the asset Prepaid Rent.
   d. All of the above would be considered adjusting entries.

PART B: Matching Sets

MATCHING SET 1

For each item (17-23) indicate which transaction (A-D) includes an account which would be used in the journal entry to close the listed item. Write the letter of your answer in the blank to the left of the number. More than one letter may be used in an answer.

TRANSACTIONS

A. Debit Income Summary
B. Credit Income Summary
C. Debit Retained Earnings
D. Credit Retained Earnings

ITEMS

_____ 17. Sales

_____ 18. Net loss

_____ 19. Dividends declared

_____ 20. Net income

_____ 21. Interest expense

_____ 22. Rent revenue

_____ 23. Income tax expense

The Accounting Cycle

MATCHING SET 2

For each statement (24-29), indicate to which step of the accounting cycle (A-H) the statement relates. Write the letter of your answer in the blank to the left of the statement.

STEPS IN ACCOUNTING CYCLE

A. Analyzing transactions and recording them in the journal
B. Posting
C. Trial balance - unadjusted
D. Worksheet
E. Financial statements
F. Journalizing and posting adjusting entries
G. Journalizing and posting closing entries
H. Postclosing trial balance

STATEMENTS

_____ 24. Prepared a working paper which included columns for the unadjusted trial balance, the adjustments, the adjusted trial balance, the balance sheet, and the income statement.

_____ 25. Purchased a machine for $20,000 cash and prepared an entry debiting the Machinery account and crediting the Cash account for $20,000.

_____ 26. Prepared a listing of the accounts in the general ledger before the adjustments were prepared.

_____ 27. Recorded a journal entry debiting Depreciation Expense and crediting Accumulated Depreciation for $1,000.

_____ 28. Transferred the $20,000 amount from item 25 to the machinery account and the cash account in the general ledger.

_____ 29. Recorded a journal entry debiting the Income Summary account and crediting the Salaries Expense account for the year-end balance in the Salaries Expense account.

PART C: Problem Situations

DIRECTIONS: For each of the questions relating to the following problem situations, select the best answer from the four alternatives. Write the letter of your answer in the blank to the left of the number.

Problem 1

Alex Company rented a building from Bates Co. for 18 months on June 1, 19XA. The amount of the rent was $3,600. Alex Company's year end is October 31. Alex Company recorded the payment of $3,600 as rent expense on June 1.

30. What is the amount of the rent expense related to this lease which should be reported on Alex Company's income statement for October 31, 19XA?

   a. $3,600
   b. $2,600
   c. $1,000
   d. $1,400

31. What is the amount of prepaid rent which should be shown on Alex Company's October 31, 19XA balance sheet?

   a. $3,600
   b. $2,600
   c. $1,000
   d. $2,200

32. On October 31, 19XA, the correct adjusting entry to record this transaction would be

   a. debit Rent Expense and credit Prepaid Rent for $1,000.
   b. debit Prepaid Rent and credit Rent Expense for $2,600.
   c. debit Prepaid Rent and credit Rent Expense for $1,000.
   d. debit Rent Expense and credit Prepaid Rent for $1,400.

33. Using the same information in questions 30-32, assume that Alex Company originally recorded the $3,600 payment as a debit to Prepaid Rent and a credit to Cash. The necessary adjusting entry would be

   a. debit Rent Expense and credit Prepaid Rent for $1,000.
   b. debit Prepaid Rent and credit Rent Expense for $1,000.
   c. debit Rent Expense and credit Prepaid Rent for $2,600.
   d. debit Prepaid Rent and credit Rent Expense for $2,600.

The Accounting Cycle

Problem 2

The following accounts and balances appear on the adjusted trial balance of Alice's Hair Salon. The accounts are not listed in chart of account order.

Accumulated Depreciation Expense	$ 300
Cash	1,764
Wages Expense	1,700
Advertising Expense	126
Revenue from Services	3,917
Equipment	3,974
Rent Expense	750
Alice Stowe, Capital	4,820
Alice Stowe, Drawing	1,200
Accounts Receivable	721
Accounts Payable	1,424
Supplies	116
Depreciation Expense	110

_____ 34. Total debits in the trial balance are

    a. $ 9,261.
    b. $10,461.
    c. $10,761.
    d. $10,161.

_____ 35. Net income for Alice's Hair Salon is

    a. $1,231.
    b. $ 931.
    c. $ 31.
    d. $1,041.

_____ 36. Total assets as shown on the balance sheet are

    a. $6,575.
    b. $7,775.
    c. $7,475.
    d. $6,275.

_____ 37. After closing entries are posted, the balance in the Alice Stowe, Capital account will be

    a. $6,051.
    b. $4,551.
    c. $4,851.
    d. $4,661.

The Accounting Cycle

Chapter 4: Solutions

PART A: Multiple-Choice Questions

	Answer	**Refer to Chapter Section**
1.	(b)	[H]
2.	(c)	[G-4]
3.	(a)	[E]
4.	(d)	[C]
5.	(d)	[H] Asset, liability, and owner's equity accounts are permanent assets. Revenue, expense, and drawing accounts are temporary accounts. Since all temporary accounts have already been closed, the postclosing trial balance includes only permanent accounts.
6.	(b)	[G]
7.	(d)	[A]
8.	(c)	[Figure 4-4]
9.	(c)	[F-3-a] Wages expense would be understated which would result in an overstatement of net income and capital and wages payable would be understated.
10.	(a)	[F-2-a(1)(a)]
11.	(c)	[F-2-a(2)(a)]
12.	(a)	[F-3-b]
13.	(a)	[C]
14.	(a)	[D]
15.	(b)	[F]
16.	(d)	[F]

PART B: Matching Sets

MATCHING SET 1

    17. (B)   [G-1]

    18. (B), (C)   [G-3]

    19. (C)   [G-4]

    20. (A), (D)   [G-3]

    21. (A)   [G-2]

    22. (B)   [G-1]

    23. (A)   [G-2]

MATCHING SET 2

    24. (D)   [D]

    25. (A)   [A]

    26. (C)   [C]

    27. (F)   [F]

    28. (B)   [B]

    29. (G)   [G]

PART C: Problem Situations

    30. (c)   [F-2-a(2)] $3,600/18 months = $200/month

                              $200/month × 5 months = $1,000 rent expense

    31. (b)   [F-2-a(2)]

    32. (b)   [F-2-a(2)]

    33. (a)   [F-2-a(1)]

The Accounting Cycle

34. (b)

[C]	dr	cr
Accumulated Depreciation		$ 300
Cash	$1,764	
Wages Expense	1,700	
Advertising Expense	126	
Revenue from Services		3,917
Equipment	3,974	
Rent Expense	750	
Alice Stowe, Capital		4,820
Alice Stowe, Drawing	1,200	
Accounts Receivable	721	
Accounts Payable		1,424
Supplies	116	
Depreciation Expense	110	
Totals	$10,461	$10,461

35. (a)

[Chapter 3, B-1]
Revenue from Services		$ 3,917
Less Expenses:		
Wages Expense	$ 1,700	
Advertising Expense	126	
Rent Expense	750	
Depreciation Expense	110	2,686
Net Income		$ 1,231

36. (d)

[Chapter 2, B-1]
Cash		$ 1,764
Accounts Receivable		721
Supplies		116
Equipment	$ 3,974	
Less Accum. Depreciation	(300)	3,674
		$ 6,275

37. (c)

[Chapter 3, D]
Alice Stowe, Capital Beg.	$ 4,820
Add: Net Income	1,231
Less: Alice Stowe, Drawing	(1,200)
Alice Stowe, Capital Ending	$ 4,851

CHAPTER 5
Accounting for Cash

OVERVIEW

Cash is an area of accounting with which candidates should be familiar. The procedures for performing a bank reconciliation for a business account are the same as the procedures used to reconcile an individual's checking account. Other aspects of accounting for cash, such as internal control and the recording of transactions, may be less familiar to the candidates.

The candidate should understand the recording of cash receipts and cash disbursements, the procedures needed for proper internal control over cash, the treatment of trade and cash discounts, the handling of a petty cash fund, the use of a voucher system, the procedures for reconciling a bank account, the types of checks, and the check register.

DEFINITION OF TERMS

BANK RECONCILIATION. A report which explains the difference between the balance per the bank statement and the balance per the general ledger cash account.

CASH. Coins, paper money, checks, money orders, and money on deposit in banks.

CASH DISBURSEMENTS JOURNAL. A special journal used to record all disbursements of cash.

CASH DISCOUNT. A reduction in the total amount due on an invoice offered if the invoice is paid within a designated period of time.

CASH RECEIPTS JOURNAL. A special journal used to record receipts of cash.

CERTIFIED CHECK. A check which is guaranteed by the depositor's bank.

CHECK REGISTER. The form of the cash disbursements journal used in conjunction with a voucher system.

CONTROL ACCOUNT. An account with a balance representing the total of all of the account balances of a related subsidiary ledger.

DEPOSITS IN TRANSIT. Bank deposits that have been recorded on the books of a company but have not yet been received and recorded by the bank.

INTERNAL CONTROLS. The methods and procedures adopted by a business to control its operations and protect its assets from waste, fraud, and theft.

NSF CHECK. A check that has been written on a bank account in which there are insufficient funds deposited to cover the amount of the check; commonly called a "bad check."

OUTSTANDING CHECKS. Checks issued by a company which have not yet been presented to the bank for payment.

PETTY CASH FUND. A fund established to pay for small expenditures which would be inconvenient to pay by check.

PURCHASES JOURNAL. A special journal used to record purchases of inventory on account. The purchases journal may also include purchases of supplies on credit.

SALES JOURNAL. A special journal used to record sales of merchandise on account.

SPECIAL JOURNAL. A journal used to record routine transactions which occur frequently. The use of special journals simplifies the posting procedure.

SUBSIDIARY ACCOUNT. A detailed account which provides supporting information about an individual balance.

TRADE DISCOUNT. A reduction from the list price of goods which is offered by manufacturers or wholesalers to their dealers; a method of determining the sales price.

VOUCHER. A business paper used in summarizing a transaction and approving it for recording and payment.

VOUCHER SYSTEM. A system of internal control over cash disbursements which requires that a voucher be prepared and verified before any payments may be made.

A. Cash Receipts

1. *Cash:* Coins, paper money, checks, money orders, and money on deposit in bank accounts. If an item would be accepted as a deposit by a bank, it should be considered to be a part of the cash of the company.

2. *Major Types of Cash Receipts:* Cash may be received for the immediate sale of merchandise, performance of services, or for payment of a sale on credit.

Accounting for Cash

- a. *Cash sales:* Cash received over the counter in exchange for sales of merchandise or the performance of a service.

- b. *Credit sales:* Cash received in payment of an outstanding account receivable balance.

3. *Internal Controls:* The procedures and rules used by a company to ensure that its assets are being used for legitimate business purposes are known as *internal controls*. Internal controls aid in the efficient operation of a business.

    - a. *Procedures and rules:* The establishment of procedures and rules by a company usually falls into the following five categories:

        (1) *Adequate separation of duties among employees:* Custody of an asset and recordkeeping for it should be separated. This helps prevent an individual from stealing assets and changing the accounting records to cover up the theft.

        (2) *Proper authorization.*

        (3) *Maintenance of adequate documents and records.*

        (4) *Limiting access to assets and to accounting records.*

        (5) *Performing independent checks on the performance of individuals.*

    - b. *Internal controls for cash receipts:* Cash is very easily misappropriated so it is essential that a business maintain good internal controls over cash receipts and disbursements. The following items are examples of good internal control procedures for cash receipts:

        (1) *Recording cash sales:* Cash sales should be recorded on a cash register.

        (2) *Depositing cash receipts:* Cash receipts should be deposited intact daily.

        (3) *Daily reconciliation of cash sales:* At the end of the day, an individual not involved in the collection of cash receipts should reconcile the total cash on hand with the record of cash sales for the day.

        (4) *Endorsement of checks received:* Any checks received should be restrictively endorsed immediately.

        (5) *Recording cash receipts:* Recording of cash receipts should be separated from custody of cash.

(5) *Recording cash receipts:* Recording of cash receipts should be separated from custody of cash.

(6) *Opening mail cash receipts:* Responsibility should be assigned for opening mail receipts. Payments on outstanding account receivable balances are typically received in the mail.

    (a) The person who is assigned responsibility for opening mail receipts should restrictively endorse all checks and prepare a list of checks received.

    (b) The individual opening the mail may prepare the bank deposit slip and make the deposit, or the checks may be forwarded to a cashier who deposits the receipts intact daily.

    (c) A copy of the list of checks received [see (6)(a)] should be sent to the accounting department.

    (d) The accounting department should receive a duplicate deposit slip which can be compared with the list of mail receipts. Any differences must be reconciled.

    (e) The accounting department enters the amounts received in the accounting records.

(7) *Preparation of bank reconciliation:* An independent bank reconciliation should be prepared monthly. The individual preparing the bank reconciliation should not be involved in the cash depositing or recording functions.

B. Subsidiary Ledgers and Special Journals

1. *Control Account:* A control account has a balance which is the total of all of the balances of a related subsidiary ledger. For example, the general ledger Accounts Receivable account is a control account because its balance shows the total amount owed to the company by its customers. The individual accounts for each customer are kept in the *subsidiary accounts receivable ledger.* The general ledger Accounts Payable account is also a control account.

2. *Subsidiary Account:* The detailed accounts of individual balances are kept in a subsidiary ledger.

    a. *The subsidiary accounts receivable ledger:* The subsidiary accounts receivable ledger contains an account for each credit customer of the company. The total of all of the individual accounts contained within the subsidiary accounts receivable ledger should be equal to the balance in the general ledger

certain customer, all payments made by that customer, and any adjustments made to the account. The balance in a single account of the subsidiary accounts receivable ledger (if it is up-to-date) represents the amount owed to the business by that particular customer. Figure 5-1 shows a sample of an account from the subsidiary accounts receivable ledger.

Figure 5-1
Subsidiary Accounts Receivable Ledger

Account Receivable

Henry Smith Acct. #66
111 W. Adams Street Credit Limit 1,000.00
Monticello, Iowa 52310

Date	Explanation	Ref	Charges Debits	Payments Credits	Current Balance
6/01	Television Tubes	S8	823.22		823.22
6/12	Payment	R10		823.22	-0-

b. *The subsidiary accounts payable ledger:* The subsidiary accounts payable ledger contains a separate account for each supplier from whom the company has purchased on account. The total of all of the balances of the individual accounts contained within the subsidiary accounts payable ledger should be equal to the balance in the general ledger Accounts Payable control account. Each individual subsidiary accounts payable account shows all credit purchases made by the company from a particular supplier, all payments made to the supplier, and any adjustments made to the account. The balance in an individual subsidiary accounts payable account represents the amount owed by the company to that supplier. Figure 5-2 shows an example of a subsidiary accounts payable ledger account.

Figure 5-2
Subsidiary Accounts Payable Ledger

Account Payable

Ajax Company Acct. #1015
642 Orange Avenue
Fairfax, Iowa 52601

Date	Explanation	Ref	Payments Debits	Charges Credits	Current Balance
6/02		P6		102.63	102.63
6/12	Check #802	D8	102.63		-0-

3. *Special Journals:* Special journals may be used in the recording of transactions which occur very frequently. In earlier chapters, all transactions were assumed to be recorded in a general journal. In reality, it is more efficient to use special journals for recording routine transactions which occur often. Many businesses have special journals to record cash receipts, cash disbursements, sales of goods on account, and purchases of inventory on account. It is possible that a company might have more special journals than these. However, these are the four most common special journals.

   a. *Cash receipts journal:* All receipts of cash are recorded in the cash receipts journal. The most common cash receipts are for cash sales and collections of accounts receivable, so the cash receipts journal usually has special columns for these two items. Other cash receipts are listed in a third general column.

Figure 5-3
Cash Receipts Journal

Page CR-10

		Debit			Credits		
Date	Explanation	Cash	Account Title	Ref	Account Receivable	Cash Sales	Other
6/12	Cash Sales	1,000.00				1,000.00	
6/12	Acct #6664	823.22	Henry Smith	X	823.22		
6/12	Acct #105	153.62	Lon Peterson	X	153.62		
6/12	Payment of note receivable	10,000.00	Note Receivable: J. Jones	18			10,000.00
		11,976.84			976.84	1,000.00	10,000.00
		(2)			(20)	(55)	(X)

Figure 5-3 shows an example of a cash receipts journal. There is a column for the date, an explanation column, a column debiting Cash (since the cash receipts journal records receipts of cash, Cash is always the debit in the entry), a column for the Account Title, and credit columns for Accounts Receivable collections, Cash Sales, and other types of transactions.

The Account Title column is used to record the name of the individual customer's account when the entry is for collection of an account receivable. This column is also used for the account to be credited when the Other transactions column is used. It is not necessary to make note of the account title when a cash sale is made because the credit entry is always made to the Sales account.

The Reference column is used to indicate that posting has occurred. A check mark or an "X" is made by the individual customer's account for payment of an account receivable indicating that the transaction was posted to the subsidiary accounts receivable ledger. The ledger account number to which the transaction has been posted is listed next to the account title for Other transactions.

At the end of the accounting period (month, week, or other length of time), the column totals are posted to the general ledger. First, the column totals are balanced ensuring that debits equal credits (==crossfooting==). Then the total of the Cash column is posted as a debit to the general ledger cash account, the total of the Accounts Receivable column is posted as a credit to the Accounts Receivable general ledger account and the total of the Cash Sales column is posted to the general ledger Sales account. The numbers in parentheses under the column totals indicate the ledger account number where the item was posted. An X or a check mark (✓) is shown under the Other column total since the column total is not posted. The transactions in the Other column must be posted individually and the relevant account number shown in the Reference column.

b. *Cash disbursements journal:* All payments of cash are recorded in the cash disbursements journal, sometimes ==called a cash payments journal==. Most disbursements are made in payment of outstanding accounts payable, so the cash disbursements journal has a special column for recording payments of accounts payable. Other cash payments are recorded in the Other accounts column. Figure 5-4 shows a simple cash disbursements journal. Postings would be made from the cash disbursements journal in a manner similar to that for the cash receipts journal.

Figure 5-4
Cash Disbursements Journal

Page D-8

| | | | Credit | | | Debits | |
Date	Explanation	Check #	Cash	Account Title	Ref	Accounts Payable	Other Accounts
6/12	Purchase order #1011	801	9,123.72	Handy Corp.	X	9,123.72	
6/12	Purchase order #1028	802	102.63	Ajax Company	X	102.63	
6/12	June rent	803	1,000.00	Rent Expense	102		1,000.00
			10,226.35			9,226.35	1,000.00
			(2)			(42)	(X)

c. *Sales journal:* Credit sales are recorded in the sales journal. Cash sales are recorded in the cash receipts journal. Figure 5-5 shows an example of a sales journal. The name of each subsidiary account receivable to be debited is listed under the Account Debited column. A check mark in the Reference column indicates that the entry was posted to the subsidiary accounts receivable ledger. On a periodic basis, often monthly, the total of the Amount column is posted as a debit to the Accounts Receivable control account and a credit to the Sales account in the general ledger.

Figure 5-5
Sales Journal

Page S-8

Date	Account Debited	Invoice Number	Terms	Ref	Amount
6/01	Henry Smith	13240	N/30	X	823.22
6/01	Alice Jerkins	13241	N/30	X	1,242.50
6/02	John Jerome	13242	N/30	X	422.60
6/02	Lon Peterson	13244	N/30	X	153.62
					2,641.94
					(20) (55)

d. *Purchases journal:* The purchases journal is used to record inventory purchases on account. Figure 5-6 shows an example of a purchases journal. The name of each accounts payable subsidiary ledger account to be credited is shown in the Account Title column. A check mark in the Reference column indicates that the entry was posted in the subsidiary accounts payable ledger. On a periodic basis, often monthly, the total of the Amount column is posted as a debit to the purchases journal and a credit to the Accounts Payable control account in the general ledger. A company might also define the purchases journal to include purchases of merchandise and supplies on account. A third alternative would be to use the purchases journal for all items purchased on account.

Figure 5-6
Purchases Journal

Page P-6

Date	Account Title	Purchase Order No.	Terms	Ref	Amount
6/01	Handy Corp.	1011	N/30	X	9,123.72
6/02	Ajax Company	1023	2/10 N/30	X	102.63
					9,226.35
					(42) (63)

e. *General journal:* When special journals are used, the general journal is used to record any transaction which does not fit in a special journal. Adjusting entries, closing entries, sales returns, and purchases returns are examples of items which would be recorded in the general journal.

C. **Cash Disbursements**

1. *Cash Disbursement Records:* In order to insure that proper control is

Accounting for Cash 113

maintained over cash disbursements, almost all cash disbursements should be made by check. Cash disbursements are usually recorded in a cash disbursements journal. (See Section B-3-b in this chapter.)

2. *Trade and Cash Discounts:*

   a. *Trade discounts:* Trade discounts are reductions from the retail list price of items in a catalog which are given by manufacturers or wholesalers to their dealers. Each dealer might have a specific discount (for example, 25%, 30%, or 40%) on items the dealer buys from the catalog. Trade discounts are not recorded on the accounting records of the buyer or of the seller. Both companies record the sale at the reduced amount. The trade discount is simply a method of determining the sales price.

   EXAMPLE: *Jones Distributing Company is a dealer of Ajax Wholesaling Company. Jones Distributing Company is given a 30% trade discount on all purchases from Ajax Wholesaling Company's catalog. Jones purchased goods with a total catalog list price of $10,000 from Ajax. The amount of the sale would be computed as follows:*

List Price	$10,000	
– Trade Discount	–3,000	($10,000 x .30)
Selling/ Purchase Price	$ 7,000	

   b. *Cash discounts:* Cash discounts encourage customers to pay their accounts promptly. Cash discounts are stated on the invoice and tell the customer how much of a discount may be taken if the bill is paid within a certain period.

   An invoice might have the terms 2/10, n/30. This means the customer will get a 2 percent discount if the bill is paid within 10 days of the invoice date and the net amount (the total amount) is due in 30 days.

   The terms 3/15, n/30 mean that the customer will get a 3 percent discount if the bill is paid within 15 days and the net amount is due in 30 days.

   The terms 3/15 EOM, n/60 mean that the customer may deduct a 3 percent discount if the invoice is paid within the first 15 days of the month following the month of the sale, and the net amount is due within 60 days from the date of the sales invoice.

   EXAMPLE: *Jones Company receives an invoice from Papper Company dated January 2, 19XA. The terms of the invoice are 2/10, n/30. The amount of the invoice is $100. If the invoice were paid on January 10, the amount due would be $98.*

Total invoice amount	$100
– Cash discount (2% x $100)	2
Amount to be paid	$ 98

Using the gross method of recording cash discounts, Jones Company's journal entry to record payment of this invoice would be:

	dr	cr
Accounts Payable	100	
Cash		98
Purchase Discounts		2

Papper Company's entry to record receipt of the payment would be:

	dr	cr
Cash	98	
Sales Discounts	2	
Accounts Receivable		100

If the invoice were paid on January 15, the ten-day discount period would have passed and the total invoice amount of $100 would be due.

Using the gross method of recording cash discounts, Jones Company's entry to record payment on January 15 would be:

	dr	cr
Accounts Payable	100	
Cash		100

Papper Company's entry to record the receipt would be:

	dr	cr
Cash	100	
Accounts Receivable		100

EXAMPLE: If an invoice is subject to both a trade and a cash discount, the cash discount is computed on the selling price after consideration of the trade discount. Jones Company received an invoice from Ajax Company. The list price of the goods purchased was $2,000. The trade discount is 30% and the terms of the cash discount are 3/10, n/30. Jones Company paid the invoice within the ten-day discount period. The amount paid was $1,358 which was computed as follows:

List Price	$2,000	
–Trade Discount	– 600	($2,000 x .30)
	$1,400	
–Cash Discount	– 42	($1,400 x .03)
Amount Paid	$1,358	

Accounting for Cash 115

3. *Imprest Petty Cash:* It is not practical for a company to write checks for small expenditures. Some items such as postage stamps, taxi fares, office supplies, and parking meter payments can be made more easily from a special fund called a *petty cash fund*. An imprest petty cash fund has one custodian, often a secretary, who is responsible for handling cash payments from the fund. The word *imprest* means an advance of money for some specified business use.

   a. *Establishing the petty cash fund:* The petty cash fund is established at some reasonable amount. Assume that a petty cash fund of $100 is to be established. A check for $100 would be written and cashed, and the money would be kept in a petty cash drawer or box. The journal entry to record the establishment of the fund is:

	dr	cr
Petty Cash	100	
Cash		100

   The only times an entry is made to the petty cash fund are when the fund is established or when the total amount of money in the fund is increased or decreased.

   b. *Making disbursements from the petty cash fund:* When disbursements are made from the fund, the custodian prepares a petty cash voucher. A petty cash voucher is a record of the expenditure which includes the date, the amount paid, the reason for the expenditure, and the signature of the person who received the money. The petty cash drawer should always contain cash and vouchers equal to the total amount of the fund. No journal entries are prepared when the disbursements are made. The entries to record the disbursements are made when the fund is replenished.

   c. *Replenishing the petty cash fund:* When the fund becomes depleted, the petty cash custodian makes a list of the petty cash vouchers and requests reimbursement. Assume that the petty cash vouchers indicate that $83.78 was disbursed from the fund. A check would be made out to the petty cash fund for $83.78. This check would be cashed and the money placed in the petty cash drawer. A journal entry would be made to record the expenditures as indicated by the petty cash vouchers. A typical journal entry to record replenishment might be:

	dr	cr
Postage Expense	42.00	
Freight In	21.00	
Transportation Expense	12.53	
Miscellaneous Expense	8.25	
Cash		83.78

   Note that the expense accounts are debited each time the fund is replenished.

d. *Reconciling petty cash:* At any time, the sum of the money and the petty cash vouchers in the petty cash drawer should equal the total amount of the fund. A periodic reconciliation should be made to ensure that this is the case. Occasional surprise audits (counts) of the fund should be made by a supervisor. This ensures that the petty cash custodian is using the fund for authorized expenditures and that vouchers are being properly completed.

4. *Checks and Check Registers:*

    a. *Check:* A check is a written document which orders a bank to pay a specific amount from the depositor's account to the payee of the check. Checks come in many different forms. Many checks have a check stub attached to the check. This stub is filled out prior to writing the check and is kept by the company writing the check. The stub may serve as a source document for recording the transaction.

    b. *Certified check:* A certified check is a check for which the bank guarantees that the depositor has enough funds in the bank account to cover the check when it is presented for payment. The depositor must take the check to the bank and have it certified prior to giving the check to the payee. The bank stamps *certified* on the check and removes the money from the depositor's account. A fee is usually charged for certifying a check. Certified checks might be issued when a large sum of money is involved.

    c. *Check register:* Check register is another term for cash disbursements journal. The check register lists all of the checks issued. When a voucher system is used, a simplified version of the cash disbursements journal may be used, and this journal is usually called a check register. (See Section C-5 of this chapter for further discussion of the check register.)

5. *The Voucher System and Recording of Accounts Payable:* A voucher system is used to obtain the maximum amount of internal control over cash disbursements, purchasing, and receiving. A voucher system requires that a voucher be prepared and verified prior to making any payments.

    a. *The voucher system:* A voucher is a document which is used to authorize payment of a liability. A voucher typically contains spaces for the voucher date, information from the supplier's invoice, the ledger accounts to be debited and credited, space for the approval signatures for each step of the verification process, and space for the signature for the approval of the liability. Figure 5-7 shows an example of a typical voucher. Vouchers are numbered consecutively, and a separate voucher is attached to each incoming invoice.

Figure 5-7
Voucher
XYZ Corporation
Voucher

Pay to: _____

_____ Date _____

_____ Date Due _____

Date of Invoice _____ Amount _____

Less Discount _____

Invoice Number _____ Amount Due _____

Accounts	Amount		
Purchases	$ _____		
Freight-in	_____		
Repairs	_____	Payment	
Utilities	_____	Check #	_____
Salaries	_____	Date	_____
_____	_____	Amount	$ _____

Credit Vouchers
   Payable (total) $ _____

Verification and approval

	Date	Approved by
Extensions and footings verified	_____	_____
Prices agree with purchase order	_____	_____
Quantities agree with receiving rep.	_____	_____
Credit terms agree with purchase order	_____	_____
Accounts	_____	_____
Approved for payment	_____	_____

b. *Recording transactions in a voucher system:*

(1) An invoice is received and a voucher is prepared by transferring all the pertinent information from the invoice to the voucher.

(2) The voucher with the invoice attached is sent to the appropriate individuals for verification.

(3) After the verification process has been completed, an employee from the accounting department indicates the accounts to be debited and credited.

(4) The voucher is approved by an official who notes that the verification procedures have been completed and the liability is valid.

(5) After approval, the voucher is entered in the voucher register. A voucher register is similar to a purchases journal, but it has more columns for the different types of asset and expense accounts to be debited. Typically a purchases journal records only purchases of inventory or inventory and supplies on account. A voucher register is used to record all types of expenditures. (A voucher register replaces the purchases journal in companies using the voucher system.) All credits in the voucher register consist of a credit to the Vouchers Payable account. Figure 5-8 shows an example of a voucher register.

(6) When payment is made, the date of the payment and the check number are recorded in the voucher register and the check is recorded in the check register. When a voucher system is used, all entries in the check register consist of a debit to Vouchers Payable and a credit to Cash. The check register contains columns for debits to Vouchers Payable, credits to Cash and credits to Purchase Discounts (for use when payment is made within the cash discount period). Figure 5-9 shows an example of a check register.

(7) The column totals from the voucher register and the check register are posted to the general ledger periodically.

(8) Paid vouchers are filed numerically in a special file.

6. *Internal Control of Cash Disbursements:* In order to maintain adequate internal control over cash disbursements, the following steps should be followed:

a. *Payments:* All cash disbursements should be made by check except for minor expenditures paid through a petty cash fund.

b. *Use of prenumbered checks:* Checks should be prenumbered, and any checks which are written incorrectly should be marked *void* and filed in numerical sequence with the other canceled checks. In this way, all check numbers will be accounted for.

c. *Authorized signatures:* The individual who is authorized to sign checks should not have the authority to approve invoices or vouchers for payment or to make entries in the accounting records.

d. *Access to cash:* The individual who records cash disbursements in the accounting records should not have access to cash.

e. *Approval of voucher or invoice:* Checks submitted for signature should be accompanied by an approved voucher or invoice. The

Figure 5-8

Voucher Register

Voucher Number	Date	Name	Payment made Date	Check #	Vouchers payable cr	Purchases dr	Freight In dr	Advertising dr	Utilities dr	Salaries dr	Supplies dr	Repair dr	Other Accts. Acct Name	Debit	Credit
1238	6/01	Arthur	6/05	891	5,232.61	5,232.61									
1239	6/01	Beany	6/05	892	922.00			922.00							
1240	6/02	Jarvis			123.22						123.22				
1241	6/02	McCallum			1,000.00								Rent	1,000.	
1242	6/05	NI Gas			8,322.00				8,332.00						

119

approved voucher or invoice should be stamped *paid* at the time the check is signed. This eliminates the possibility of paying the same invoice twice.

Figure 5-9
Check Register

Date	Check Number	Payee	Voucher Number	Vouchers Payable dr	Purchase Discounts cr	Cash cr
6/05	891	Arthur Wholesaling	1238	5,232.61	104.65	5,127.96
6/05	892	Beany Adv. Co.	1239	922.00		922.00

7. *Cash Over and Short:* Small errors may occur in making change during over-the-counter sales to customers. When this happens, the total of the daily cash register tapes will not be equal to the total cash collected. If there is more cash available than that reported on the total cash register tape (overage), the Cash Over and Short account is credited. If there is less cash available than that reported on the total cash register tape (shortage), the Cash Over and Short account is debited.

EXAMPLE: *Jones Company collected $1,010.25 in cash for over-the-counter sales on March 1. The total cash sales per the cash register tapes on March 1 were $1,011.38. The entry to record the day's sales would be as follows:*

	dr	cr
Cash	1,010.25	
Cash Over and Short	1.13	
Sales		1,011.38

D. **Bank Statements and Cash Balance**

Every month the bank provides each depositor with a bank statement for each bank account. This bank statement includes any checks paid by the bank and charged to the depositor's account and any deposit slips showing amounts that have been credited to the depositor's account. The bank statement is the bank's record of their account payable to the depositor. See Figure 5-10 for an example of a bank statement.

1. *Reconciliation:* When the bank statement is received, the depositor should prepare a reconciliation which explains any differences between the bank statement and the cash account in the ledger. In most circumstances, the balance per the bank statement will not agree with the cash balance per the general ledger. Preparation of a bank reconciliation by a party independent of recording cash, handling cash, or preparing checks is an important internal control tool.

Accounting for Cash

Figure 5-10
Bank Statement

THE FIRST NATIONAL BANK

MONTHLY STATEMENT OF ACCOUNT

PAGE 1

Jones Company
6491 Alameda Drive
Chicago, Illinois 60101

ACCOUNT NUMBER
31-484-6
STATEMENT DATE
11/29/19XA
LAST STATEMENT DATE
10/31/19XA

YOUR LAST CHECKING STATEMENT BALANCE WAS	From Which is Subtracted CHECKS/DEBITS/ PAYMENTS	And Added DEPOSITS/CREDITS/ ADVANCES	YOUR SERVICE CHARGE IS	RESULTING IN A CHECKING BALANCE OF
$10,423.82	$15,633.28	$16,752.41	$5.00	$11,537.95

DATE	CHECKS/DEBITS/PAYMENTS		DEPOSITS/CREDITS/ ADVANCES	BALANCE
11/1	101.23			
11/2	1,320.24			2,423.82
11/3	916.13		4,422.21	
11/5	212.10		33.24	
11/7	98.80			
11/8	100.00		893.26	4,513.17
11/10	87.50			
11/12	3,212.10		105.40	
11/13	108.20			3,123.22
11/14	56.43		157.22	
11/16	82.18			
11/18	99.50		3,310.12	2,100.10
11/19	71.33			
11/21				1,822.16
11/26	63.25 DM		182.84	2,769.94
11/29	5.00 SC			

DM = Debit Memo, NSF Check.
SC = Service Charge

a. *Transactions not recorded by bank:* Transactions could have been recorded by the depositor which have not yet been recorded by the bank. Examples of these types of transactions are:

(1) *Deposits in transit:* Deposits recorded on the books of the depositor and sent to the bank which have not yet been recorded by the bank.

(2) *Outstanding checks:* Checks written and recorded on the books of the depositor which have not yet been paid by the bank and recorded on the books of the bank.

b. *Transactions not recorded by depositor:* Transactions could have been recorded by the bank which have not yet been recorded in the general ledger of the depositor. Examples of these types of transactions are:

(1) *Service charges:* The bank may charge a service charge for

handling the depositor's account. Prior to receiving the bank statement, the depositor has no record of the amount of the service charge and it will not have been recorded on the depositor's books.

(2) *Notes collected by the bank:* The bank might have collected a note receivable for the depositor. If this is done, the bank usually charges a collection fee.

(3) *NSF checks:* NSF checks are nonsufficient funds checks. An NSF check is a check which has been received by the depositor company and deposited in its account. This check was returned to the bank because the account on which the check was written did not contain sufficient funds to cover the amount of the check. The bank returns the check to the depositor along with a debit memo indicating that the depositor's account was reduced by the amount of the check the bank was unable to collect.

(4) *Miscellaneous debit or credit memos:* There may be other miscellaneous types of debit or credit memos not recorded by the depositor, such as check printing costs or stop payment order charges.

2. *Detection and Correction of Errors:* The bank reconciliation may be complete after consideration of the reconciling items discussed in Section D-1. It is possible that the bank or the depositor may have made an error in recording the transactions for the month. If an error was made, it would be necessary to correct the error in order to reconcile the bank statement balance and the general ledger balance. Common types of errors are:

   a. A check or a deposit is recorded with an incorrect amount.

   b. The depositor has more than one bank account and records a check or a deposit in the wrong account.

   c. The bank has made an error. Notify the bank immediately so the error can be corrected. There is no need to make an entry on the depositor's books since they are correct.

   If the depositor made an error in recording a transaction, a correcting journal entry must be made to bring the account balance to the proper amount.

3. *Preparation of a Bank Reconciliation:* A bank reconciliation is a report which explains the difference between the bank's balance shown on the bank statement issued by the bank and the balance shown in the general ledger Cash account. Here is a typical form that may be followed in preparing a bank reconciliation.

Accounting for Cash

BANK RECONCILIATION

Balance per Bank	*Balance per Books*
Add: Deposits in Transit	Add: Notes collected by the bank less service charge
Deduct: Outstanding checks	Deduct: Service charges
Add or Deduct: Bank errors if any	NSF checks
	Other bank debits
	Add/Deduct: Book errors
Adjusted Balance per Bank =	Adjusted Balance per Books

EXAMPLE OF BANK RECONCILIATION: Jones Company received the bank statement shown in Figure 5-10 on December 5, 19XA. They found that the bank had not yet recorded a deposit of $1,322.93 which was mailed on November 28 and that five checks totaling $2,020.89 had not yet been presented to the bank for payment.

The outstanding checks were:

Check Number	*Date*	*Amount*
1933	11/20	$ 33.25
1938	11/25	282.65
1941	11/29	1,050.87
1942	11/29	200.00
1943	11/29	454.12
		$2,020.89

The $63.25 debit memo was for an NSF check issued by G-Var Company to Jones Company. The bookkeeper of Jones Company had recorded check number 1930 to the gas company as $65.43 in the records. The correct amount of the check was $56.43. This type of error is called a transposition error (when two figures of a number are transposed). The difference resulting from a transposition error is always divisible by 9, and this fact can be used to help in locating errors. The bank reconciliation for Jones Company is shown in Figure 5-11.

Figure 5-11
Bank Reconciliation for Jones Company

Balance per bank statement		11,537.95	Balance per books		10,899.24
Add: Deposit in transit		1,322.93	Add: Transposition error		9.00
		12,860.88			
Less:			Less: Service charge	5.00	
Outstanding checks			NSF check	63.25	
No. 1933	$33.25				
No. 1938	288.65		Total		68.25
No. 1941	1,050.87				
No. 1942	200.00				
No. 1943	454.12	$2,020.89			
Adjusted Bank Balance		$10,839.99	Adjusted Book Balance		$10,839.99

4. *Journal Entries to Record Reconciling Items:* The additions and deductions necessary to go from the balance per bank to the adjusted balance per bank and from the balance per books to the adjusted balance per books are called reconciling items. It is necessary to record journal entries for all reconciling items under the Balance Per Books. No journal entries are necessary for the reconciling items which relate to the balance per bank, since they refer to the bank's records rather than the company's records. The journal entries to record the reconciling items on the Jones Company bank reconciliation are as follows:

   a. *Transposition errors:* The transposition error resulted in an overstatement of Utilities Expense of $9.00 and an understatement of Cash of $9.00. The entry to correct the transposition error would be:

	dr	cr
Cash	9.00	
Utilities Expense		9.00

   b. *Service charges:* The service charge was not yet recorded on the books of Jones Company. The entry to record the service charge would be:

	dr	cr
Bank Service Charge Expense	5.00	
Cash		5.00

   c. *NSF check:* The NSF check was originally recorded as a cash receipt. Since there were not sufficient funds to cover the check, it is not really a cash receipt but an account receivable from the customer. Jones Company would make the following entry to record the receipt of the NSF check.

	dr	cr
Accounts Receivable—G-Var	63.25	
Cash		63.25

Accounting for Cash

Chapter 5: Review Questions

PART A: Multiple-Choice Questions

DIRECTIONS: Select the best answer from the four alternatives. Write the letter of your answer in the blank to the left of the number.

_____ 1. The total amount owed by Jones Company to Company X is represented by

   a. the balance in Jones Company's subsidiary accounts payable account for Company X.
   b. the balance in Jones Company's subsidiary accounts receivable account for Company X.
   c. the amount in the general ledger Accounts Payable control account.
   d. the amount in the general ledger Accounts Receivable control account.

_____ 2. Trade discounts are

   a. reductions from the list price of goods which are used in determining selling price.
   b. only allowed if the invoice is paid within a specified time period.
   c. recorded at the time of payment for the goods.
   d. all of the above.

_____ 3. Which of the following items should be classified as cash?

   a. Postage stamps
   b. Certificates of deposit
   c. Money orders
   d. IOUs

_____ 4. When the petty cash fund is reimbursed

   a. petty cash is debited.
   b. petty cash is credited.
   c. cash is debited.
   d. expenses are debited.

_____ 5. Which of the following procedures would not be considered a good internal control procedure for cash?

   a. All cash receipts should be deposited intact daily.
   b. All disbursements should be made by check (except for minor items paid from petty cash)
   c. The person assigned to open cash receipts should restrictively endorse all checks immediately.
   d. The bank reconciliation should be prepared by the same person who records cash receipts and disbursements since this person is familiar with the records.

6. The terms 3/15, n/60 on an invoice mean that

   a. a discount of 15 percent may be taken if the invoice is paid in 60 days.
   b. a discount of 3 percent may be taken if the invoice is paid within 15 days of the invoice date and the net amount of the invoice is due within 60 days.
   c. if the invoice is paid within 60 days, 3/15 of the invoice may be deducted.
   d. a discount of 3 percent may be taken if the invoice is paid by the fifteenth day of the month following the month of purchase.

7. Which of the following procedures should be followed to ensure good internal control over cash disbursements?

   a. Disbursements made from the petty cash fund should be recorded on petty cash vouchers which are signed by the recipient of the cash.
   b. The same individual who signs checks should approve vouchers for payment.
   c. The individual who signs the checks should also record them in the check register.
   d. Vouchers should be stamped paid when the canceled check is returned with the bank statement.

8. Nonsufficient funds checks are

   a. checks that have been canceled by the bank to show that they have been paid.
   b. checks that are guaranteed by the depositor's bank.
   c. checks written by a customer and returned by the bank as uncollectible because there were insufficient funds in the customer's account.
   d. checks issued by a company which have not yet been presented to the bank for payment.

9. A business paper used in summarizing a transaction and approving it for recording and payment is called a/an

   a. invoice.
   b. special journal.
   c. control account.
   d. voucher.

10. The Cash Over and Short account might be used to record

    a. a transposition error made in recording a check in the cash disbursements journal.
    b. a bank service charge.
    c. small errors made in making change in the petty cash fund.
    d. all of the above.

Accounting for Cash

_____ 11. When a voucher system is used

    a. an obligation should not be recorded as a liability until a check is written for payment.
    b. vouchers are prepared only for large invoices.
    c. Petty Cash is debited and Vouchers Payable is credited when the petty cash fund is reimbursed.
    d. all credits in the voucher register are made to the Vouchers Payable account.

_____ 12. Which of the following procedures would not be considered a good internal control procedure for cash?

    a. Use of a voucher system.
    b. Use of a cash register.
    c. Verification of the amount on an invoice before payment.
    d. Checks should be numbered only after they have been written to avoid having a number assigned to a check written incorrectly.

_____ 13. After completing a bank reconciliation, it is necessary to make journal entries to record

    a. errors made by the bank.
    b. all reconciling items.
    c. the reconciling items which explain the difference between the balance per bank and the adjusted balance per bank.
    d. the reconciling items which explain the difference between the balance per books and the adjusted balance per books.

_____ 14. The correct journal entry to record a check returned as NSF by the bank would be

    a. debit Accounts Receivable, credit Cash.
    b. debit Bad Debt Expense, credit Cash.
    c. debit Cash, credit Accounts Receivable.
    d. debit NSF Expense, credit Cash.

PART B: Matching Sets

MATCHING SET 1

Determine which journal (A-E) should be used to record each transaction (15-25). Write the letter of your answer in the blank to the left of each number.

JOURNALS

A. Cash Receipts Journal
B. Cash Disbursements Journal
C. Purchases Journal*
D. Sales Journal
E. General Journal

TRANSACTIONS

_____ 15. Contributions of cash by owners.

_____ 16. Payment of rent.

_____ 17. Purchase of inventory on account.

_____ 18. Purchase of supplies for cash.

_____ 19. Sales of merchandise on account.

_____ 20. Collection of an account receivable.

_____ 21. Sales of merchandise for cash.

_____ 22. Payment of an account payable.

_____ 23. Recording of depreciation expense.

_____ 24. Withdrawals by an owner.

_____ 25. Closing the interest revenue account.

*Assume the purchases journal is used to record only purchases of merchandise and supplies on account.

Accounting for Cash

MATCHING SET 2

Indicate the appropriate location (A-E) for each of the items listed on a company's bank reconciliation (26-32). Write the letter of your answer in the blank to the left of each number.

LOCATIONS

A. Addition to the book balance of cash
B. Deduction from the book balance of cash
C. Addition to the bank statement balance
D. Deduction from the bank statement balance
E. The item should not be included on the bank reconciliation.

ITEMS ON BANK RECONCILIATION

_____ 26. A bank service charge.

_____ 27. A check written by the company but not yet paid or returned by the bank.

_____ 28. A check returned with the bank statement marked *NSF*.

_____ 29. A deposit mailed to the bank on the last day of the year which is not yet recorded on the bank statement.

_____ 30. A check paid by the bank at its correct amount of $350 but recorded in the cash disbursements journal at $530.

_____ 31. A check listed on last month's reconciliation which was paid by the bank this month and returned with this month's statement.

_____ 32. A note collected for the company by the bank.

PART C: Problem Situations

DIRECTIONS: For each of the questions relating to the following problem situations, select the best answer from the four alternatives. Write the letter of your answer in the blank to the left of the number.

Problem 1

Merry Co. purchased items with a list price of $10,000 on May 1, 19XA. Merry Co. was given trade discounts of 20% and 10%. The terms of the invoice were 2/10, n/30.

_____ 33. Assuming that Merry Co. paid the invoice on May 9, the amount of the payment would be

a. $6,860.
b. $9,800.
c. $7,056.
d. $7,200.

_____ 34. Assuming that Merry Co. paid the invoice on June 10, 19XA, the amount of payment would be

a. $10,000.
b. $6,860.
c. $7,056.
d. $7,200.

_____ 35. Assuming that Merry Co. paid the invoice on May 9, the journal entry to record payment would include

a. a debit to Accounts Payable, a debit to Purchase Discounts, and a credit to Cash.
b. a debit to Accounts Payable, a credit to Purchase Discounts, and a credit to Cash.
c. a debit to Cash, a credit to Accounts Payable, and a credit to Purchase Discounts.
d. a debit to Accounts Payable and a credit to Cash.

Accounting for Cash

Problem 2

Good Company wrote a check for $639.25 to Jones Company in payment for office equipment. The bookkeeper erroneously recorded the check in the cash disbursements journal for $369.25. The accounts used were correct; only the amount recorded was in error. The error was discovered when the monthly bank reconciliation was prepared.

_____ 36. The item should be shown on the bank reconciliation as

      a. an addition to the balance per books.
      b. a deduction from the balance per books.
      c. an addition to the balance per bank.
      d. a deduction from the balance per bank.

_____ 37. The journal entry to correct the error would be

      a. a debit to Office Equipment and a credit to Cash for $270.
      b. a debit to Cash and a credit to Office Equipment for $270.
      c. a debit to Error Correction and a credit to Cash for $270.
      d. a debit to Cash and a credit to Error Correction for $270.

_____ 38. This type of error is called

      a. a slide error.
      b. a posting error.
      c. a balancing error.
      d. a transposition error.

Accounting for Cash

Chapter 5: Solutions

PART A: Multiple-Choice Questions

	Answer	Refer to Chapter Section
1.	(a)	[B-2-b]
2.	(a)	[C-2-a]
3.	(c)	[A-1]
4.	(d)	[C-3-c]
5.	(d)	[A-3-b(7)]
6.	(b)	[C-2-b]
7.	(a)	[C-3-b]
8.	(c)	[D-1-b(3)]
9.	(d)	[C-5-a]
10.	(c)	[C-7]
11.	(d)	[C-5-b(5)]
12.	(d)	[A-3 and C-6-b]
13.	(d)	[D-4]
14.	(a)	[D-4-c]

PART B: Matching Sets

MATCHING SET 1

15.	(A)	[B-3-a] Any receipt of cash is recorded in the cash receipts journal.
16.	(B)	[B-3-b]
17.	(C)	[B-3-d]
18.	(B)	[B-3-b] Every disbursement of cash is recorded in the cash disbursements (payments) journal.
19.	(D)	[B-3-c]
20.	(A)	[B-3-a]
21.	(A)	[B-3-a]
22.	(B)	[B-3-b]
23.	(E)	[B-3-e] All adjusting entries are recorded in the general journal.

134   Accounting for Cash

  24. (B)   [B-3-b] Cash withdrawals made by an owner are a disbursement of cash.

  25. (E)   [B-3-e] All closing entries are recorded in the general journal.

MATCHING SET 2

  26. (B)   [D-3]

  27. (D)   [D-3] This is an outstanding check.

  28. (B)   [D-3]

  29. (C)   [D-3] This is a deposit in transit.

  30. (A)   [D-3] Due to the error, cash was reduced by $180 too much when the check was originally recorded. In order to compensate for the error, the cash balance per the books must be increased by $180.

  31. (E)   [D-3] This check was an outstanding check on last month's bank reconciliation, but it is no longer outstanding. It would be checked off in last month's reconciliation.

  32. (A)   [D-3]

PART C: Problem Situations

  33. (c)   [C-2-a, C-2-b] The correct solution is calculated as follows:

$10,000		
− 2,000	($10,000 x .20)	Trade Discount
$ 8,000		
− 800	($8,000 x .10)	Trade Discount
$ 7,200		
− 144	($7,200 x .02)	Cash Discount
$ 7,056		

  34. (d)   [C-2-a, C-2-b] The cash discount is not allowed because the invoice was paid after the cash discount period. The trade discounts would be calculated in the same fashion as they were in question 33.

  35. (b)   [C-2-b]

  36. (b)   [D-3] Due to the error, the book balance of cash is overstated by $270. In order to compensate for the error, the cash account per the books must be decreased by $270.

  37. (a)   [D-4-a] When the original entry was made, the office equipment account was debited for $270 too little and the cash account was credited for $270 too little. A correcting journal entry debiting Office Equipment and crediting Cash for $270 will fully correct the error.

  38. (d)   [D-4-a]

CHAPTER 6

Accounting for Investments

OVERVIEW

This section is intended to introduce the candidate to the basics of accounting for investments. Topics such as bond premium, discount amortization, and the equity method of accounting for investments in common stock are explained in the chapter. It is not important that the candidate fully understand these topics; however, knowledge that the various methods exist and when they are used will be useful.

The candidate should understand the three major categories of investments and the appropriate accounting procedures for each. Accounting for stocks and bonds at cost should be emphasized over the other methods discussed.

DEFINITION OF TERMS

BOND. A debt security issued in stated dollar denominations with a stated interest rate and maturity date. The most commonly stated dollar value is $1,000.

BOND DISCOUNT. The difference between the face value of a bond and the amount it sells for when the bond sells for less than its face value.

BOND PREMIUM. The difference between the face value of a bond and the amount it sells for when the bond sells for more than its face value.

CONSOLIDATED STATEMENTS. The combination of two or more accounting entities into one entity for financial reporting purposes. This is done when one entity possesses a controlling interest over the other entity or entities.

EQUITY METHOD. A method used to account for investments in common stock where the investor has significant control over the operations of the investee.

INVESTMENT. An asset which is not used in the operations of a business but is held in the hope of earning a return on the amount invested.

PARENT COMPANY. A company that owns the majority of the voting stock of another company.

STOCK DIVIDEND. A dividend distributed in the form of additional shares of stock.

SUBSIDIARY COMPANY. A company that is controlled by a parent company.

A. Introduction to Investments

Investments are assets held by a company which are not used in the operations of the business. These assets are held for investment purposes in the hope of earning a return or profit on the amount invested. The treatment of accounting for investments differs depending upon whether the investments are of a short-term or long-term nature.

1. *Short-term Investments:* Short-term investments, which the company intends to hold for less than one operating cycle, are classified as *temporary* investments (or marketable securities). Marketable securities are classified as current assets on the balance sheet.

2. *Long-term Investments:* Long-term investments are investments which are intended to be held for longer than one operating cycle. Long-term investments are classified as *investments* on the balance sheet. There are three basic types of investments: real estate, bonds, and stocks. Bond sinking funds and cash surrender value of life insurance are also classified as long-term investments.

B. Real Estate

Investments in real estate are usually long term in nature. The accounting treatment for investments in real estate is the same whether the investments are of a short-term or long-term nature. An example of a real estate investment would be land held for future development of the business. The land is not currently used in the business but is being held for future expansion. The land would be carried at cost on the records of the business. A gain or loss would be recorded when the land is sold if it is sold for an amount different from its cost.

EXAMPLE: Selzig Corp. holds 10 acres of land for investment purposes. The cost of the land was $100,000. The land is sold for $150,000. The entry to record the sale would be:

	dr	cr
Cash	150,000	
Investment: Land		100,000
Gain on Sale of Land		50,000

To record sale of 10 acres of land held for investment purposes.

Accounting for Investments

C. **Bonds and Interest Income**

Bonds are debt securities issued by the government or a corporation in order to raise large sums of money. Most individual bond certificates have a stated face value of $1,000. Bonds pay interest at a fixed rate based upon the stated face value. Bond interest is normally paid every six months. The fixed interest rate paid by a bond is called the contract rate.

1. *Issuance of Bonds:* When bonds are issued, they may be sold for an amount greater or less than their face value. If a bond sells for less than its stated face value, it is selling at a discount. If it sells for more than its stated face value, it is selling at a premium. Bonds will sell for face value when the contract rate and the market rate are equal.

   a. *Discount:* If the market rate of interest (for bonds of the same quality) at the time the bonds are sold is higher than the contract rate paid by the bonds, the bonds will sell at a discount.

   b. *Premium:* If the market rate of interest at the time the bonds are sold is lower than the coupon (contract) rate paid by the bonds, the bonds will sell at a premium.

2. *Accounting for Bonds and Interest Income:*

   a. *Short-term investments:* Short-term investments in bonds are carried at cost.

   b. *Purchase of bonds between interest dates:* The price paid for a bond includes a portion for purchased interest if the bond is purchased between interest dates. Commissions paid in acquiring a bond are considered to be a part of the cost.

      (1) If a bond is purchased exactly on an interest payment date, the full purchase price is considered to be the cost of the bond (that is, no "interest receivable" is purchased).

      EXAMPLE: *Selzig Corp. sold $10,000 (face value) of bonds to Petit Company. The bonds had a 10% coupon rate and paid interest on December 1 and June 1. Petit Company purchased the bonds on December 1 for $9,558. A $100 broker's commission was paid. The entry to record the bond purchase would be:*

		dr	cr
Dec. 1	Investment in Bonds of Selzig Corp.	9,658	
	Cash		9,658

      To record purchase of $10,000 (face value) of Selzig Corp. bonds for $9,558 plus $100 commission.

(2) If a bond is purchased between interest dates, the buyer must pay the seller for any interest which has accrued on the bond. The buyer then receives the full amount of the interest payment on the next interest payment date.

EXAMPLE: Assume that Petit Company purchased the Selzig Corp. bonds on February 1 instead of on December 1. Petit Company still paid $9,658 for the bonds. However, $166.67 of the purchase price would have been for accrued interest. The interest portion was calculated as follows:

$10,000	Face Value
× .10	Coupon Rate
$ 1,000	Interest per Year
× 2/12	Portion of Year
$166.67	Interest for 2 Months

The entry to record the purchase of the bonds would be:

		dr	cr
Feb. 1	Investment in Bonds	9,491.33	
	Interest Receivable	166.67	
	Cash		9,658.00

When the semiannual interest payment is received, Petit Company would make the following entry:

		dr	cr
June 1	Cash	500.00	
	Interest Receivable		166.67
	Interest Income		333.33

To record semiannual interest receipt ($10,000 × .10 × 6/12 months).

c. *Interest income:* The interest income earned on bonds accrues from day to day. Bond interest is paid every six months. Therefore, it might be necessary to record an adjusting entry to recognize accrued interest receivable at the end of the accounting period.

EXAMPLE: Assume that Petit Company's year end is October 31. The Selzig Corp. bonds pay interest on June 1 and December 1. Petit Company purchased the bonds on December 1. The journal entry to record the June 1 receipt of interest would be:

	dr	cr
Cash	500.00	
Interest Income		500.00

To record semiannual receipt of bond interest ($10,000 × .10 × 6/12 months).

It would be necessary for Petit Company to record an adjusting entry to recognize the interest which has been earned from June 1 through October 31. The adjusting journal entry to record the interest accrual would be:

	dr	cr
Accrued Interest Receivable	416.67	
Interest Income		416.67

To record interest accrued on Selzig bond from June 1 through October 31 ($10,000 × .10 × 5/12 months).

3. *Amortization of Premium or Discount on Long-term Bonds:* A premium or discount is ignored in the measurement of interest revenue for short-term bonds since the bonds are not intended to be held to maturity. The effect of any premium or discount on interest revenue should be recognized when the bonds are to be held for a long period of time. A bond premium or discount results when the market rate of interest is different from the contract rate of interest. The premium or discount paid for the bond effectively adjusts the rate of interest received on the bond to the market rate. Amortization of bond premium or discount is used to adjust the interest received to approximate the effective amount of interest earned on the investment. Amortization of bond premium decreases interest income and amortization of bond discount increases interest income.

   a. *Amortizing bond premium or discount:* When long-term bonds are acquired at a premium or discount, they are recorded at cost. As interest is received over the life of the bond, any premium or discount is amortized. This brings the carrying value (book value) of the bond closer to its face value. By the maturity date of the bond, it will be valued at face value.

   b. *Methods of bond premium or discount amortization:* There are two methods of bond premium or discount amortization: the straight-line method and the effective interest method. The effective interest method is more exact and should be used whenever the difference which results from using the straight-line method instead of the effective interest method is material. The straight-line method is illustrated in the two examples that follow:

   EXAMPLE: *Ryan Company purchased $200,000 (face value) of Jones Corporation bonds for $210,000 on January 1, 19XA. A total bond premium of $10,000 was paid. The bonds pay 10% interest on January 1 and July 1. The bonds are due in 10 years. The entry to record the purchase of the bonds would be:*

		dr	cr
Jan. 1	Investment in Bonds	210,000	
	Cash		210,000

Purchased 200 10% bonds of Ryan Company.

The entries to record the interest receipt on July 1 would be as follows:

	dr	cr
July 1 Cash	10,000	
Interest Income		10,000

To record receipt of semiannual interest payment (200,000 × .10 × 1/2).

	dr	cr
July 1 Interest Income	500	
Investment in Bonds		500

To amortize 1/20 of the $10,000 bond premium.

Since Ryan Company paid more than $200,000 for the bonds, the effective interest rate which they are receiving on the bonds is less than 10%. The amortization of the bond premium reflects this reality. Ryan Company's year end is December 31. It is necessary for them to prepare the following adjusting entries on December 31:

	dr	cr
Dec. 31 Accrued Interest Receivable	10,000	
Interest Income		10,000

To accrue bond interest income through December 31.

	dr	cr
Dec. 31 Interest Income	500	
Investment in Bonds		500

To amortize 1/20 of the $10,000 bond premium.

EXAMPLE: Assume Ryan Company purchased $200,000 (face value) of Jones Corporation bonds for $190,000 on January 1, 19XA. The bonds pay 10% interest on January 1 and July 1. The bonds are due in 10 years. The total amount of the bond discount is $10,000. The entries to record the investment in the bonds for the first year would be:

	dr	cr
Jan. 1 Investment in Bonds	190,000	
Cash		190,000

To record purchase of 100 Jones Corp. Bonds.

July 1 Cash	10,000	
Interest Income		10,000

To record semiannual interest receipt.

July 1	Investment in Bonds	500	
	Interest Income		500

To amortize 1/20 of $10,000 bond discount.

Dec. 31	Accrued Interest Receivable	10,000	
	Interest Income		10,000

To accrue interest through December 31.

Dec. 31	Investment in Bonds	500	
	Interest Income		500

To amortize 1/20 of $10,000 bond discount.

4. *Accounting for Sale of Bond Investment:*

   a. *Sale of bonds at maturity:* If bonds are held to maturity, the holder receives the face value of the bonds from the company which issued the bonds.

   b. *Sale of bonds prior to maturity:* If a bond investment is sold prior to its maturity date, a gain or loss will probably occur. If the bonds are sold between interest dates, the purchaser must pay the seller for any interest which has accrued. If the bonds are classified as long term, any premium or discount on the bonds should be amortized up to the date of sale. There is no premium or discount amortization recorded for short-term bond investments. Any selling commission should be deducted from the selling price of the bonds.

   EXAMPLE: ABC Co. held $10,000 (face value) of XYZ Corp. bonds. The bonds were purchased at face value. The coupon rate of interest is 15%, and the bonds pay interest on April 1 and October 1. ABC Co. sold the bonds on May 1 for $10,750. A sales commission of $50 was paid. The entry to record the sale would be:

		dr	cr
May 1	Cash	10,700	
	Investment in Bonds		10,000
	Interest Revenue		125
	Gain on Sale of Bonds		575

   To record sale of 10 XYZ Corp. bonds for $10,750 less a broker's commission of $50. Accrued interest was $125.

D. **Stocks and Dividend Income**

   1. *Recording Investment in Stock:* Investments in stock are usually recorded at cost. Commissions paid in acquiring stocks are considered to be part of the cost of the stock.

a. *Short-term investment:* Short-term investments in stock of other companies are called marketable equity securities. Marketable equity securities are recorded in the balance sheet at the lower of cost or market. Short-term investments in stock are valued at cost in the balance sheet unless the aggregate market value of all short-term equity securities is less than their cost. If the aggregate market value is less than cost, the securities are valued at market.

EXAMPLE: Jones Corporation has the following portfolio of marketable equity securities:

	Cost	Market
Equity Security 1	$100,000	$ 90,000
Equity Security 2	150,000	170,000
Equity Security 3	50,000	30,000
Equity Security 4	60,000	60,000
Total	$360,000	$350,000

Since the total market value of the portfolio is less than the total cost, the marketable equity securities would be reported in the balance sheet at the cost of $360,000 less an allowance for decline in market value of $10,000 to yield a carrying amount of $350,000. Note that the carrying amount is based on the comparison of total cost and total market value of the portfolio, rather than the lower of cost or market for each individual equity security.

b. *Long-term investment:* Long-term investments in stock are accounted for differently depending upon the amount of stock which the investor owns and the resulting amount of control which the investor can exercise over the operations of the investee. This amount of control is measured by the percentage of the investee's voting common stock which is owned by the investor. The three classifications which are used in accounting are:

(1) *Ownership of more than 50 percent of common stock:* The investor owns greater than 50 percent of the voting stock of the investee corporation. (Usually common stock is the stock which confers the right to vote.) In this case, the investor is said to own a controlling interest in the investee, and the financial statements of the two companies are combined into a *consolidated* set of financial statements by the parent company. When financial statements are consolidated, the two accounting entities are treated as if they were one accounting entity for financial statement purposes. The investor company which owns more than 50 percent of the voting stock in the investee company is called the *parent company*. The investee company which is controlled by the parent company is called the *subsidiary company*. The procedures for consolidating financial statements are beyond the scope of this module.

(2) *Ownership of 20 to 50 percent of common stock:* The investor owns between 20 and 50 percent of the investee's voting stock. In this case, the investor is *assumed* to have significant influence over the operations of the investee corporation. Due to the assumption of significant influence, the investor should account for the investment using the equity method. Under the equity method, the investment is originally recorded at cost. When the investee corporation reports earnings, the investor recognizes its share of the investee's reported earnings by debiting the Investment account and crediting Earnings. The amount recorded is based on the percentage of the stock held by the investor. Dividends and the investor's proportionate share of net losses are recorded as a reduction in the investment account. The earnings or loss account recorded by the investor for its proportionate share of the investee's income is shown on the income statement as investment income or loss.

EXAMPLE: In January, 19XA, James Co. purchased 2,000 shares (25%) of PRO, Inc. common stock for a total cost of $80,320. The entry to record the purchase on James Co.'s books is:

		dr	cr
Jan. 1	Investment in PRO, Inc.	80,320	
	Cash		80,320

Purchased 2,000 shares of stock.

On December 31, 19XA, PRO, Inc. reported net income of $100,000. The entry to record James Co.'s share of PRO, Inc.'s net income is:

		dr	cr
Dec. 31	Investment in PRO, Inc	.25,000	
	Earnings from Investment		
	in PRO, Inc		.25,000

To record 25% equity in PRO, Inc.'s net income of $100,000.

On January 20, 19XB, PRO, Inc. paid James Co. $5,000 in dividends. (The total dividend declaration was $20,000.) The entry to record the receipt of the dividend is:

		dr	cr
Jan. 20	Cash	5,000	
	Investment in PRO, Inc.		5,000

To record receipt of dividends paid by PRO, Inc.

On December 31, 19XB, PRO, Inc. reported a net loss of $28,000. The entry to record James Co.'s share of PRO, Inc.'s net loss is:

	dr	cr
Dec. 31 Loss from Investment in PRO, Inc.	7,000	
Investment in PRO, Inc.		7,000

To record 25% equity in PRO, Inc.'s net loss of $28,000.

(3) *Ownership of less than 20 percent of common stock:* The investor owns less than 20 percent of the voting stock of the investee corporation. When less than 20 percent of the common stock is owned, the investor is assumed to have little influence over the operations of the investee. In this case, the investment is accounted for at cost using the lower of cost or market. If the aggregate market value of the long-term investment portfolio declines below the aggregate cost of the portfolio, long-term investments should be valued in the balance sheet at market. Lower of cost or market for long-term investments is similar to that for short-term marketable securities. See Section D-1 of this chapter. Lower of cost or market is used to satisfy the conservatism principle.

(4) *Ownership of preferred stock:* Investments in preferred stock are accounted for at cost using lower of cost or market.

2. *Recording Dividend Income:*

   a. *Recording receipt of dividends:* Dividend income does not accrue as interest income does. Dividends are income when received by the investor and are usually not recorded until they are received. The entry to record the receipt of dividends when stock ownership is less than 20 percent is:

	dr	cr
Cash	XXX	
Dividend Income		XXX

   b. *Recording receipt of stock dividends:* Stock dividends are distributions in the form of additional shares of stock instead of cash. Stock dividends do not represent income to the recipient. The investor apportions the original cost of the shares over the new total amount of shares owned.

   EXAMPLE: If XYZ Corp. owned 1,000 shares of Ajax Corp. common stock and a 5% stock dividend was paid by Ajax Corp., XYZ Corp. would receive an additional 50 shares of Ajax Corp. stock.

Accounting for Investments

Assume that XYZ Corp. paid $10,000 for the 1,000 shares which it originally owned. After the stock dividend is received, that $10,000 is apportioned over the new number of shares owned ($10,000/1,050 shares = $9.524). The new cost per share of stock would be approximately $9.524 per share. If any of the shares of stock are sold after the stock dividend is received, the gain or loss on the sale must be computed using the new cost of $9.524 per share.

3. *Sale of Investments in Stock:* When an investment in stock is sold, the book value of the investment (which in most cases is cost) is compared to the selling price in order to determine any gain or loss on the sale. Any selling commissions are treated as a deduction from the total selling price.

EXAMPLE: Jones Corporation sold 10 shares of Baines Corp. common stock for $1,000. The carrying value of the stock was $800 which was its cost. Selling commissions on the sale amounted to $25. The journal entry to record the sale would be:

	dr	cr
Cash	975	
Investment in Baines Corp. Stock		800
Gain on Sale of Stock		175

To record sale of 10 shares of Baines Corp. stock for $100/share less $25 broker's commission.

Accounting for Investments

Chapter 6: Review Questions

PART A: Multiple-Choice Questions

DIRECTIONS: Select the best answer from the four alternatives. Write the letter of your answer in the blank to the left of the number. (For simplicity, when calculating interest in this set of questions, assume 360 days per year and 30 days per month.)

__c__ 1. A long-term debt security which normally has a face value of $1,000 and pays semiannual interest at a stated rate is called a/an

  a. note.
  b. account receivable.
  c. bond.
  d. preferred stock.

__b__ 2. If bonds are sold between interest dates

  a. the seller must pay the buyer the accrued interest to the date of sale.
  b. the buyer must pay the seller the accrued interest to the date of sale.
  c. the bonds will sell at a premium.
  d. the seller is allowed to deduct the interest which accrued prior to the date of purchase from the next semiannual interest payment.

__b__ 3. When a bond sells for more than its face value, the difference between the face value of the bond and the selling price is called

  a. bond discount.
  b. bond premium.
  c. additional paid-in debt.
  d. amortization.

_____ 4. When bonds receivable which were purchased at a discount are classified as long-term investments

  a. the bond investment account should be debited for the face value of the bonds purchased.
  b. the carrying value of the bonds (the book value in the investment account) will remain unchanged over the life of the bond.
  c. any discount on the purchase of the bond should be amortized over the life of the bond.
  d. accrual of bond interest at year end is not necessary.

_a_   5. Land held by a business for future sale should be valued in the balance sheet at

   a. cost.
   b. lower of cost or market.
   c. market value.
   d. replacement cost.

_____   6. Puscas Co. purchased 10 shares of Schmaus Co. common stock for $100 per share. Puscas Co. paid a $50 brokerage commission on this transaction. The investment account should be debited for

   a. $150.
   b. $950.
   c. $1,000.
   d. $1,050.

_c_   7. Short-term marketable equity securities should be reported in the balance sheet at

   a. cost.
   b. market value.
   c. lower of cost or market.
   d. replacement cost.

_b_   8. A real estate investment which had a book value of $20,000 was sold for $22,000. The journal entry to record the sale would include

   a. a credit to Cash for $22,000.
   b. a credit to a gain account for $2,000.
   c. a debit to the Investment account for $20,000.
   d. a debit to Cash for $20,000.

_a_   9. When the equity method is used to account for an investment in another company

   a. the investor is assumed to have significant influence over the operations of the investee.
   b. dividends are recorded as income.
   c. the basis of the investment on the company's books remains at cost.
   d. dividends are recorded by the investor company as an increase in the investment account.

_c_   10. A company that owns more than 50 percent of the voting stock of another corporation is called the

   a. primary company.
   b. subsidiary company.
   c. parent company.
   d. controlling company.

Accounting for Investments

11. Bart Co. sold 10 shares of Ajax Corporation preferred stock for $826 in cash. The carrying value of the stock on Bart Co.'s books was $900. Selling commissions on the transaction were $30. The journal entry to record the sale would be:

	dr	cr
a. Loss on Sale of Stock	44	
Commissions Expense	30	
Cash	826	
Investment in Ajax Corp.		900
b. Investment in Ajax Corp.	900	
Cash		826
Gain on Sale of Stock		74
c. Cash	826	
Loss on Sale of Stock	74	
Investment in Ajax Corp.		900
d. Cash	796	
Loss on Sale of Stock	104	
Investment in Ajax Corp.		900

12. Financial statements which combine the results of a parent company with its subsidiaries for financial reporting purposes are called

    a. parent statements.
    b. consolidated statements.
    c. combined statements.
    d. subsidiary statements.

13. Which of the following items would not be classified as a long-term investment?

    a. Bond sinking fund.
    b. An investment in bonds which is expected to be held for more than one year.
    c. A building used in the business.
    d. Land held for future expansion of the business.

14. Which of the following statements about dividend income is true?

    a. Dividends are recorded as income regardless of the percentage of voting stock of the investee held by the investor.
    b. Dividends should be accrued at year end based on historical dividend rates.
    c. Dividends are considered to be income when they are received by the investor company if the investor owns less than 20 percent of the voting shares of the investee.
    d. Stock dividends increase the basis per share of stock owned by the investor.

15. Axel Co. owned 400 shares of common stock which were purchased for $4,400. Axel Co. received a common stock dividend of 40 shares of this stock. What was the carrying value per share of stock after the stock dividend was received?

   a. $11
   b. $110
   c. $9
   d. $10

PART B: Matching Sets

MATCHING SET 1

Determine which method of accounting for long-term investments in stock (A-C) is appropriate for each of the investments listed (16-20). Assume that common stock is the only form of voting stock outstanding. Write the letter of your answer in the blank to the left of the number.

METHODS OF ACCOUNTING

A. Lower of Cost or Market
B. Equity Method
C. Consolidation

INVESTMENTS

16. Morrisey Co. owns 62 percent of the common stock of Bell Co.

17. Burns Co. owns 23 percent of the common stock of Lyle Co.

18. Alexander Co. owns 10 percent of the common stock of Merry Merry Music Co.

19. Jones Co. owns 48 percent of the common stock of Long Co.

20. Sun Co. owns 22 percent of the preferred stock of Line Co.

Accounting for Investments   151

MATCHING SET 2

For each of the long-term bond investment transactions listed (21-23), determine whether the bonds will sell at a premium, at a discount, or for face value (A-C). Write the letter of your answer in the blank to the left of the number.

BASIS FOR SALE

A. The bonds will sell at a premium.
B. The bonds will sell at a discount.
C. The bonds will sell at face value.

INVESTMENT TRANSACTIONS

_____ 21. ABC Co. purchases bonds issued by XYZ Co. The bonds have a contract rate of interest of 10 percent. The market rate of interest for investments of similar risk is 10 percent.

_____ 22. ABC Co. purchases bonds issued by XYZ Co. The bonds have a contract rate of 10 percent. The market rate of interest for investments of similar risk is 9 percent.

_____ 23. ABC Co. purchased bonds issued by XYZ Co. The bonds have a contract rate of 10 percent. The market rate for investments of similar risk is 11 percent.

PART C: Problem Situations

DIRECTIONS: For each of the questions relating to the following problem situations, select the best answer from the four alternatives. Write your answer in the blank to the left of the number. (For simplicity, when calculating interest in this set of questions, assume 360 days per year and 30 days per month.)

Problem 1

Assume Kan Co. purchased $300,000 of Lily Corp. 12% bonds for face value on April 1, 19XA. The bonds pay interest on January 1 and July 1. Kan Co.'s year end is August 31.

_____ 24. The total amount of cash which Kan Co. paid for the bonds on April 1 was

a. $300,000.
b. $318,000.
c. $291,000.
d. $309,000.

25. The amount of the interest payment Kan Co. will receive on July 1 is

   a. $18,000.
   b. $ 9,000.
   c. $36,000.
   d. $18,540.

26. The adjusting entry which Kan Co. should make on August 31 is:

   a. Debit Bond Interest Receivable and credit Bond Interest Revenue for $6,000.
   b. Debit Bond Interest Revenue and credit Bond Interest Receivable for $6,000.
   c. Debit Bond Interest Receivable and credit Bond Interest Revenue for $9,000.
   d. No adjusting entry should be made.

Problem 2

On January 1, 19XA, Box Co. purchased 5,000 shares (40%) of Bag Co.'s common (voting) stock for a total cost of $100,000. On December 31, 19XA, Bag Co. reported net income of $100,000. On January 5, 19XB, Bag Co. declared a $10,000 dividend on its common stock.

27. The entry to record the purchase of Bag Co. stock by Box Co. would be:

   a. Debit Cash and credit Investment in Bag Co. for $100,000.
   b. Debit Investment in Bag Co. and credit Cash for $100,000.
   c. Debit Investment in Bag Co. and credit Cash for $40,000.
   d. None of the above.

28. The entry to record the receipt of the dividend by Box Co. would be:

   a. Debit Cash and credit Dividend Income for $10,000.
   b. Debit Cash and credit Dividend Income for $4,000.
   c. Debit Cash and credit Investment in Bag Co. for $4,000.
   d. Debit Cash and credit Investment in Bag Co. for $10,000.

29. The entry by Box Co. to record the earnings of Bag Co. would be:

   a. Debit Investment in Bag Co. and credit Earnings from Investment in Bag Co. for $40,000.
   b. Debit Investment in Bag Co. and credit Earnings from Investment in Bag Co. for $100,000.
   c. Debit Cash and credit Earnings from Investment in Bag Co. for $40,000.
   d. No journal entry would be made to recognize Bag Co.'s income.

Accounting for Investments 153

___d___

30. Jayne Co. has the following portfolio of marketable equity securities:

	Cost	Market
Equity Security 1	$ 5,000	$ 6,000
Equity Security 2	10,000	5,000
Equity Security 3	6,000	6,000

The marketable equity securities should be reported on the balance sheet at

a. $21,000.
b. $16,000.
c. $19,000.
d. $17,000.

Accounting for Investments

Chapter 6: Solutions

PART A: Multiple-Choice Questions

	Answer	Refer to Chapter Section
1.	(c)	[C]
2.	(b)	[C-2-b(2)]
3.	(b)	[C-1]
4.	(c)	[C-3-a]
5.	(a)	[B]

6. (d) [D-1] Commissions paid in acquiring stock are included as part of the cost of the stock.

Cash paid for the stock	$1,000	($10 x 100)
+ Commission paid	50	
Amount to be debited	$1,050	

7. (c) [D-1-a]

8. (b) [B]

Selling Price	$22,000
- Book Value	−20,000
Gain on Sale	$ 2,000

The entry to record the transaction would be:

	dr	cr
Cash	22,000	
Gain on Sale of Investment		2,000
Investment		20,000

9. (a) [D-1-b(2)]

10. (c) [D-1-b(1)]

11. (d) [D-3]

Selling Price	$826
− Selling Commission	−30
Amount for computing gain or loss	$796
Book Value	$900
− Proceeds	−796
Loss on Sale	$104

12.	(b)	[D-1-b(1)]
13.	(c)	[A]
14.	(c)	[D-2-a and D-1-b(2)]
15.	(d)	[D-2-b]

$$\frac{\text{Total Original Cost}}{\text{Total Number of Shares Owned after Stock Dividend}} = \text{Cost per Share}$$

$$\frac{\$4,400}{440} = \$10$$

PART B: Matching Sets

MATCHING SET 1

16.	(C)	[D-1-b(1)]
17.	(B)	[D-1-b(2)]
18.	(A)	[D-1-b(3)]
19.	(B)	[D-1-b(2)]
20.	(A)	[D-1-b(4)]

MATCHING SET 2

21.	(C)	[C-1]
22.	(A)	[C-1-b]
23.	(B)	[C-1-a]

PART C: Problem Situations

24. (d) [C-2-b(2)] Since the bonds were purchased between interest dates, Kan Co. had to pay for the accrued interest as well as the face value of the bonds.

$300,000   Face Value
   9,000   Accrued Interest ($300,000 x .12 x 3/12)
$309,000

25. (a) [C-2-b(2)] The amount of the semiannual interest payment is $18,000 ($300,000 x .12 x 6/12).

Accounting for Investments

26. (a) [C-2-c] Kan Co. must make an adjusting entry to accrue the interest earned for the months of July and August. The computation of accrued interest is $300,000 \times .12 \times 2/12 = \$6,000$. This entry would debit Bond Interest Receivable and credit Bond Interest Revenue.

27. (b) [D-1-b(2)]

28. (c) [D-1-b(2)] Dividends reduce the investment account under the equity method. Box Company's share of the dividend was $4,000 ($10,000 × .40). The entry would include a debit to Cash and a credit to Investment in Bag Co.

29. (a) [D-1-b(2)] Under the equity method, the investor records its proportionate share of the investee's net income as an increase in the investment account. Box Company's share of Bag Company's net income is $40,000 ($100,000 × .40).

30. (d) [D-1-a]

	Cost	Market
Equity Security 1	$ 5,000	$ 6,000
Equity Security 2	10,000	5,000
Equity Security 3	6,000	6,000
Totals	$21,000	$17,000

Since the aggregate market value of the portfolio as a whole is less than the aggregate cost, marketable equity securities should be reported on the balance sheet at market value of $17,000.

CHAPTER 7
Accounting for Inventories

OVERVIEW

This chapter is intended to introduce the candidate to the accounting procedures used in valuing and recording inventories. Inventories are often one of the most important and largest current assets held by a company. Therefore, an understanding of the area is important.

The candidate should understand the three methods of pricing inventories, how to apply the lower of cost or market theory, how to determine cost of goods sold, and the effects which inventory valuation and inventory errors have on net income. The candidate should thoroughly review the periodic inventory system.

DEFINITION OF TERMS

FIFO. The *first-in, first-o*ut method of valuing inventory which assumes that the earliest units purchased are sold first and that ending inventory is made up of the latest purchases.

GROSS PROFIT METHOD. A method of inventory estimation which is based on the use of the past gross profit percentage experienced by the company.

LIFO. The *last-in, first-o*ut method of valuing inventory which assumes that the latest units purchased are sold first and that ending inventory is made up of the earliest units purchased.

LOWER OF COST OR MARKET. The rule that requires certain assets (such as inventory and temporary investments) be recorded at market value if their

159

market value is below their cost.

PERIODIC INVENTORY SYSTEM. A system of accounting for inventory which requires the use of a physical count of inventory at the end of the accounting period in order to determine ending inventory and to calculate cost of goods sold.

PERPETUAL INVENTORY SYSTEM. A system of accounting for inventory which maintains a continuous record of all inventory transactions.

WEIGHTED-AVERAGE METHOD. The method that uses a weighted-average unit cost to value ending inventory and cost of goods sold.

A. Types of Inventory Systems

1. *Perpetual Inventory Systems:* When a perpetual inventory system is used, a continuous record is maintained of all inventory transactions.

    a. *Merchandise inventory account:* A Merchandise Inventory account is kept. Inventory purchases are recorded as increases in the Inventory account, and sales of inventory are recorded as decreases in the Inventory account. The cost of goods sold is recorded as units are sold.

    b. *Use of perpetual inventory system:* A perpetual inventory system is often used by businesses which sell merchandise with a high per unit value. Manufacturing firms often use a perpetual inventory system since they need accurate and timely information about costs. As computers make the processing of data easier, more companies are using perpetual inventory systems.

    EXAMPLE: Assume that Nelson Co., which sells minicomputers, has 10 units of inventory on hand on January 1, 19XA. These 10 units originally cost $10,000. The 10 units would be included in the Merchandise Inventory account.

    Merchandise Inventory

1/1/XA	10,000		
2/2	7,700	6,000	2/10
Balance	11,700		

    Cost of Goods Sold

2/10	6,000	

    On February 2, 19XA, the company purchased seven more units at $1,100 each. The journal entry to record the purchase would be:

			dr	cr
Feb. 2	Merchandise Inventory		7,700	
	Accounts Payable			7,700
	Purchased 7 units of inventory			
	P.O. #2182			

On February 10, 19XA, the company sold six of the original ten units for $2,500 each. The entries to record this transaction would be:

		dr	cr
Feb. 10	Accounts Receivable	15,000	
	Sales		15,000

To record sale of six units.

Feb. 10	Cost of Goods Sold	6,000	
	Merchandise Inventory		6,000

To record cost of goods sold for 6 units sold on February 10.

    c. *End-of-period inventory procedure:* At the end of the period, the balance in the Inventory account should represent the cost of the inventory which is on hand. The Cost of Goods Sold account should contain the cost of all units sold during the period. A periodic physical count of inventory is taken to verify the balance of the Inventory account. This count will reveal any "shrinkage."

2. *Periodic Inventory Systems:* When a periodic inventory system is used, purchases of inventory are recorded in a Purchases account. Ending inventory is determined by taking a physical count of the goods on hand at the end of the period. A value is then determined for the ending inventory which is on hand. The cost of goods sold is computed by subtracting the ending inventory from the goods available for sale. Goods available for sale is determined by adding total purchases for the period to the beginning inventory.

    a. *Use of a periodic inventory system:* Many businesses which sell a variety of low-cost items use a periodic inventory system. A perpetual inventory system is more difficult and costly to maintain than a periodic inventory system.

        EXAMPLE: Use the same facts as in the previous example, with the Nelson Co. using a periodic inventory system. The beginning inventory consists of 10 units which cost $10,000.

Merchandise Inventory	
Bal 1/1 10,000	

Purchases	
2/2 7,700	

The entry to record the purchase on February 2 would be as follows:

		dr	cr
2/2	Purchases	7,700	
	Accounts Payable		7,700

To record purchase of 7 units of inventory P.O. #2182.

The entry to record the sale on February 10 would be as follows:

		dr	cr
2/10	Accounts Receivable	15,000	
	Sales		15,000

To record sale of six units.

b. *Merchandise inventory account:* When a periodic system is used, the Merchandise Inventory account remains unchanged for the period. Purchases of inventory are recorded in the Purchases account, and no entry is made which affects inventory when a sale is made.

EXAMPLE: Assume that Nelson Co. made no other purchases or sales during the month of February. Financial statements will be prepared as of February 28. In order to do so, a physical count of the inventory must be taken to determine the quantity on hand. The physical count indicated that 11 units were on hand. Nelson Co. assumed that these 11 units were made up of the seven units purchased on February 2 and four units from beginning inventory (FIFO). The value of the ending inventory ($11,700) was calculated as follows:

```
 7 units @ $1,000 = $ 7,700
 4 units @ $1,000 =   4,000
11 units          = $11,700
```

In order to determine cost of goods sold, Nelson Co. made the following calculation:

Accounting for Inventories

Beginning Inventory	$10,000
+ Purchases	7,700
= Goods Available for Sale	$17,700
− Ending Inventory	11,700
= Cost of Goods Sold	$ 6,000

B. Inventory Pricing

In order to value ending inventory, the company must make an assumption about the cost flow of the goods out of the inventory account. Four basic inventory cost flow assumptions are used in accounting: FIFO, LIFO, weighted average, and specific identification. (The implementation of various cost-flow assumptions with a perpetual inventory system will not be discussed in this module.)

1. *FIFO (First-In, First-Out):* When a FIFO inventory pricing assumption is used, the units purchased first are assumed to be the first units sold. The units left in ending inventory are made up of the units purchased last.

   EXAMPLE: Petit Company uses a periodic inventory system and uses the FIFO method of inventory pricing. The periodic inventory count indicated that 60 units were on hand on January 31. The January 31 inventory valuation and cost of goods sold for January is calculated as follows:

   Units Available for Sale:

   50 units from beginning inventory @ $2.00/unit
   20 units from January 3 purchase @ $2.20/unit
   30 units from January 5 purchase @ $2.30/unit
   50 units from January 30 purchase @ $2.50/unit
   150 units available

   If there are 60 units in ending inventory, then 90 units must have been sold. Using a FIFO pricing assumption, the cost of goods sold would be calculated in this way:

50 units in beginning inventory @ $2.00/unit	$100.00
20 units from January 3 purchase @ $2.20/unit	44.00
20 units from January 5 purchase @ $2.30/unit	46.00
	$190.00

   Ending Inventory:

10 units from January 5 purchase @ $2.30/unit	$ 23.00
50 units from January 30 purchase @ $2.50/unit	125.00
	$148.00

2. *LIFO (Last-In, First-Out):* When a LIFO inventory pricing assumption is used, the units purchased last are assumed to be the first units sold. The units remaining in ending inventory consist of the units which were acquired earliest.

EXAMPLE: *Using the facts in the previous example, assume that Petit Co. now uses a LIFO inventory pricing assumption. The January 31 inventory and cost of goods sold for January would be calculated as follows:*

Units Available for Sale:

    50 units from beginning inventory @ $2.00/unit
    20 units from January 3 purchase @ $2.20/unit
    30 units from January 5 purchase @ $2.30/unit
    <u>50</u> units from January 30 purchase @ $2.50/unit
    150 units available

Using a LIFO pricing assumption, the cost of goods sold would be calculated in this way:

50 units from January 30 purchase @ $2.50/unit	$125.00
30 units from January 5 purchase @ $2.30/unit	69.00
10 units from January 3 purchase @ $2.20/unit	22.00
	$216.00

Ending Inventory:

50 units from beginning inventory @ $2.00/unit	$100.00
10 units from January 3 purchase @ $2.20/unit	22.00
	$122.00

Note: The IRS requires that if LIFO is used for income tax purposes, it *must* be used for financial reporting purposes. In Canada, LIFO is not acceptable for income tax purposes.

3. *Weighted Average:* When a weighted-average inventory pricing assumption is used, a weighted-average unit cost is determined by dividing the cost of goods available for sale by the total units available for sale (units in beginning inventory + total units purchased). The cost of ending inventory is determined by multiplying the total number of units in the ending inventory by the weighted-average unit cost. The cost of the units sold is determined by multiplying the number of units sold by the weighted-average unit cost.

EXAMPLE: *Using the facts in the previous example, assume that the Petit Company uses the weighted-average inventory pricing assumption. The January 31 inventory valuation and the cost of goods sold for January would be determined as follows:*

	Units Available for Sale		Cost of Goods Available for Sale
Beginning inventory	50 units x $2.00	=	$100.00
January 3 purchase	20 units x $2.20	=	44.00
January 5 purchase	30 units x $2.30	=	69.00
January 30 purchase	<u>50</u> units x $2.50	=	<u>125.00</u>
	150 units		$338.00

The weighted-average unit cost is computed as follows:

$$\frac{\text{Cost of Goods Available for Sale}}{\text{Units Available for Sale}} = \frac{\$338.00}{150.00} = \$2.2533\text{/unit}$$

The cost of goods sold would be calculated as follows:

Units available for sale	150
− Units in ending inventory	60
= Units sold	90

Cost of Goods Sold = Units Sold × Weighted Average per Unit Cost
$202.80   = 90 units × $2.2533/unit
Ending Inventory = 60 units × $2.2533/unit = $135.20

4. *Specific Identification:* When a company is able to identify each item in inventory with a specific purchase, specific invoice prices may be used to assign costs to the units in ending inventory.

EXAMPLE: Using the facts in the previous example, assume that Petit Co. now uses specific invoice prices to cost ending inventory. Of the 60 units in ending inventory, they have determined that 30 units are from the January 30 purchase, 20 units are from the January 5 purchase, and 10 units are from the January 3 purchase.

Ending inventory would be valued as follows:

30 units @ $2.50/unit	=	$75.00
20 units @ 2.30/unit	=	46.00
10 units @ 2.20/unit	=	22.00
Total ending inventory	=	$143.00

Cost of goods sold:

50 units @ $2.00/unit	=	$100.00
10 units @ 2.20/unit	=	22.00
10 units @ 2.30/unit	=	23.00
20 units @ 2.50/unit	=	50.00
Cost of goods sold	=	$195.00

C. **Applying Lower of Cost or Market**

Inventory is normally reported in the balance sheet at cost. If a permanent decline in the value of the inventory occurs, the conservatism principle requires that the inventory be reported at a lower value than cost. A permanent decline in the value of inventory may occur when the goods become obsolete, damaged, or shopworn or if there is a general price decline for goods of that type. When the market value of inventory is lower than its cost, the inventory should be reported at its market value.

1. *Cost of Inventory:* The historical cost of the inventory is used as the cost of goods included in the inventory.

2. *Market Value of Inventory:* In accounting, the market value of inventory is determined in one of the following ways:

a. *Replacement cost:* Replacement cost is the amount for which the goods could be purchased on the market today.

b. *Net realizable value:* The net realizable value (NRV) is equal to the selling price of the inventory less the cost of marketing it.

   NRV = Selling Price - Cost of Marketing
   NRV = Market Value Ceiling

   The net realizable value is considered to be the *ceiling* for the market price, that is, the market value is not allowed to go above NRV.

c. *Net realizable value less a normal profit margin:* The net realizable value less a normal profit margin which would be earned on the inventory is another method of determining the market value of inventory.

   NRV - Normal Profit = Market Value Floor

   The NRV less normal profit is considered to be the *floor* for the market price, that is, market value is not allowed to go below NRV less a normal profit margin.

   Market value is defined as replacement cost unless replacement cost is higher than NRV or lower than NRV less a normal profit margin.

   (1) If replacement cost is higher than NRV, NRV should be used as the market price to be compared with the cost.

   (2) If replacement cost is lower than NRV less a normal profit margin, NRV less a normal profit should be used as the market price to be compared with the cost.

   Note: Market value to be chosen is the middle amount among replacement cost, net realizable value (the ceiling), and net realizable value less a normal profit margin (the floor).

   EXAMPLE 1: *ABC Company has 2,000 units of inventory on hand. The cost of each unit was $9. There has been a general price decline for this type of item so the inventory should be valued at the lower of cost or market. ABC Company used the following information in order to determine the market value to be compared with the cost:*

Unit Cost	$ 9
Replacement Cost	7
Selling Price	10
Cost of Marketing	2
Normal Profit per Unit	2

ABC Company then determined the market price to be $7 as follows:

Replacement Cost	$ 7
Net Realizable Value ($10-$2)	8
NRV - Normal Profit ($8-$2)	6

The replacement cost is between the ceiling and the floor; therefore, market value is determined to be replacement cost of $7. The market value of $7 is below the cost of $9 so the inventory should be valued at market value. The entry to record the decline in value would be:

	dr	cr
Loss from Decline in Inventory Value	4,000	
Allowance for Decline in Inventory Value		4,000

To write down the cost of 2,000 units of inventory from $9 to $7.

The Allowance for Decline in Inventory Value account is a contra-asset account which is reported in the balance sheet as a deduction from the inventory account. The Loss from Decline in Inventory Value is shown on the income statement.

EXAMPLE 2: Assume the same facts as Example 1, except that the selling price of the goods is now $8.50. The market value of the goods would be $6.50, which is computed as follows:

Replacement Cost	$7.00
Net Realizable Value ($8.50-$2)	6.50
NRV - Normal Profit ($6.50-$2)	4.50

Since replacement cost of $7 is higher than NRV of $6.50, NRV is used as the market value of the inventory. The entry to record the decline in value would be:

	dr	cr
Loss from Decline in Inventory Value	5,000	
Allowance for Decline in Inventory Value		5,000

To write down the cost of 2,000 units of inventory from $9 to $6.50.

EXAMPLE 3: Assume the same facts as Example 1, except the replacement cost of the inventory is $5. The market value of the goods would be $6 which is computed as follows:

Replacement Cost	$5
NRV ($10-$2)	8
NRV - Normal Profit ($8-$2)	6

Since replacement cost is below NRV less normal profit, NRV less normal profit is used as the market value of the inventory which is compared to the cost. Since the market value of the inventory is lower than its cost, market would be used to record the inventory in the balance sheet.

    d. *Application of lower of cost or market value:* When a company has more than one type of inventory and lower of cost or market is used in valuing the inventory, the accountant may choose to apply the lower-of-cost-or-market rules in one of three ways:

        (1) Lower of cost or market may be applied to individual items of inventory.

        (2) Lower of cost or market may be applied to classes or categories of inventory items.

        (3) Lower of cost or market may be applied to the entire inventory as a whole.

EXAMPLE: *Schedule A shows the application of lower of cost or market to individual items of inventory. Schedule B shows the application of lower of cost or market to the inventory as a whole.*

SCHEDULE A

Description	Quantity	Unit Cost Price	Unit Market Price	Cost	Lower of Cost or Market
Product A	100 units	$10.00	$9.00	$1,000	$ 900
Product B	200 units	8.00	9.00	1,600	1,600
Product C	200 units	5.00	6.00	1,000	1,000
				$3,600	$3,500

The inventory would be valued at the lower of cost or market of $3,500.

SCHEDULE B

Description	Quantity	Unit Cost Price	Unit Market Price	Cost	Lower of Cost or Market
Product A	100 units	$10.00	$9.00	$1,000	$ 900
Product B	200 units	8.00	9.00	1,600	1,800
Product C	200 units	5.00	6.00	1,000	1,200
				$3,600	$3,900

The inventory would be valued at the lower of cost of $3,600 since cost is lower than market.

D. Determining Cost of Goods Sold

    1. *Periodic Inventory System:* When a periodic inventory system is used, the cost of goods sold is determined as follows:

Accounting for Inventories

Cost of Goods Sold:

Beginning Inventory
+ Net Purchases
Goods Available for Sale
- Ending Inventory
= Cost of Goods Sold

Net Purchases:

Purchases
+ Transportation (Freight) In
- Purchases Discounts
- Purchase Returns and Allowances
= Net Purchases

EXAMPLE: Sullivan Co. had beginning inventory for 19XA of $105,000. The balance in the purchases account as of the year end was $1,120,000. The ending inventory valued at LIFO was $110,000. Cost of goods sold for 19XA is:

Beginning Inventory	$ 105,000
+ Purchases	1,120,000
Goods Available for Sale	$1,225,000
- Ending Inventory	110,000
Cost of Goods Sold	$1,115,000

2. *Perpetual Inventory System:* When a perpetual inventory system is used, the balance in the Cost of Goods Sold account should represent the cost of goods sold for the period, unless a physical count detects "shrinkage."

3. *Estimate as Percentage of Sales:* Cost of goods sold is sometimes estimated as a percentage of sales. This method may be used when monthly financial statements are prepared and taking a physical count is too costly. Inventory estimation may also be necessary if inventory has been stolen or destroyed by fire.

4. *Gross Profit Method:* The income statement format is:

Sales
- Cost of Goods Sold
Gross Profit
- Operating Expenses
Net Operating Income

The gross profit divided by sales revenue is called the *gross profit ratio*.

If a company's gross profit ratio is consistent from period to period, that ratio can be used to estimate the cost of goods sold. Once the cost of goods sold is estimated, ending inventory can also be computed.

EXAMPLE: Crass Company's gross profit ratio is 40 percent and is relatively consistent from period to period. Crass Co. wishes to estimate ending inventory and cost of goods sold for the month of June. Sales for June are estimated at $100,000. Beginning inventory was $30,000 and purchases were $72,000. Figure 7-1 shows the calculation of estimated inventory and cost of goods sold.

Figure 7-1
Calculation/Gross Profit

Goods Available for Sale	$102,000
− Estimated Cost of Goods Sold	60,000
Estimated Ending Inventory	$ 42,000

Sales		$100,000	100%
Less: Cost of Goods Sold			
Beginning Inventory	$ 30,000		
+ Purchases	72,000		
Goods Available for Sale	$102,000		
− Estimated Ending Inventory	42,000		
− Estimated Cost of Goods Sold		60,000	60%
Gross Profit		$ 40,000	40%

If the gross profit percentage (ratio) is 40 percent, the average percentage for cost of goods sold is 60 percent. If sales are $100,000, cost of goods sold is estimated to be $60,000 and gross profit is estimated to be $40,000. Once cost of goods sold is estimated to be $60,000, an estimate of ending inventory can be made as follows:

Goods Available for Sale	$102,000
− Estimated Cost of Goods Sold	− 60,000
Estimated Ending Inventory	$ 42,000

5. *Retail Inventory Method:* The retail inventory method is often used by retail businesses to compute inventory valuations. Records are kept of merchandise acquired at both cost and retail selling price. The ratio of cost to selling price is used to convert inventory from retail value to approximate cost. This method is complex, and the details of the method will not be discussed in this module.

E. **Evaluating Effect of Inventory on Net Income**

1. *Inventory Valuation:* It is important that inventory be valued accurately. An error in the ending inventory valuation will affect both the balance sheet (through inventory) and the income statement (through cost of goods sold). Since the ending inventory of one period is the beginning

inventory of the next period, the income statement of the next year will also be incorrect. However, the error will cancel itself over two accounting periods.

a. *Overstatement of ending inventory:* If ending inventory is overstated, cost of goods sold will be understated and net income for the period will be overstated.

b. *Understatement of ending inventory:* If ending inventory is understated, cost of goods sold will be overstated, and net income will be understated.

c. *Overstatement of beginning inventory:* If beginning inventory is overstated, cost of goods available for sale is overstated, cost of goods sold is overstated and net income is understated.

d. *Understatement of beginning inventory:* If beginning inventory is understated, cost of goods available for sale will be understated, cost of goods sold will be understated, and net income will be overstated.

EXAMPLE: Sullivan Corp. made an error in the ending inventory in 19XA. Ending inventory was overstated by $20,000. Due to this error, cost of goods sold for 19XA was understated by $20,000 and net income was overstated by $20,000. Figure 7-2 shows the effects of the error on the income statement for 19XA.

Figure 7-2
Sullivan Corporation
Income Statement for 19XA

			Including Error		Without Error
Sales			1,000,000		1,000,000
Less:	Cost of Goods Sold				
	Beginning Inventory	100,000		100,000	
	+ Purchases	700,000		700,000	
	Goods Available for Sale	800,000		800,000	
	− Ending Inventory	100,000		80,000	
Cost of Goods Sold			700,000		720,000
Gross Profit			300,000		280,000
Less: Operating Expenses			200,000		200,000
Net Operating Income			100,000		80,000

If it were not corrected, the error would carry through to the income statement of 19XB since beginning inventory would be overstated. Beginning inventory would be overstated by $20,000, cost of goods available for sale would be overstated by $20,000, cost of goods sold would be overstated by $20,000, and net income would be understated by $20,000. Figure 7-3 shows the effects of the error on the income statement for 19XB.

Figure 7-3
Sullivan Corporation
Income Statement for 19XB

		Including Error		Without Error	
Sales			1,100,000		1,100,000
Less:	Cost of Goods Sold				
	Beginning Inventory	100,000		80,000	
	+ Purchases	800,000		800,000	
	Goods Available for Sale	900,000		880,000	
	− Ending Inventory	110,000		110,000	
Cost of Goods Sold			790,000		770,000
Gross Profit			310,000		330,000
Less: Operating Expenses			210,000		210,000
Net Operating Income			100,000		120,000

2. *Method of Inventory Valuation Used:* The method of inventory valuation used has an effect on the amount recorded in the inventory account and also an effect on cost of goods sold, which influences the amount of net income reported by the company.

   a. *Rising Prices:* During a period of rising prices, the use of FIFO normally results in a higher reported net income and a higher ending inventory valuation than LIFO.

   b. *Falling Prices:* During a period of falling prices, the use of LIFO normally results in a higher reported net income and higher ending inventory valuation than FIFO.

   c. *Use of weighted-average method:* The weighted-average method will always produce an amount of net income and an inventory valuation which is between the amounts determined using the FIFO and LIFO methods.

Accounting for Inventories

Chapter 7: Review Questions

PART A: Multiple-Choice Questions

DIRECTIONS: Select the best answer from the four alternatives. Write the letter of your answer in the blank to the left of the number.

_____ 1. Net realizable value is

   a. the price for which an item can be expected to sell.
   b. the floor amount which can be used for market value when lower of cost or market is used.
   c. the price for which an item can be expected to sell less the expected costs of selling the item.
   d. replacement cost less a normal profit margin.

_____ 2. A perpetual inventory system is

   a. a method where cost of goods sold is recorded after each sale and the inventory account is updated for each purchase and sale transaction.
   b. a method of estimating inventory value using the historical gross profit percentage.
   c. a method which updates the inventory account only one time each period after a physical count of the inventory is taken.
   d. a method which requires that records be kept of merchandise acquired both at cost and at retail selling price.

_____ 3. A periodic inventory system

   a. is most often used by companies selling numerous small inexpensive items.
   b. uses a purchases account for recording inventory acquisitions.
   c. requires a physical inventory count be taken in order to determine the ending inventory valuation.
   d. all of the above.

4. The method of inventory estimation which is based on the company's historical gross profit percentage is called the

   a. retail method.
   b. perpetual method.
   c. periodic method.
   d. gross profit method.

5. Inventory should not be valued at

   a. more than net realizable value minus a normal profit margin.
   b. less than net realizable value.
   c. market value when market value exceeds cost.
   d. cost when market value exceeds cost.

6. The amount for which items in inventory could be purchased on the market today is called

   a. net realizable value.
   b. historical cost.
   c. price level adjusted cost.
   d. replacement cost.

7. Jana Co. had beginning inventory of $200,000. Ending inventory is $100,000 and cost of goods sold for the year is $1,000,000. Net purchases made during the year were

   a. $1,000,000.
   b. $900,000.
   c. $1,100,000.
   d. The answer cannot be determined from the information given.

8. Sales are $100,000; goods available for sale are $90,000; and the gross profit ratio is 30 percent. The estimate of ending inventory using the gross profit method is

   a. $20,000.
   b. $30,000.
   c. $60,000.
   d. $27,000.

Accounting for Inventories 175

9. Merz Company had beginning inventory for 19XA of $95,000. The balance in the purchases account as of year end is $900,000. The ending inventory valued at FIFO is $90,000. The purchase discounts account has a balance of $5,000; the purchase returns account has a balance of $2,000; and the freight-in account has a balance of $10,000. Cost of goods sold is

   a. $888,000.
   b. $908,000.
   c. $813,000.
   d. $898,000.

10. Obsolete or damaged inventory

    a. should be excluded from inventory.
    b. should be included in inventory at historical cost.
    c. should be included in inventory at market value if market value is lower than cost.
    d. should be included in inventory at its expected selling price.

11. Which of the following statements is false?

    a. A major objective in accounting for inventories is to properly match revenues and expenses.
    b. The use of lower of cost or market to value inventory is an example of an application of the conservatism principle.
    c. When a periodic inventory system is used, an error that understates the ending inventory of 19XA will result in an understatement of net income in 19XB.
    d. When LIFO is used for tax purposes, the IRS requires that it also be used for financial reporting purposes (in the United States).

PART B: Matching Sets

MATCHING SET 1

Match each description (12-17) with the appropriate inventory pricing method (A-C). Write the letter of your answer in the blank to the left of the number.

> INVENTORY PRICING METHODS
>
> A. FIFO
> B. LIFO
> C. Weighted Average
>
> DESCRIPTIVE STATEMENTS

_____ 12. Inventory is priced using the assumption that the last items received were the first items sold.

_____ 13. A method of valuing ending inventory by computing an average unit price of goods available for sale and multiplying by the number of units on hand.

_____ 14. The method of inventory pricing which results in the highest net income under conditions of rising prices.

_____ 15. The method of inventory pricing that results in the lowest inventory value under conditions of falling prices.

_____ 16. The method of inventory pricing that results in the lowest net income under conditions of rising prices.

_____ 17. Inventory is priced using the assumption that the first items received were the first items sold.

Accounting for Inventories

MATCHING SET 2

Determine the effect on net income for the year (A-C) resulting from each of the following inventory errors (18-23). Write the letter of your answer in the blank to the left of the number.

NET INCOME EFFFECTS

A. Net income will be overstated.
B. Net income will be understated.
C. Net income will not be misstated.

INVENTORY ERRORS

_____ 18. Jones Company failed to record an item purchased on December 28, 19XA, in the purchases journal until January, 19XB. The goods were correctly counted and included in the ending inventory for 19XA. What would be the effect on 19XA net income?

_____ 19. In 19XA, Jones Company incorrectly included 50 units of inventory on consignment from another company in their year-end inventory valuation. What would be the effect on 19XA net income?

_____ 20. Beginning inventory was understated by $10,000 due to an error in last year's inventory valuation.

_____ 21. Ending inventory was understated due to a failure to correctly count widgets on hand.

_____ 22. Both beginning inventory and ending inventory were overstated by $5,000.

_____ 23. Beginning inventory was overstated by $5,000 and ending inventory was understated by $3,000.

PART C: Problem Situations

DIRECTIONS: For each of the questions pertaining to the following problem situations, select the best answer from the four alternatives. Write the letter of your answer in the blank to the left of the number.

Problem 1

Hanes Company began a year ago and purchased merchandise as follows:

Jan. 1	Beginning Inventory	20 units @ $10.00
Feb. 15	Purchased	90 units @ $11.00
May 26	Purchased	50 units @ $11.50
Aug. 10	Purchased	80 units @ $12.00
Nov. 30	Purchased	60 units @ $12.50

Hanes uses a periodic inventory system, and there are 65 units in ending inventory.

_____ 24. Assuming that Hanes Company uses FIFO to value inventory, the amount of cost of goods sold for the year would be

a. $2,665.
b. $ 810.
c. $ 695.
d. $2,780.

_____ 25. Assuming that Hanes Company uses LIFO to value inventory, ending inventory for the year would be valued at

a. $2,780.
b. $ 695.
c. $2,665.
d. $ 810.

_____ 26. Assuming that Hanes Company uses the weighted-average method to value inventory, ending inventory for the year would be valued at (rounded to the nearest dollar)

a. $ 760.
b. $ 741.
c. $2,725.
d. $ 753.

Accounting for Inventories 179

Problem 2

Fin Company had 200 units in ending inventory. Fin Company sells only one type of item. The information for calculating lower of cost or market for Fin Company's inventory is as follows:

    Cost $20/unit
    Replacement Cost $15/unit
    Selling Price $18/unit
    Selling Costs $ 2/unit
    Normal Profit $ 3/unit

_____ 27. The net realizable value of the 200 units in total is

    a. $2,600.
    b. $3,600.
    c. $3,200.
    d. $3,000.

_____ 28. The floor for valuing market price per unit is

    a. $13.
    b. $10.
    c. $15.
    d. $12.

_____ 29. The inventory should be valued on the balance sheet at a total amount of

    a. $3,200.
    b. $3,000.
    c. $4,000.
    d. $2,600.

Accounting for Inventories

Chapter 7: Solutions

PART A: Multiple-Choice Questions

	Answer	Refer to Chapter Section
1.	(c)	[C-2-b]
2.	(a)	[A-1-a]
3.	(d)	[A-2]
4.	(d)	[D-4]
5.	(c)	[C]
6.	(d)	[C-2-a]

7. (b)   [D-1] The following computations show how net purchases is derived:

Beginning Inventory	$ 200,000 (given)
+ Net Purchases	900,000[a]
Goods Available for Sale	$1,100,000[b]
- Ending Inventory	100,000 (given)
Cost of Goods Sold	$1,000,000 (given)

8. (a)   [D-4] The estimate of ending inventory is computed as shown here:

Goods Available for Sale	$90,000
- Estimated Cost of Goods Sold	70,000[c]
Estimated Ending Inventory	$20,000

The estimated cost of goods sold percentage is 70%.
Sales % - Gross Profit % = 100% - 30% = 70%

[a]$1,000,000 - $100,000
[b]$1,100,000 + $200,000
[c]($100,000 x .7) = $70,000

9. (b)   [D-1] The following computations show how the cost of goods solds is derived:

Beginning Inventory		$ 95,000
+	Net Purchases	
Purchases	$900,000	
Add: Freight In	10,000	
Deduct: Purchase Discounts	- 5,000	
Deduct: Purchase Returns	- 2,000	903,000
Goods Available for Sale		$998,000
- Ending Inventory		- 90,000
Cost of Goods Sold		$908,000

10. (c)   [C]

11. (c)   [E-1-d] An understatement of ending inventory in 19XA results in an understatement of beginning inventory in 19XB. When beginning inventory is understated, net income will be overstated.

PART B: Matching Sets

MATCHING SET 1

12. (B)   [B-2]

13. (C)   [B-3]

14. (A)   [E-2-a]

15. (A)   [E-2-b]

16. (B)   [E-2-a]

17. (A)   [B-1]

MATCHING SET 2

18. (A)   [E-1] This error results in an understatement of purchases. When purchases are understated, cost of goods available for sale will be understated. Since ending inventory includes these units, cost of goods sold will be understated. When cost of goods sold is understated, net income is overstated.

19. (A)   [E-1-a] This error results in an overstatement of ending inventory which causes cost of goods sold to be understated and net income to be overstated.

20. (A)   [E-1-d]

Accounting for Inventories 183

21. (B)   [E-1-b]

22. (C)   [E-1] An overstatement of beginning inventory of $5,000 results in an understatement of net income of $5,000. An overstatement of ending inventory of $5,000 results in an overstatement of net income of $5,000. The two errors offset one another, and net income for the year is correct.

23. (B)   [E-1-c and E-1-b] If beginning inventory is overstated by $5,000, net income will be understated by $5,000. If ending inventory is understated by $3,000, net income will be understated by $3,000. The total effect on net income for the year is an understatement of $8,000.

PART C: Problem Situations

24. (a)   [B-1] Goods available for sale were:

		In Units	$ Value
Jan. 1	Beg. Inventory	20 units @ $10	$ 200
Feb. 15	Purchased	90 units @ $11	990
May 26	Purchased	50 units @ $11.50	575
Aug. 10	Purchased	80 units @ $12	960
Nov. 30	Purchased	60 units @ $12.50	750
Goods available for sale		300 units	$3,475

Under FIFO ending inventory would be:
60 units @ $12.50 = $750
5 units @ $12.00 =   60
Ending inventory = $810

Cost of Goods Sold = Goods Available - Ending
                                 for Sale   Inventory
      $2,665   = $3,475 $810

25. (b)   [B-2] Ending inventory under LIFO would be:
20 units @ $10.00 = $200
45 units @ $11.00 =   495
Ending Inventory = $695

26. (d)   [B-3] The weighted-average cost per unit is:
$3,474/300 = $11.5833.
Ending inventory using the weighted-average method would be:
$11.5833/unit x 65 units = $752.91 or $753.

27. (c) [C-2-b]
NRV/unit = Selling Price/Unit - Selling Cost/Unit
$16 = $18 - $2
NRV in total is $16/unit x 200 units = $3,200.

28. (a) [C-2-c]
The floor is NRV minus the normal profit.
$16/unit - $3/unit = $13/unit

29. (b) [C] Replacement cost should be used in determining market value since it is lower than net realizable value (ceiling) but higher than net realizable value less the normal profit (floor). Total market value is $15/unit x 200 units = $3,000. Since market value is lower than cost, the ending inventory should be valued at market.

CHAPTER 8

Property, Plant, and Equipment Records

OVERVIEW

Property, plant, and equipment records are the records which relate to the fixed assets of the company. This section is intended to introduce the candidate to the recording of transactions involving property, plant, and equipment.

The candidate should understand what is considered to be part of the cost of a fixed asset and know the procedures for calculating depreciation and depletion, accounting for repairs of fixed assets, and recording the sale or exchange of a fixed asset.

DEFINITION OF TERMS

ACCELERATED DEPRECIATION METHOD. A depreciation method which assigns more depreciation expense to the earlier years of an asset's useful life than to its later years of useful life.

DEPLETION. The amount a natural resource is reduced due to usage, for example, cutting timber, mining ore, or pumping oil.

DOUBLE-DECLINING-BALANCE DEPRECIATION (DDB). An accelerated depreciation method which uses a depreciation rate which is twice the straight-line rate.

EXTRAORDINARY REPAIRS. Repairs which either prolong the useful life of the asset or change the quality of service provided by the asset.

INFLATION. A general increase in the prices which must be paid for goods and services.

MODIFIED ACCELERATED COST RECOVERY SYSTEM (MACRS). An accelerated method of depreciation required for income tax purposes in the United States.

PRICE INDEX. A measure of the changes in prices of a particular group of goods and services.

SALVAGE VALUE. The residual value an asset is expected to have when its useful life is over.

STRAIGHT-LINE DEPRECIATION. A depreciation method which assigns an equal amount of depreciation expense to each period of the asset's useful life.

SUM-OF-THE-YEARS' DIGITS DEPRECIATION (SYD). An accelerated depreciation method which uses a decreasing fraction as the depreciation rate which is used to allocate the cost less salvage value of an asset over its useful life.

UNITS-OF-PRODUCTION METHOD. A depreciation method which computes depreciation expense based on the total estimated productive output of the asset.

A. Acquisition Cost

The first thing which must be determined when a fixed asset is acquired is the cost of the asset.

1. *Cost of Fixed Assets:* Cost of a fixed asset includes all expenses necessary to acquire the asset and to prepare the asset for its use in the operations of the business. The cost of a fixed asset should include only amounts which are reasonable and necessary. Examples of items which would be included in the cost of a fixed asset are the cash paid to acquire the asset, freight-in, insurance on the asset while in transit, installation costs, and any trial runs necessary to determine the asset's readiness for use. *Freight-in* is the term used to refer to the transportation cost of an asset when it is paid by the buyer. If a fixed asset is purchased with a note which has an interest provision, any interest paid should be recorded as interest expense rather than as a part of the cost of the asset.

2. *Cost of Acquiring Land:* If land is purchased, the cost of the land must be separated from the cost of any depreciable buildings or improvements which are situated on the land since land is not depreciable. If land is purchased for use in the business and there is an existing structure on the land which must be removed, the cost of removing the structure should be included as part of the cost of the land. Any surveying or grading costs should also be included in the cost of the land if these costs are necessary to make the land suitable for its intended use. If a building is to be constructed on the land, any excavation costs associated with the construction of the building should not be included in the cost of the land. These costs are considered part of the cost of the building. Any commissions paid to brokers, legal fees, and title fees would also be included as a part of the cost of the land. Land improvements which may

Property, Plant, and Equipment Records 187

have a limited life such as driveways, fences, and parking lots should be recorded in a separate land improvements account. Land improvements have a limited life and, as such, are subject to depreciation.

B. Allocation of Costs: Depreciation and Depletion

1. *Depreciation:* Depreciation is the systematic and rational allocation of the cost of an asset over its useful life. In order to determine the amount of depreciation to charge to specific periods, it is necessary to perform the following steps:

    a. *Cost of the asset:* The cost of the asset to be depreciated must first be determined.

    b. *Useful life of the asset:* The length of the useful life of the asset is estimated.

    c. *Salvage value:* Salvage value is the residual value an asset is expected to have when its estimated useful life is over. The amount of salvage value anticipated needs to be estimated. Often, no residual value is assigned because it is indeterminable.

    EXAMPLE: *Jones Co. purchases a truck for $20,000. The useful life of the truck is estimated to be eight years. At the end of eight years, Jones Co. expects to be able to sell the truck for $2,000. $2,000 is the salvage value of the truck.*

    d. *Selection of depreciation method to be used:* Depreciation expense is an approximation which is based on a number of estimates. There are many methods of computing depreciation. As long as a depreciation method is systematic and rational, it is normally an acceptable method. There are four basic depreciation methods that you should be familiar with.

        (1) *Straight-line depreciation method:* The straight-line depreciation method assumes that an equal amount of depreciation should be taken for each year of the asset's useful life. The formula for computing straight-line depreciation is:

        Depreciation Rate x (Cost - Salvage Value)

        The depreciation rate which is used with straight-line depreciation is

        $$\frac{100\% \text{ (or } 1.00)}{\text{Number of Periods of Useful Life}}$$

        Therefore, straight-line depreciation would be computed in this way:

$$(\text{Cost} - \text{Salvage Value}) \times \frac{100\% \text{ (or } 1.00)}{\text{Number of Periods of Useful Life}}$$

EXAMPLE: Lox Company purchases a machine for $10,000. Freight-in on the machine was $100 and installation charges were $100. The salvage value of the machine is estimated to be $1,200. The useful life is estimated to be five years. The asset was purchased on January 1, 19XA. The calculation of depreciation for each year of useful life is shown below:

Depreciation Schedule
Straight-Line Depreciation Method

Year	Computation	Depreciation Expense	Accumulated Depreciation	Book Value
1	(9,000[a] x .20[b])	1,800	1,800	8,400
2	(9,000 x .20)	1,800	3,600	6,600
3	(9,000 x .20)	1,800	5,400	4,800
4	(9,000 x .20)	1,800	7,200	3,000
5	(9,000 x .20)	1,800	9,000	1,200
		9,000		

[a] Cost   Salvage Value
 $10,200 - 1,200 = $9,000

[b] 1/5 = 20% (or .20)

The journal entry to record the depreciation expense for each year would be:

	dr	cr
Dec. 31 Depreciation Expense	1,800	
Accumulated Depreciation		1,800

(2) *Double-declining-balance method:* Some assets produce more benefits in the early years of their useful life than in the later years. For example, some machines might require substantial repair as they become older. These types of assets might be depreciated using an accelerated depreciation method. Accelerated depreciation methods assign a larger amount of depreciation expense to the earlier years of an asset's useful life than to its later years. The double-declining-balance (DDB) method is an example of an accelerated depreciation method. The DDB depreciation method uses a constant depreciation rate applied to a declining asset base.

(a) The depreciation rate used in DDB depreciation is twice or 200 percent of the straight-line rate. In the previous Lox Company example, the straight-line rate

Property, Plant, and Equipment Records 189

was 1/5 or 20%, so the DDB rate would be 40%.

(b) In order to obtain depreciation expense for a period, the DDB depreciation rate is multiplied by the book value of the asset at the beginning of the period for which depreciation is to be calculated.

(c) Note that salvage value is not considered when computing depreciation using the DDB method. When the DDB method is used, however, an asset should not be depreciated below its salvage value.

EXAMPLE: Assume the same facts as were used in the Lox Company example except that Lox Company wishes to use the double-declining-balance depreciation method.

Depreciation Schedule
Double-Declining-Balance Depreciation Method

Year	Computation	Depreciation Expense	Accumulated Depreciation	Book Value
				10,200
1	(10,200 x .40)[b]	4,080	4,080	6,120
2	(6,120 x .40)	2,448	6,528	3,672
3	(3,672 x .40)	1,469	7,997	2,203
4	(2,203 x .40)	881	8,878	1,322
5		122[c]	9,000	1,200
		9,000[c]		

[b] .40 = 2 x straight-line rate of 20% (.20).
[c] Under DDB depreciation, we do not depreciate below the estimated salvage value amount. Note that the amount of the depreciation expense recorded each year declines from that reported in the previous year.

(3) *Sum-of-the-years' digits method:* The sum-of-the-years' digits (SYD) method is also an accelerated depreciation method. When the sum-of-the-years' digits method is used, a decreasing rate is applied to a constant asset base.

(a) The asset base to be depreciated in the SYD method is the cost of the asset minus the salvage value of the asset (as with straight-line depreciation).

(b) The decreasing rate is achieved by using a fraction, with the numerator representing the number of years remaining to be written off and the denominator representing the sum of the years' digits.

In the Lox Company example, the sum of the years'

digits would be 15 years (5 years + 4 years + 3 years + 2 years + 1 year). An easy formula for calculating the sum-of-the-years' digits is [N(N+1)]/2 where N is the number of years of useful life. (This number is the denominator.)

In the Lox Company example, the depreciation rate in the first year would be 5/15; in the second year, 4/15; in the third year, 3/15; in the fourth year, 2/15; and in the fifth year, 1/15. By the end of the fifth year, the entire asset base will have been written off: 5/15 + 4/15 + 3/15 + 2/15 + 1/15 = 15/15.

EXAMPLE: Assume the same facts as were used in the Lox Company straight-line depreciation example, except that Lox Company now uses the SYD method of computing depreciation expense.

Depreciation Schedule
Sum-of-the-Years' Digits Method

Year	Computation	Depreciation Expense	Accumulated Depreciation	Book Value
				$10,200
1	(5/15 x 9,000)a	3,000	3,000	7,200
2	4/15 x 9,000	2,400	5,400	4,800
3	3/15 x 9,000	1,800	7,200	3,000
4	2/15 x 9,000	1,200	8,400	1,800
5	1/15 x 9,000	600	9,000	1,200
		9,000		

aCost   Salvage Value
$10,200 - 1,200 = $9,000

Note that the amount of the depreciation expense which is recorded declines in each successive year.

(4) *Units-of-production method:* The units-of-production method of calculating depreciation may be used when the total units of service which an asset will provide can be estimated accurately.

The formula used to calculate units-of-production depreciation is:

$$\frac{\text{Total Units Produced During the Period}}{\text{Total Estimated Units of Production}} \times (\text{Cost} - \text{Salvage Value})$$

Property, Plant, and Equipment Records

EXAMPLE: *XYZ Company bought a new truck. It is expected that the truck will have a useful life of 100,000 miles. The cost of the truck was $20,000 and salvage value is expected to be $2,000. During the first year the truck was driven 25,000 miles. The depreciation expense for the first year would be calculated as follows:*

$$\frac{25,000}{100,000} \times (\$20,000 - \$2,000) = \$4,500$$

2. *Depletion:* Assets which are natural resources such as timber, iron ore, gold, or oil reserves are subject to depletion since the total quantity available will eventually be used up.

   a. *Estimating quantity of natural resources:* First, the company must estimate the amount of the natural resource which will be available for use. This estimate is likely to change as time progresses and the company is more aware of the actual amount of the resource left.

   b. *Calculating depletion:* The calculation of depletion is similar to the calculation of the units-of-production method.

   c. *Formula for computing depletion:* The formula for computing depletion is:

$$\frac{\text{Quantity of Resource Used in Current Year}}{\text{Estimated Quantity of the Resource Available}} \times (\text{Cost} - \text{Salvage Value of Natural Resource})$$

   d. *Expensing depletion cost:* Depletion is an inventoriable cost. Depletion cost should be added to the cost of extracting the resource. These costs should be expensed as the product is sold.

   EXAMPLE: *The Sylvan Silver Co. owns a silver mine in Alaska. It is estimated that 30,000 tons of silver ore will be able to be extracted from the mine. During the past year, 5,000 tons of silver ore were mined. The cost of the silver mine was $20,000 and the salvage value of the mine is estimated to be $5,000. The calculation of depletion for the period would be:*

$$\frac{5,000}{30,000} \times (\$20,000 - \$5,000) = \$2,500$$

C. **Repairs**

Ordinary repairs are amounts spent to maintain an asset in its normal operating condition. Ordinary repairs include regular maintenance, painting, cleaning, and repair of minor parts. Ordinary repairs performed on fixed assets are considered to be expenses for the period in which they are incurred. Extraordinary repairs should be capitalized and depreciated over the remainder of the asset's life. Repairs are extraordinary when they change the quality of service provided by an asset or extend its useful life beyond the original estimate.

1. *Extraordinary Repairs:* An extraordinary repair which increases the service life of an asset is recorded by debiting Accumulated Depreciation and crediting Cash. An extraordinary repair which materially increases the productivity of the asset is debited directly to the asset account.

2. *Effect on Depreciation:* When extraordinary repairs occur, the current year's depreciation and all future periods' depreciation are affected. (No changes are made to the depreciation expense which was recorded in the past.)

   EXAMPLE: *Geni Co. purchased a truck for $18,000. The truck had a six-year estimated useful life. After five years Geni Co. decided to install a new engine in the truck which would extend its useful life to a total of 10 years. The new engine cost $10,000 including installation. Prior to the extraordinary repairs, the accounts appeared as follows (straight-line depreciation was used):*

Truck #4		Accumulated Depreciation	
18,000			15,000

   Geni Co. recorded the extraordinary repairs as follows:

	dr	cr
(a) Accumulated Depreciation/Truck #4	10,000	
Cash		10,000

   To record installation of new engine in Truck #4.

   Then, the accounts appeared as follows:

Truck #4		Accumulated Depreciation	
18,000			15,000
		(a) 10,000	
			5,000

The new book value of the truck is $13,000. This amount should be depreciated over the new remaining useful life of the asset which is five years. The depreciation expense on the truck for each of the next five years (assuming straight-line depreciation is used) would be $13,000/5 = $2,600 per year (no salvage value is assumed).

D. Disposition of Property Items

Assets may be disposed of in one of the following three ways: sale, exchange, or abandonment. If an asset is disposed of at any time other than the end of an accounting period, depreciation should be calculated for the portion of the year for which the asset was held.

EXAMPLE: Floit Company sold a machine on June 30, 1991. The company purchased the machine on January 1, 1984, for $20,000 and estimated depreciation on the machine using the straight-line method over a 10-year period. Floit Company's year end is December 31. The entry to record the partial-year depreciation to date of sale would be:

		dr	cr
June 30	Depreciation Expense	1,000	
	Accumulated Depreciation		1,000

To record 6 months' depreciation prior to
disposal of machine (6/12 months x $2,000).

1. *Sale of a Property Item:* When a property item is sold, the book value of the asset is compared to the proceeds generated by the sale of the asset.

    a. *Gain:* If an asset is sold for more than its book value, a gain is recorded.

    b. *Loss:* If an asset is sold for less than its book value, a loss is recorded.

    EXAMPLE 1: Assume that Floit Company sold the machine in the previous example for $10,000 cash. The book value of the asset is computed as follows:

$20,000.00	Cost
-15,000.00	Less Accumulated Depreciation
$ 5,000.00	Book Value

The gain on the sale is computed as follows:

$10,000.00   Proceeds
− 5,000.00   Book Value
$ 5,000.00   Gain

The journal entry to record the sale is:

		dr	cr
June 15	Cash	10,000.00	
	Accumulated Depreciation	15,000.00	
	Machine		20,000.00
	Gain on Sale of Machine		5,000.00

Sold machine on June 15 for $10,000.

EXAMPLE 2: *Assume that Floit Company sold the machine for $4,000 cash. The loss on the sale of the asset is calculated as follows:*

$ 4,000.00   Proceeds
− 5,000.00   Book Value
($1,000.00) Loss on Sale

The entry to record the sale is:

		dr	cr
June 15	Cash	4,000.00	
	Loss on Sale of Machine	1,000.00	
	Accumulated Depreciation	15,000.00	
	Machine		20,000.00

Sold machine on June 15 for $4,000.

2. *Exchange of Property Items:* Often a business trades in an old asset when a new one is purchased. These transactions are treated as exchanges of assets. Exchanges of assets are treated either as an exchange of unlike assets or an exchange of like assets.

   a. *Exchange of unlike assets:* An example of an exchange of unlike assets would be the exchange of a machine for a new truck. The two assets are to be used for different purposes within the business. Gains or losses on exchanges of unlike assets are calculated, based upon the *fair value* of the asset given up. The fair value of the asset given up is the market value of that asset on the day it is exchanged. If no fair value can be determined, book value is assumed to be fair value. Trade-in value is often used as a measure of the fair value of the asset.

EXAMPLE: *Villa Corporation traded in a stamping machine on a new truck. The stamping machine has a cost of $10,000, accumulated depreciation of $6,000, and a fair value of $4,500. The stamping machine is exchanged for a new truck with a list price of $15,000. A trade-in value of $4,500 is allowed on the exchange. The company must pay the balance of $10,500 in cash. The entry to record this transaction is:*

	dr	cr
Truck	15,000	
Accumulated Depreciation/ Stamping Machine	6,000	
Stamping Machine		10,000
Cash		10,500
Gain on Exchange of Stamping Machine		500

Exchanged stamping machine for truck.

b. *Exchange of like assets:* An example of an exchange of like assets would be the exchange of an old truck for a new truck or the exchange of an old calculator for a new calculator. No gain is reported when like assets are exchanged. Since no gain is recorded, the company must adjust the cost of the new asset. Losses are recorded on exchanges of like assets in order to satisfy the conservatism principle.

EXAMPLE 1: *No Gain on Exchange of Like Assets*
Villa Corporation exchanged an old calculator with a cost of $500 and accumulated depreciation of $300 for a new calculator with a list price of $800. The seller allowed a $300 trade-in allowance for the old calculator (the trade-in value was equal to the fair value). The entry to record this transaction would be:

	dr	cr
Office Equipment (new calculator)	700	
Accumulated Depreciation/Office Equipment (old calculator)	300	
Office Equipment (old calculator)		500
Cash		500

Exchanged old calculator for new calculator.

EXAMPLE 2: *Loss on Exchange of Like Assets*
Assume that Villa Corporation exchanged the old calculator for a new one and all of the facts are the same except that the trade-in allowance was $100 instead of $300. The entry to record this transaction would be:

	dr	cr
Office Equipment (new calculator)	800	
Accumulated Depreciation/Office Equipment (old calculator)	300	
Loss on Exchange of Calculator	100	
Office Equipment (old calculator)		500
Cash		700

Exchanged old calculator for new calculator.

Note: For federal income tax purposes, losses on exchanges of like assets are not deductible.

3. *Abandonment of Property Items:* If fully depreciated assets are abandoned, a journal entry must be made debiting Accumulated Depreciation and crediting the asset account which results in the writing off of the asset. If an asset which is not yet fully depreciated is abandoned, a loss due to the abandonment must be recorded.

If fully depreciated assets are still being used in the business, no further depreciation should be taken on the asset but the full amount of the asset and the accumulated depreciation related to it should be left on the records of the company.

E. **Depreciation for Income Tax Purposes**

In 1981, the U.S. tax provisions included a new system of depreciation known as the Accelerated Cost Recovery System (ACRS). In 1986, Congress modified the ACRS system. Under the Modified ACRS system (MACRS), an asset is assigned to a class of property which has a defined life for income tax depreciation purposes. The asset is depreciated over that statutory life at an assigned rate per year. Tables of class lives and depreciation rates for each year are published by the Internal Revenue Service. Although the Modified ACRS should be used for income tax purposes, it is not in accord with generally accepted accounting principles and should not normally be used for financial accounting purposes. Some small businesses may use MACRS depreciation for both financial reporting and tax purposes when the differences between MACRS and conventional methods are not material.

F. **Price-Level Indexing**

Financial statements are based on the historical cost principle, which makes use of the stable dollar concept (refer to Chapter I, Section A-3). Stable dollar financial statements fail to account for the effects of inflation. *Inflation* is an increase in the general price level which causes a decline in the purchasing power of the dollar. There are a number of different approaches to accounting for inflation. One of these approaches is the use of *price- level indexing*. Price-level indexes can be constructed based on a general market basket of goods, or they can be constructed based on a specific group of goods used in a particular industry. The Consumer Price Index is an example of a general price-level index which is based on a very broad range of goods.

1. *Construction of a Price Index:* To construct a price index, one year is selected as the base year. The cost of purchasing the selected basket of goods in the base year is assigned a value of 100. An index number for other years is then calculated as a percentage of the base year's cost.

   EXAMPLE: The cost of purchasing the selected basket of goods (X, Y, and Z) was as follows:

19XA	$ 8.00
19XB	9.00
19XC	10.15
19XD	12.00

   Assume that 19XA is selected as the base year. The $8.00 cost in 19XA is then assigned the value of 100. The index numbers for 19XA through 19XD are calculated as follows:

   19XA $ 8.00/$8.00 x 100 = 100%
   19XB $ 9.00/$8.00 x 100 = 112.5%
   19XC $10.15/$8.00 x 100 = 126.875%
   19XD $12.00/$8.00 x 100 = 150%

2. *Using a Price Index:* One way a price index might be used is to restate a historical dollar amount to the current price level. The formula for restating an amount is:

   $$\text{Historical Cost} \times \frac{\text{Price-Level Index of Year Converting To}}{\text{Price-Level Index of Year Converting From}}$$

   EXAMPLE: If in 19XA $2,000 was spent on goods X, Y, and Z, the 19XA cost restated in terms of 19XD prices is:

   $$\$2{,}000 \times \frac{150}{100} = \$3{,}000$$

In 1979, the Financial Accounting Standards Board (FASB) passed a statement which required large publicly held companies to report inflation-adjusted amounts as supplemental financial statement information. The financial statements were still prepared on a historical cost basis with the inflation information as a supplement. This requirement was part of an experiment to determine the usefulness of the additional information. In 1986, the FASB made the disclosure of the inflation-adjusted amounts voluntary, and few companies have continued to disclose this information. Further discussion of price-level indexing is beyond the scope of this module.

Chapter 8: Review Questions

PART A: Multiple-Choice Questions

DIRECTIONS: Select the best answer from the four alternatives. Write the letter of your answer in the blank to the left of the number.

_____   1. Any depreciation method which assigns more depreciation expense in the early years of an asset's life and less in later years is called

   a. double-declining-balance depreciation.
   b. an accelerated depreciation method.
   c. sum-of-the-years' digits depreciation.
   d. modified accelerated cost recovery system.

_____   2. Jones Company bought a plot of land with an old building located on it. The old building was demolished in order to pave the land for a parking lot. The cost of demolishing the building should be

   a. capitalized as a part of the building account.
   b. charged to demolition expense.
   c. capitalized as part of the parking lot improvement account.
   d. capitalized as a part of the cost of the land.

_____   3. Which of the following items should not be included as part of the cost of a new machine?

   a. Sales tax paid on the purchase of the machine.
   b. Installation cost of the machine.
   c. Cost of repairing damage to the machine caused when it was dropped from a forklift while carrying it into the building.
   d. Freight-in on the delivery of the machine.

_____   4. Which of the following items may correctly be included as part of the land account?

   a. Fences
   b. Title fees
   c. Excavation costs incurred during construction of a building
   d. Concrete parking lot

5. The amount a natural resource is reduced as a result of usage is called

    a. depreciation.
    b. amortization.
    c. depletion.
    d. accumulation.

6. A repair which is treated as an expense in the period in which it is incurred is a/an

    a. extraordinary repair.
    b. capital item.
    c. betterment.
    d. ordinary repair.

7. The residual value an asset is expected to have when its useful life is over is called

    a. book value.
    b. depreciated value.
    c. salvage value.
    d. current value.

8. The general increase in the prices which must be paid for goods and services is called

    a. current cost.
    b. inflation.
    c. price-level index.
    d. deflation.

9. When like assets are exchanged

    a. gains or losses on the exchange should not be recognized.
    b. gains on the exchange should be recognized for financial reporting purposes, but losses should not be recognized.
    c. losses on the exchange should be recognized for financial reporting purposes, but gains should not be recognized.
    d. both gains and losses on the exchange should be recognized.

Property, Plant, and Equipment Records   201

_____ 10. Rohas Co. purchased a new machine for $50,000 which they estimated would be able to produce 100,000 units of product C. During the current year, they produced 10,000 units of product C. The machine is expected to last eight years and have a salvage value of $2,000. Assuming that Rohas Co. uses the units-of-production method, depreciation expense for the current period is

   a. $6,000.
   b. $5,000.
   c. $5,102.
   d. $4,800.

_____ 11. If a fixed asset is sold for less than its book value

   a. a loss is recorded.
   b. a gain is recorded.
   c. no gain or loss is recorded.
   d. Cash is credited.

_____ 12. Extraordinary repairs

   a. should be recorded as an increase in accumulated depreciation.
   b. result in a decrease in the value of the fixed asset repaired.
   c. result in a prior period adjustment of depreciation taken in earlier years.
   d. often extend the useful life of the asset.

_____ 13. Using U.S. tax law, which of the following statements is true?

   a. Gains are not recognized on exchanges of unlike assets.
   b. Depletion should be treated as an expense when the natural resource is extracted.
   c. No journal entry is necessary when fully depreciated assets are abandoned.
   d. Losses on exchanges of like assets are not deductible for federal income tax purposes.

_____ 14. An accelerated method of depreciation prescribed in United States law for assets placed in service after 1986 is

   a. accumulated cost recovery system.
   b. double declining balance.
   c. modified accelerated cost recovery system.
   d. sum-of-the-years' digits.

PART B: Matching Sets

MATCHING SET 1

Determine the appropriate depreciation method (A-D) which matches the following descriptions (15-19). Write the letter of your answer in the blank to the left of the number.

> DEPRECIATION METHODS
>
> A. Straight-Line Method
> B. Double-Declining-Balance Method
> C. Sum-of-the-Years' Digits Method
> D. Units-of-Production Method
>
> DESCRIPTIONS

_____ 15. A depreciation method which applies twice the straight-line rate to the beginning-of-period book value of the asset in order to obtain the depreciation expense for the period.

_____ 16. A depreciation method that allocates depreciation to each year in a plant asset's life by using a decreasing fraction times the cost less the salvage value of the asset.

_____ 17. A depreciation method which does not consider salvage value in the formula for calculation of yearly depreciation expense.

_____ 18. A depreciation method which results in equal amounts of depreciation being taken in each full year of the life of the asset.

_____ 19. A depreciation method that allocates the cost less the salvage value of an asset based on the relation of the units produced in a given period to the total units expected to be produced over the asset's life.

Property, Plant, and Equipment Records

MATCHING SET 2

Determine whether each of the following items (20-26) should be capitalized and depreciated over the life of the asset (A) or expensed in the current period (B). Write the letter of your answer in the blank to the left of the number.

TREATMENT OF COST

A. Capitalize the cost and depreciate it over the life of the asset.
B. Expense the entire cost in the current period.

ITEMS

_____ 20. Insurance on an asset while it is in transit.

_____ 21. Cost of a trial run needed to establish the settings on a machine before it could be used.

_____ 22. Interest paid on a note used to acquire land.

_____ 23. Commissions paid to a broker in acquiring land.

_____ 24. Cost of changing the oil and tires on a vehicle.

_____ 25. Cost of adding an air conditioner to a truck.

_____ 26. Cost of painting a room.

PART C: Problem Situations

DIRECTIONS: For each of the questions pertaining to the following problem situations, select the best answer from the four alternatives. Write the letter of your answer in the blank to the left of the number.

Problem 1

Nelson Company sold a truck for $14,000 on August 1, 19XD. The cost of the truck was $30,000 and the balance in the Accumulated Depreciation/Truck account on January 1, 19XD, was $9,000. The truck had an estimated useful life of 10 years with no salvage value.

_____ 27. The sale resulted in

    a. a gain of $14,000.
    b. a loss of $5,250.
    c. a loss of $7,000.
    d. a gain of $7,000.

Problem 2

On January 1, 19XA, Hawk Co. purchased equipment for $60,000. The equipment was expected to last eight years and have a salvage value of $4,000. Hawk Co.'s year end is December 31.

_____ 28. Assuming that Hawk Co. uses straight-line depreciation, the balance in the accumulated depreciation account on January 1, 19XC, would be

    a. $ 7,000.
    b. $14,000.
    c. $ 7,500.
    d. $15,000.

_____ 29. Assuming that Hawk Co. uses the double-declining-balance method, depreciation expense for 19XB would be

    a. $10,500.
    b. $15,000.
    c. $30,000.
    d. $11,250.

Property, Plant, and Equipment Records   205

_____ 30. Assuming that Hawk Co. uses the sum-of-the-years' digits method, depreciation expense for 19XC would be (rounded to the nearest dollar)

  a. $12,444.
  b. $ 9,333.
  c. $12,000.
  d. $10,000.

_____ 31. Assuming that Hawk Co. uses the sum-of-the-years' digits method, the book value of the equipment on December 31, 19XB, (after closing) would be (rounded to the nearest dollar)

  a. $32,667.
  b. $10,889.
  c. $36,667.
  d. $25,000.

Problem 3

On January 1, 19XA, Rose Co. purchased new equipment which had a list price of $50,000. Rose Co. traded in some *like* equipment. The cost of the equipment traded in was $40,000, and the accumulated depreciation on this equipment as of January 1, 19XA, was $15,000.

_____ 32. Assuming that Rose Co. received a trade-in allowance of $30,000 (which is equal to fair value), the journal entry to record this transaction should include

  a. a debit to the equipment account for $50,000.
  b. a credit to the accumulated depreciation account for $15,000.
  c. a debit to the equipment account for $45,000.
  d. a credit to a gain account for $5,000.

_____ 33. Assuming that Rose Co. received a trade-in allowance of $20,000 (which is equal to fair value), the journal entry to record this transaction should include

  a. a debit to a loss account for $5,000.
  b. a debit to the new equipment account for $55,000.
  c. a credit to a gain account for $5,000.
  d. a credit to the old equipment account for $25,000.

Problem 4

The cost of purchasing a given market basket is:

Year	Price
19XA	$10.00
19XB	11.00
19XC	12.00
19XD	13.00

_____ 34. Using 19XA as the base year, the price index for 19XC is

   a. 110.
   b. 120.
   c. 83.33.
   d. 109.1.

_____ 35. In 19XA a car cost $10,000. If the price index in 19XA was 110 and in 19XD the price index was 125, the cost of the car in 19XD dollars is (rounded to the nearest dollar)

   a. $12,500.
   b. $11,000.
   c. $11,364.
   d. $ 8,800.

Chapter 8: Solutions

PART A: Multiple-Choice Questions

	Answer	Refer to Chapter Section
1.	(b)	[B-1-d(2)]
2.	(d)	[A-2]
3.	(c)	[A-1]
4.	(b)	[A-2]
5.	(c)	[B-2]
6.	(d)	[C]
7.	(c)	[B-1-c]
8.	(b)	[F]
9.	(c)	[D-2-b]
10.	(d)	[B-1-d(4)] The calculation of depreciation using the units-of-production method is: $\frac{10,000}{100,000} \times (\$50,000 - 2,000)$.
11.	(a)	[D-1-b]
12.	(d)	[C]
13.	(d)	[D-2-b]
14.	(c)	[E]

PART B: Matching Sets

MATCHING SET 1

    15. (B)   [B-1-d(2)]

    16. (C)   [B-1-d(3)]

    17. (B)   [B-1-d(2)(c)]

    18. (A)   [B-1-d(1)]

    19. (D)   [B-1-d(4)]

MATCHING SET 2

    20. (A)   [A-1]

    21. (A)   [A-1]

    22. (B)   [A-1]

    23. (A)   [A-2]

    24. (B)   [C]

    25. (A)   [C]

    26. (B)   [C]

PART C: Problem Situations

    27. (b)   [D-1-b] The book value of the truck was:

$30,000	Cost
-10,750	Accumulated Depreciation[a]
$19,250	Book Value

The selling price of the asset is less than the book value so there was a loss on the sale of $5,250 ($19,250 - $14,000).

    28. (b)   [B-1-d(1)] Straight-line depreciation expense is $7,000 per year. [($60,000 - 4,000) x .125] or [($60,000 - 4,000)/8]

Accumulated depreciation as of January 1, 19XC would have a balance of $14,000 ($7,000 for 19XA and $7,000 for 19XB).

[a]Accumulated depreciation as of January 1, 19XD + depreciation for the current year through August 1, 19XD ($3,000 year x 7/12).

29. (d)   [B-1-d(2)] Double-declining-balance depreciation would be computed as follows:

	Beg. of Period Carrying Value	Rate[b]	Depreciation Expense	End of Period Carrying Value
19XA	$60,000	.25	$15,000	$45,000
19XB	$45,000	.25	$11,250	$33,750

30. (b)   [B-1-d(3)] Sum-of-the-years' digits depreciation would be computed as follows:

Year	Fraction	x	Cost-Salvage Value	=	Depreciation Expense
19XA	8/36[c]		$60,000 - $4,000	=	$12,444
19XB	7/36		$60,000 - $4,000	=	$10,889
19XB	6/36		$60,000 - $4,000	=	$ 9,333

31. (c)   [B-1-d(3)] Book value as of December 31, 19XB, is:

Cost	-	Accumulated Depreciation	=	Book Value
$60,000	-	$23,333[d]		$36,667

32. (c)   [D-2-b] Book value of the old equipment is $25,000 ($40,000 - 15,000). Since the trade-in allowance of $30,000 is greater than the book value of $25,000, there is a $5,000 gain on the transaction. Gains on the exchange of like assets are not recognized for financial reporting purposes. The entry to record the transaction would be:

	dr	cr
Equipment (new)	45,000[e]	
Accumulated Depreciation/ Equipment	15,000	
Equipment (old)		40,000
Cash		20,000[f]

[b] Straight-line rate = 1/8 = .125. Double-declining-balance rate = .125 x 2 = .25.

[c] The denominator is the sum-of-the-years' digits, which can be computed using the formula $n(n+1)/2$. The computation is 8(9)/2 = 36.

[d] $12,444 + $10,889 (see solution to question 30).

[e] $50,000 cost minus $5,000 gain not recognized.

[f] $50,000 cost minus $30,000 trade-in allowance.

33. (a) [D-2-b] Since the trade-in allowance of $20,000 is less than the book value of $25,000, there is a $5,000 loss on the exchange. For financial reporting purposes, losses are recognized on the exchange of like assets. The entry to record this transaction would be:

	dr	cr
Equipment (new)	50,000	
Accumulated Depreciation/ Equipment	15,000	
Loss on Exchange of Equipment	5,000	
Equipment (old)		40,000
Cash		30,000[g]

34. (b) [F-1] $\dfrac{\$12}{\$10} \times 100 = 120$

35. (c) [F-2] $\$10,000 \times (125/110) = \$11,364$

[g]$50,000 cost - $20,000 trade-in allowance.

CHAPTER 9
Other Assets

OVERVIEW

This chapter covers the accounting for the rest of the asset categories. Some of the topics such as the calculation of interest and treatment of prepaid expenses have already been discussed in Chapter 4. The candidate should review Chapter 4 if necessary.

The candidate should be familiar with the recording of notes receivable and interest revenue for both interest-bearing and noninterest-bearing notes, the process of discounting a note receivable with a bank, accounting for accounts receivable and bad debts, types of insurance, co-insurance, and the recording of adjusting entries for prepaid insurance, accounting for office supplies and accounting for intangible assets including amortization of intangible assets.

DEFINITION OF TERMS

AGING OF ACCOUNTS RECEIVABLE. A method of estimating the amount of the allowance for uncollectible accounts and bad debt expense. This method groups the individual accounts according to the length of time they have been outstanding. The amount of uncollectible accounts is then estimated for each group.

AMORTIZATION. The systematic writing off as an expense of the balance in an account over a period of time. Amortization is usually associated with intangible asset accounts.

CASUALTY INSURANCE. Insurance coverage which is primarily for the liability of a party which results from negligent acts or omissions resulting in bodily injury and/or property damage to another party.

CO-INSURANCE. A provision in some insurance contracts which requires the insured party to insure property for at least a specified minimum percentage of its fair market value, or to share the loss proportionately with the insurance company.

CONTINGENT LIABILITY. A potential liability that could become an actual liability only if certain events occur.

DIRECT WRITE-OFF METHOD. A method of recording bad debt expense which does not use an allowance for uncollectible accounts or attempt to match bad debt expense with related revenue. When the direct write-off method is used, worthless accounts are written off as a debit to Bad Debt Expense and a credit to Accounts Receivable. This method does not conform to GAAP.

DISCOUNTING OF A NOTE RECEIVABLE. When a note receivable is discounted, it is sold to a bank for cash. The seller remains contingently liable for payment of the note if the maker defaults.

FIDELITY BOND. Insurance that guarantees that the insurance company will pay for losses of money or property that result from the dishonest acts of bonded employees.

INTEREST-BEARING NOTE RECEIVABLE. A note receivable which requires payment of the principal of the note plus a stated amount of interest on the maturity date.

LIFE AND HEALTH INSURANCE. Business life and health coverage provides funds for normal maintenance of a business in the event of a loss of a key person.

MATURITY DATE OF A NOTE. The date on which a note and any interest are due and payable.

NONINTEREST-BEARING NOTE RECEIVABLE. A note in which no provision is included for the payment of interest; only the payment of principal is required.

PROPERTY INSURANCE. Insurance protection of the property (assets) of the company from damage or destruction by fire, smoke, vandalism, etc.

SURETY BOND. A contract under which one party agrees to make good the debt or default of another party.

A. Notes Receivable

A note receivable is a legal document signed by the borrower which promises to pay the lender the principal amount of the note. Notes receivable normally specify that a certain interest rate will be paid on the principal.

1. *Interest-Bearing Note Receivable:* A note receivable which requires payment of both the principal and a stated rate of interest is called an interest-bearing note receivable.

    EXAMPLE: Moomey Company accepted a $5,000 60-day 10% note receivable from Joe Pone in exchange for merchandise on June 1. The *journal entry to record the receipt of the note would be:*

		dr	cr
June 1	Note Receivable	5,000	
	Sales Revenue		5,000

Received 60-day 10% note from Joe Pone in exchange for merchandise.

The journal entry to record the collection of the note receivable would be:

		dr	cr
July 31	Cash	5,083	
	Note Receivable		5,000
	Interest Revenue		83

Collected Joe Pone note; interest = $5,000 x .10 x 60/360 = $83.

2. *Noninterest-Bearing Note Receivable:* A note receivable which has no provision for the payment of interest on the principal of the note is called a noninterest-bearing note receivable. Since money has a time value, the principal amount received on the due date includes an amount for implied interest. Generally accepted accounting principles require that interest be imputed on long-term noninterest-bearing notes. Imputing interest refers to the process of recognizing the implied interest through an approximation process. Short-term noninterest-bearing notes are recorded at face value since the implied interest on the note is immaterial. In order to determine the amount of imputed interest associated with a noninterest-bearing note, the following steps are used:

   a. *Rate of imputed interest:* Determine the rate of interest which is usually charged on transactions of the same nature as the one involving the noninterest-bearing note.

   b. *Present value of note:* Find the present value of the note using the following formula:

   $$\frac{\text{Face Value of the Note}}{(1 + r)^n} = \text{Present Value of the Note}$$

   In this formula, r is the interest rate and n is the number of interest periods.

   c. *Discount:* Find the amount of the discount to be recorded on the note using the following formula:

   Face Value - Present Value = Discount on Note Receivable

The discount amount represents the interest which is implied in the note. This amount is recorded in a Discount on Notes Receivable account. The discount account is a contra-asset account and is deducted from the face value of the note on the balance sheet. The balance in the discount account is written off to interest income over the life of the note. The amount of interest to be recorded in any given period is based on the beginning of the period carrying value of the note (Notes Receivable - Discount on Notes Receivable), times the interest rate, times the period of time for which interest is to be accrued.

EXAMPLE: Moomey Company accepted a $10,000 two-year noninterest-bearing note receivable from Zebo Company on January 1, 19XA. The note was taken in exchange for merchandise. The interest rate normally charged in this type of transaction is 10 percent. The computation of interest to be imputed is:

$$\frac{\$10,000}{(1+.1)^2} = \frac{\$10,000}{1.21} = \$8,264$$

The discount on the note would be $1,736 ($10,000 - 8,264).

The journal entry to record the receipt of the note would be:

		dr	cr
Jan. 1	Notes Receivable	10,000	
	Discount on Notes Receivable		1,736
	Sales		8,264

Received a two-year, noninterest-bearing note from Zebo Co. Interest was imputed at 10%.

The journal entry to record the first year's interest on the note would be:

		dr	cr
Dec. 31	Discount on Notes Receivable	826	
	Interest Income (Revenue)		826

To record interest accrued on the Zebo Co. note receivable. (Carrying value x interest rate x time) ($8,264 x .10 x 1 year)

The journal entry to record the collection of the note on December 31, 19XB, would be:

Other Assets 215

	dr	cr
Dec. 31 Cash	10,000	
Discount on Notes Receivable	910	
Interest Income (Revenue)		910
Notes Receivable		10,000

To record collection of the Zebo Co. note and to write off the balance in the discount account to interest income.

    d. *Imputing interest on notes:* Interest should be imputed whenever a long-term (more than one year) note is noninterest-bearing or has an interest rate which is unreasonably low under the circumstances.

3. *Recording Accrued Interest Receivable:* If financial statements are prepared before a note receivable is collected, the amount of accrued interest receivable must be recorded.

    a. *Interest-bearing notes receivable:* For interest-bearing notes receivable, interest is accrued in the same fashion as for bonds receivable (see Chapter 6).

    b. *Noninterest-bearing notes receivable:* For noninterest-bearing notes receivable, an adjusting entry records the interest revenue which was accrued and writes off the portion of the discount which has been earned. (See the December 31 entries in the example in A-2-c.)

4. *Discounting of Notes Receivable:* A company may discount (sell) its notes receivable to a bank if the company needs cash immediately and does not want to hold the notes to maturity. The bank buys the note and holds it until maturity. At the time the note matures, the bank collects the principal and interest earned on the note from the maker.

The seller of the note is liable to the bank for payment of the maturity value if the maker does not pay the note. This liability to pay the bank if the maker fails to do so is called a contingent liability. A contingent liability might become a liability at a future date but is not a liability at the present time. Contingent liabilities are potential liabilities, but they are not currently legal obligations. Contingent liabilities are usually reported in footnotes on financial statements.

The amount which a company will receive from the bank when a note is discounted may be calculated as follows:

    a. *Maturity value of note:* The maturity value of the note (the principal plus the interest) is determined.

b. *Discount on note:* The amount of interest the bank will charge for the note is calculated. This is called the *discount* on the note. The formula for calculating the discount is:

> Maturity Value × Bank Discount Rate
> × Portion of a year for which the bank = Discount
> will hold the note

c. *Proceeds:* The maturity value less the discount is equal to the proceeds which the bank will pay to the seller.

> Maturity Value - Discount = Proceeds

d. *Interest expense:* If the proceeds received from the bank are less than the face value of the note, the seller will record the difference as *interest expense.*

e. *Interest revenue:* If the proceeds received from the bank are more than the face value of the note, the seller will record the difference as *interest revenue.*

EXAMPLE 1: *Lackey Co. discounted a $10,000 8% 90-day note receivable with the bank. The note was issued on June 1, and Lackey Co. discounted the note with the bank on July 1. The bank charges a 10% discount rate. The calculation of the proceeds to be received by Lackey Co. follows:*

Principal	$10,000
+ Interest ($10,000 × .08 × 90/360)	200
Maturity Value	$10,200
Less: Discount ($10,200 × .10 × 60/360)	170
Proceeds to Lackey Co.	$10,030

Lackey Co. would record the receipt of the proceeds as follows:

		dr	cr
July 1	Cash	10,030	
	Notes Receivable		10,000
	Interest Revenue		30

Discounted note receivable with the bank.

EXAMPLE 2: *Assume the same facts as in Example 1, except that Lackey Co. discounted the note on June 1 rather than holding it until July 1. The calculation of the proceeds to be received by Lackey Co. is made as follows:*

Maturity Value		$10,200
Less: Discount ($10,200 x .10 x 90/360)		255
Proceeds to Lackey Co.		$ 9,945

Lackey Co. would record the receipt of the proceeds as follows:

		dr	cr
June 1	Cash	9,945	
	Interest Expense	55	
	Notes Receivable		10,000

    f. *Default in payment of discounted note:* If the maker of a discounted note defaults, the bank requests payment from the seller. The journal entry to record payment on a defaulted note would be a debit to Accounts Receivable and a credit to Cash. The seller would then be responsible for collection of the note from the maker.

EXAMPLE: Assume that the maker of the note Lackey Co. discounted with the bank defaulted and that the bank charged a $25 protest fee. Lackey Co. would make the following entry to record the payment to the bank of the maturity value:

	dr	cr
Accounts Receivable	10,225	
Cash		10,225

To record payment of defaulted notes receivable and bank protest fee.

B. Accounts Receivable and Bad Debts

Accounts receivable are amounts owed to a business for sales of merchandise or services which are sold on credit. Many businesses have a credit department which analyzes prospective customers before credit is issued to them. Even if a business has a credit department which screens credit customers, some of the accounts receivable of the business will prove to be uncollectible. An allowance for uncollectible accounts (or allowance for doubtful accounts) is set up to report accounts receivable on the balance sheet at the amount which is expected to be collected.

    Total Accounts Receivable Balance
    <u>Less: Allowance for Uncollectible Accounts</u>
    = Net Realizable Value of Accounts Receivable

Using an allowance for uncollectible accounts results in a better matching of the expense related to uncollectible accounts with the sales revenue recorded when the initial sales took place. It also reports accounts receivable at a more conservative amount (net realizable value). There are a number of different methods for estimating the amount of bad debt expense to be recorded and the amount to be included in the allowance for uncollectible accounts.

1. *Aging of Accounts Receivable:* When an aging of accounts receivable is prepared, individual customers' account balances are categorized according to the length of time they have been outstanding. Based upon past experience, the company estimates the probability of accounts not being collected for each category. The estimated losses in each category are totaled to determine the total amount of estimated uncollectible accounts. The aging-of-accounts-receivable method provides the best estimate of uncollectible accounts. Figure 9-1 shows an example of an aging-of-accounts-receivable schedule.

Figure 9-1
Aging of Accounts Receivable

Nelson Company
Aging of Accounts Receivable
December 31, 19XA

Account Name	Account Balance	Not Yet Due	1-30 Days Past Due	30-60 Days Past Due	Over 60 Days Past Due
Aronson	2,500	2,500			
Bellows Co.	10,122	8,000	2,122		
Bird	8,310	8,310			
Cafen Co.	503				503
Crane	12,200	10,000		2,200	
Dulow Corp., etc.	5,110		5,110		
Total	100,000	65,000	20,000	10,000	5,000
Percentage estimated to be uncollectible from past experience			1%	3%	8%	15%
Amount estimated to be uncollectible	2,800	650	600	800	750

EXAMPLE: Assume that Nelson Company's Accounts Receivable control account had a $100,000 debit balance and the company's Allowance for Uncollectible Accounts account had a $200 credit balance prior to adjustment.

Accounts Receivable (Control)

Balance 12/31   100,000

Other Assets

Allowance for Uncollectible Accounts	
	200 Balance 12/31
	2,600 12/31
	(Adjusting Entry)
	2,800

The entry to record bad debt expense based upon the aging schedule in Figure 9-1 would be:

		dr	cr
12/31	Bad Debt Expense	2,600	
	Allowance for Uncollectible Accounts		2,600

To record bad debt expense.

2. *Percentage of Accounts Receivable:* The percentage-of-accounts-receivable method estimates the balance of the Allowance for Uncollectible Accounts based upon a percentage of the ending accounts receivable balance.

   EXAMPLE: Assume that based upon past experience Nelson Company estimates that uncollectible accounts are about 2.5 percent of total ending accounts receivable. Nelson Company would estimate that their Allowance for Uncollectible Accounts balance should be $2,500 ($100,000 x .025). Since the allowance account already has a balance of $200, the entry to record bad debt expense, assuming the percentage-of-accounts-receivable method is used, would be:

		dr	cr
Dec. 31	Bad Debt Expense	2,300	
	Allowance for Uncollectible Accounts		2,300

To record bad debt expense.

3. *Percentage of Credit Sales:* The percentage-of-credit-sales method assumes that a certain percentage (based on past experience) of credit sales for the year will prove to be uncollectible. When the percentage-of-sales method is used, the company estimates the amount of bad debt expense rather than the amount of the allowance for uncollectible accounts as in the other two methods. The amount already recorded in the Allowance for Uncollectible Accounts does not affect the adjusting entry when the percentage-of-credit-sales method is used. Bad debt expense might also be estimated using a percentage of net sales rather than credit sales.

   EXAMPLE: Assume that Nelson Company had credit sales of $900,000 during 19XA. Nelson Company estimates that .3 percent of its credit *sales will be uncollectible. The entry to record bad debt expense, assuming that the percentage-of-credit-sales method is used, would be:*

		dr	cr
Dec. 31	Bad Debt Expense Allowance for Uncollectible Accounts	2,700	2,700

To record bad debt expense ($900,000 x .003).

Note that the balance in the allowance account did not affect the entry which was made, since the percentage-of-sales method was used.

4. *Writing Off an Uncollectible Account:* When it is determined that an individual account has become uncollectible, that account must be written off. In order to write off an account, the Allowance for Uncollectible Accounts is debited and the Accounts Receivable account is credited. The procedure for writing off an uncollectible account is the same regardless of the method used to estimate bad debt expense and the allowance for uncollectible accounts. The writing off of a bad debt does not affect the net realizable value of accounts receivable since both accounts receivable and the allowance for uncollectible accounts are reduced by an equal amount.

EXAMPLE: Assume that Nelson Company determines, on May 1, 19XA, that Cafen Co.'s account is uncollectible. The entry to write off the account would be:

		dr	cr
May 1	Allowance for Uncollectible Accounts Accounts Receivable	503	503

To write off Cafen Co.'s uncollectible account.

5. *Collection of Uncollectible Account:* It is possible that an account which has previously been written off will be collected. When this happens, it is necessary to restore the account as a part of the accounts receivable balance before recording the collection of the account.

EXAMPLE: Assume that on May 5, 19XB, Nelson Company collects a $300 account from J.D. Corporation which was written off in 19XA. On May 5, 19XB, the entries necessary to record the transaction would be:

		dr	cr
May 5	Accounts Receivable Allowance for Uncollectible Accounts	300	300

To restore J.D. Corporation account which was previously written off.

Other Assets

		dr	cr
May 5	Cash	300	
	Accounts Receivable		300

To record collection of J.D. Corporation account receivable.

If a collection agency were used to help collect the account, its commission would need to be shown as a part of the cash received.

6. *Direct Write-Off:* When the direct write-off method is used, a company does not record an allowance for doubtful accounts or attempt to match bad debt expense with the related revenues. When an account is determined to be uncollectible, an entry is made directly to Bad Debt Expense and Accounts Receivable. No adjusting entry is made at the end of the period. From an accounting standpoint, the direct write-off method is deficient because no attempt is made to match revenues and expenses, and the accounts receivable balance in the balance sheet is overstated, except where the company ordinarily would not have any bad accounts.

EXAMPLE: Sullivan Co. uses the direct write-off method of recording bad debts. On October 1, 19XA, the $500 account of J. B. Harding was determined uncollectible. The entry to write off the account would be:

		dr	cr
Oct. 1	Bad Debt Expense	500	
	Accounts Receivable		500

To write off the J. B. Harding account as uncollectible.

C. **Prepaid Expenses**

Prepaid expenses consist of the cost of supplies or services bought for use in the business which are not used up at the end of the accounting period.

1. *Insurance:* Insurance policies usually cover a set period of time, and frequently they are paid for in advance. When the period of time covered by an insurance policy extends beyond one accounting period, prepaid insurance should be recorded. When payment is made on an insurance policy which covers more than one accounting period, the payment may be recorded in two alternate ways:

    a. *Recording original payment:* The original payment for insurance may be recorded in either of the following ways:

    (1) The original payment may be recorded as a debit to the Insurance Expense account. When this is done, an adjusting entry must be made at the end of the period to record any

remaining prepaid insurance benefits. (See Chapter 4, Section F-2-a(2)(b), for an example of the recording of the adjusting entry which must be made.)

(2) The original payment may be recorded as a debit to the Prepaid Insurance account. When this is done, an adjusting entry must be made at the end of the period to record the portion of the benefits which have expired (that is, have become an expense of the period). (See Chapter 4, Section F-2-a(1)(a), for an example of the recording of the necessary adjusting entry.)

b. *Numerous insurance policies:* A company might have a number of insurance policies which cover one or more accounting periods. When this is the case, the Prepaid Insurance account includes the total of all of the prepaid insurance benefits for all of the policies.

c. *Types of insurance:* The major types of insurance available for businesses today include property insurance, casualty insurance, life and health insurance, fidelity bond insurance, surety bonding, and co-insurance.

(1) *Property insurance:* Insurance protection of the property (assets) of the company from damage or destruction by fire, smoke, vandalism, and so forth, is provided through property insurance policies.

(2) *Casualty insurance:* Casualty insurance is insurance coverage that is primarily for the liability of a party which results from negligent acts or omissions resulting in bodily injury and/or property damage to another party.

(3) *Life and health insurance:* Business life and health insurance coverage provides funds for the normal maintenance of a business in the event of the loss of a key person. This is often called *key man insurance.*

(4) *Fidelity bond insurance:* This type of insurance guarantees that the insurance company will pay for losses of money or property that result from the dishonest acts of bonded employees. The employees are named specifically or by position. The bond covers dishonest acts whether employees act alone or in collusion. Many companies feel bonding is beneficial; as well as paying for losses, bonding provides a deterrent to fraud. The bonding company can uncover dishonesty in the work history of a new employee, and many employees feel that the bonding company is certain to prosecute if they are caught performing dishonest acts.

Other Assets

(5) *Surety bond:* This is a contract under which the surety agrees to make good the debt or default of the principal.

(6) *Co-insurance:* A provision is included in some insurance contracts which requires the insured party to insure property for at least a specified minimum percentage of its fair market value or to share the loss proportionately with the insurance company.

2. *Supplies:* Office supplies are often purchased in large quantities and kept on hand for use in the business when needed. Any supplies on hand at the end of an accounting period represent a prepaid expense of the company. The original purchase of office supplies may be recorded in two alternate ways:

   a. *Debit to asset account:* When the supplies are purchased, the asset account Supplies Inventory may be debited. When this is done, an adjusting entry must be made at the end of the period to record supplies expense for the supplies which were used. (See Chapter 4, Section F-2-a(1)(b), for an example of the recording of an adjusting entry of this type.)

   b. *Debit to expense account:* When the supplies are purchased, an expense account may be debited. When this is done, an adjusting entry must be made at the end of the period to record any supplies on hand as an asset. (See Chapter 4, Section F-2-a(2)(a), for an example of the recording of an adjusting entry of this type.)

D. **Intangible Assets and Amortization**

Intangible assets are long-lived assets which have no tangible existence. Examples of intangible assets are patents, copyrights, trademarks, franchises, leaseholds, and goodwill.

1. *Value of Intangible Assets:* Intangible assets are valued at cost. A company could have intangible assets which were acquired at no cost to the company. These assets which have no cost should not be recorded on the balance sheet.

2. *Capitalization of Intangible Assets:* An intangible asset should be capitalized and shown on the balance sheet *only* if a future benefit can be expected to be derived from that intangible asset.

3. *Amortization of Intangible Assets:* Intangible assets should be amortized over their useful lives. Amortization expense is recorded by debiting amortization expense and crediting the intangible asset account. Amortization is always recorded on a straight-line basis.

a. *Limited legal life:* Some intangible assets, such as patents or copyrights, have a limited legal life. Patents and copyrights should be amortized over their legal life or their useful life if it is shorter than their legal life. Patents have legal life of 17 years, and copyrights have legal life of 50 years beyond the creator's lifetime.

b. *Indefinite useful life:* Some intangible assets such as trademarks, organization costs, or goodwill have indefinite useful lives. If an intangible asset has an indefinite useful life, it should be amortized over a period which does not exceed 40 years.

EXAMPLE: ABC Co. has a patent which cost $10,000. The legal life of the patent is 17 years, but the expected useful life is 10 years. The journal entry to record amortization of the patent for each of its 10 years of useful life would be:

	dr	cr
Amortization Expense	1,000	
Patent		1,000

To amortize the cost of the patent over its useful life ($10,000/10 years).

Other Assets   **225**

Chapter 9: Review Questions

PART A: Multiple-Choice Questions

DIRECTIONS: Select the best answer from the four alternatives. Write the letter of your answer in the blank to the left of the number. Assume 360 days per year in all interest calculations.

_____ 1. A note receivable which requires payment of principal only with no provision for interest is called

   a. an interest-bearing note receivable.
   b. a noninterest-bearing note receivable.
   c. an imputed note receivable.
   d. a discounted note receivable.

_____ 2. What is the interest on a $40,000 interest-bearing note at 9% for 120 days?

   a. $3,600
   b. $1,800
   c. $1,200
   d. $5,333

_____ 3. Arnold Company accepted a $10,000 three-year noninterest-bearing note from Mary Mealy. The interest rate which Arnold Company charged for similar transactions was 10%. The amount of the discount on notes receivable which Arnold Company should have recorded is (rounded to the nearest dollar)

   a. $7,513.
   b. $9,090.
   c. $3,030.
   d. $2,487.

_____ 4. In the United States, interest should be imputed on a note receivable

   a. when the note is noninterest bearing regardless of the due date of the note.
   b. when the interest rate on the note is unreasonably low and the note has a due date more than one year in the future.
   c. Both (a) and (b) are true.
   d. Neither (a) nor (b) is true.

5. Selling a note receivable to a bank

   a. is called discounting the note.
   b. results in the seller assuming a contingent liability to pay the bank if the maker of the note defaults.
   c. results in a credit to Interest Income when the proceeds of the sale exceed the face value of the note.
   d. All of the above are correct responses.

6. The maturity value of an interest-bearing note receivable is

   a. equal to the face value.
   b. equal to the face value plus the interest due on the maturity date of the note.
   c. the amount a bank will pay for a note if it is discounted with the bank.
   d. the principal amount of the note.

7. The writing off of a worthless account receivable when the allowance method of recording bad debt expense is used

   a. results in a decrease in the total assets of the company.
   b. should include a debit to Bad Debt Expense.
   c. decreases the net realizable value of accounts receivable for the firm.
   d. should include a debit to the Allowance for Uncollectible Accounts.

8. Which of the following items would not be included as an intangible asset?

   a. Patent
   b. Copyright
   c. Prepaid rent
   d. Goodwill

9. ABC Co. owns a patent which has a legal life of 17 years and an expected useful life of 10 years. The patent should be amortized over

   a. 17 years.
   b. 5 years.
   c. 12 years.
   d. 10 years.

Other Assets   227

_____ 10. Ajax Co. purchased a two-year insurance policy on June 1, 19XA, for $600. On June 1, Ajax Co. debited Prepaid Insurance and credited Cash for $600. On December 31, 19XA (Ajax Co.'s year end), Ajax Co. should

   a. include the $600 on the balance sheet as a prepaid expense.
   b. make an adjusting entry debiting Prepaid Insurance and crediting Insurance Expense for $175.
   c. make an adjusting entry debiting Insurance Expense and crediting Prepaid Insurance for $175.
   d. make an adjusting entry debiting Insurance Expense and crediting Prepaid Insurance for $425.

_____ 11. On the balance sheet, the Allowance for Uncollectible Accounts

   a. should be included as a current liability.
   b. should be shown as an addition to the accounts receivable balance.
   c. should be shown as a deduction from the balance in the accounts receivable account.
   d. should not be shown on the balance sheet since it is an income statement account.

_____ 12. If the Interest Income account has a $400 credit balance before the year-end adjustments are made, and there are adjustments for $50 of accrued interest on notes receivable, the income statement should show interest earned of

   a. $350.
   b. $450.
   c. $400.
   d. $ 50.

_____ 13. Sun Co. uses the allowance method of recording bad debt expense. In 19XA, Sun Co. wrote off the account of Susan Wendel as uncollectible. During 19XB, Susan Wendel paid Sun Co. the amount that had been owed. Sun Co. should

   a. not record the collection since the account was previously written off.
   b. credit Bad Debt Expense for the amount received.
   c. first reinstate the account of Susan Wendel by debiting Accounts Receivable and crediting Allowance for Uncollectible Accounts; then record the collection.
   d. record the amount received as miscellaneous revenue in 19XB.

14. After aging the accounts receivable at the end of the year, Ring Co. estimated that $100,000 of the accounts receivable would be uncollectible. The balance in Allowance for Uncollectible Accounts prior to adjustment was a $2,000 debit. The correct adjusting entry would include a debit to Bad Debt Expense of

    a. $ 98,000.
    b. $102,000.
    c. $100,000.
    d. $ 2,000.

15. Which of the following statements about intangible assets is true?

    a. Intangible assets should be amortized over their useful lives.
    b. Intangible assets with indefinite lives should be amortized over a period not exceeding 50 years.
    c. Intangible assets which are acquired at no cost should be recorded on the balance sheet at estimated market value.
    d. All of the above are true.

Other Assets

PART B: Matching Sets

MATCHING SET 1

Match the following definitions (16-19) with the appropriate term (A-F). Write the letter of your answer in the blank to the left of the number.

        TERMS

        A. Contingent Liability
        B. Net Realizable Value of Accounts Receivable
        C. Amortization
        D. Intangible Assets
        E. Prepaid Expenses
        F. Allowance for Uncollectible Accounts

        DEFINITIONS

_____ 16. The balance in the Accounts Receivable control account less the Allowance for Uncollectible Accounts which represents the expected amount of cash to be received from the collection of accounts receivable.

_____ 17. Long-lived assets that do not have any tangible existence. Their value stems from the rights resulting from their ownership.

_____ 18. The systematic writing off as an expense of the balance in an intangible asset account.

_____ 19. A potential liability that could become an actual liability if certain events occur.

MATCHING SET 2

Match each of the following descriptions (20-25) with the appropriate method of recording bad debt expense (A-C). Write the letter of your answer in the blank to the left of the number.

METHODS OF RECORDING BAD DEBT EXPENSE

A. Direct Write-off Method
B. Allowance Method Using Aging of Accounts Receivable
C. Allowance Method Using Percentage of Credit Sales

DESCRIPTIONS

_____ 20. Bad Debt Expense is debited when an account is written off.

_____ 21. Individual customers' accounts are grouped according to the length of time they have been outstanding.

_____ 22. The balance in Allowance for Uncollectible Accounts must be considered in determining the amount of the year-end adjusting entry.

_____ 23. This method fails to appropriately match revenues and expenses.

_____ 24. The balance in Allowance for Uncollectible Accounts is not considered in the determination of the amount of the year-end adjusting entry.

_____ 25. The amount of the year-end adjusting entry is based on a percentage of credit sales for the period.

MATCHING SET 3

Match each of the following definitions (26-29) with the appropriate insurance term (A-F). Write the letter of your answer in the blank to the left of the number.

INSURANCE TERMS

A. Property Insurance
B. Casualty Insurance
C. Life and Health Insurance
D. Fidelity Bond
E. Surety Bond
F. Co-insurance

DEFINITIONS

_____ 26. A provision in some insurance contracts which requires the insured party to insure property for at least a specified minimum percentage of its fair market value or to share the loss proportionately with the insurance company.

_____ 27. Insurance coverage which provides funds for the normal maintenance of a business in the event of a loss of a key person.

_____ 28. Insurance protection of the property of a company from damage or destruction by fire, smoke, or vandalism.

_____ 29. Insurance that guarantees that the insurance company will pay for losses resulting from the dishonest acts of bonded employees.

PART C: Problem Situations

DIRECTIONS: For each of the questions pertaining to the following problem situations, select the best answer from the four alternatives. Write the letter of your answer in the blank to the left of the number. Assume 360 days per year in all interest calculations.

Problem 1

Millikin Co. had credit sales of $2,000,000 in 19XA. The year-end Accounts Receivable balance was $588,000. The Allowance for Uncollectible Accounts had a credit balance of $1,000 prior to adjustment.

_____ 30. Assuming that Millikin Co. uses the percentage-of-credit-sales method of estimating bad debt expense and that past experience indicates 1 percent of credit sales will be uncollectible, the year-end adjusting entry should include

   a. a debit to Bad Debt Expense for $21,000.
   b. a debit to Bad Debt Expense for $19,000.
   c. a debit to Bad Debt Expense for $20,000.
   d. none of the above.

_____ 31. Assuming that Millikin Co. uses the percentage-of-accounts-receivable method of estimating uncollectible accounts and that past experience indicates that 3.5 percent of the total accounts receivable prove to be uncollectible, the year-end adjusting entry should include

   a. a debit to Bad Debt Expense for $19,580.
   b. a credit to Allowance for Uncollectible Accounts of $20,580.
   c. a debit to Bad Debt Expense for $21,580.
   d. none of the above.

_____ 32. Assuming that Millikin Co. uses the direct write-off method of recording bad debts, the year-end adjusting entry should include

   a. a debit to Bad Debt Expense and a credit to Accounts Receivable.
   b. a debit to Accounts Receivable and a credit to Bad Debt Expense.
   c. a debit to Bad Debt Expense and a credit to Allowance for Uncollectible Accounts.
   d. No adjusting entry would be made under the direct write-off method.

Problem 2

Frank Co. accepted a $10,000 10% 90-day note receivable from Alex Co. on June 1, 19XA. On July 1, 19XA, Frank Co. discounted the note with ABC Bank. The bank discount rate is 12%.

_____ 33. The maturity value of the note is

   a. $11,000.
   b. $10,300.
   c. $10,250.
   d. $11,200.

_____ 34. The proceeds received by Frank Co. from ABC Bank were (rounded to the nearest dollar)

   a. $10,079.
   b. $ 9,500.
   c. $10,000.
   d. $10,045.

_____ 35. Assuming that the proceeds received in question 34 were $9,500, the entry to record the receipt of the proceeds would include

   a. a debit to Cash, a credit to Notes Receivable, and a credit to Interest Income.
   b. a debit to Cash, a debit to Interest Expense, and a credit to Notes Receivable.
   c. a debit to Notes Receivable, a credit to Cash, and a credit to Interest Income.
   d. a debit to Cash and a credit to Notes Receivable.

_____ 36. On September 5, 19XA, Frank Co. received a notice from ABC Bank that Alex Co. had dishonored the note. The bank charged a $50 protest fee. The entry to record Frank Co.'s payment to the bank would include

   a. a debit to Notes Receivable for $10,000 and a credit to Cash for $10,000.
   b. a debit to Accounts Receivable for $10,050 and a credit to Cash for $10,050.
   c. a debit to Accounts Receivable for $10,300 and a credit to Cash for $10,300.
   d. a debit to Notes Receivable for $10,250 and a credit to Cash for $10,250.

Other Assets   235

Chapter 9: Solutions

PART A: Multiple-Choice Questions

	Answer	**Refer to Chapter Section**
1.	(b)	[A-2]
2.	(c)	[A-1] Interest = Principal x Rate x Time $1,200 = $40,000 x .09 x 120/360
3.	(d)	[A-2] The present value of the note is computed using the following formula: $$\frac{\text{Face Value of Note}}{(1 + r)^n} = \frac{\$10,000}{(1 + .1)^3} = \$7,513$$ The discount to be recorded is the difference between the face value and the present value of the note ($10,000 - 7,513 = $2,487).
4.	(b)	[A-2-d]
5.	(d)	[A-4]
6.	(b)	[A-4-a]
7.	(d)	[B-4] When an individual worthless account is written off, there is no change in total assets or the net realizable value of accounts receivable.
8.	(c)	[D]
9.	(d)	[D-3]
10.	(c)	[C-1-a(1) and F-2-a(1)(a)] $600/24 months = $25/month $25/month x 7 months = $175 insurance expense
11.	(c)	[B]
12.	(b)	[A-3]

13. (c) [B-5]

14. (b) [B-1] Since Allowance for Uncollectible Accounts has a $2,000 debit balance, the adjusting journal entry must be made for $102,000 in order to have an ending balance of $100,000 in Allowance for Uncollectible Accounts after adjustment.

15. (a) [D-3]

PART B: Matching Sets

MATCHING SET 1

16. (B) [B]

17. (D) [D]

18. (C) [D-3]

19. (A) [A-4]

MATCHING SET 2

20. (A) [B-6]

21. (B) [B-1]

22. (B) [B-1]

23. (A) [B-6]

24. (C) [B-3]

25. (C) [B-3]

MATCHING SET 3

26. (F) [C-1-c(6)]

27. (C) [C-1-c(3)]

28. (A) [C-1-c(1)]

29. (D) [C-1-c(4)]

Other Assets

PART C: Problem Situations

30. (c) [B-3] $2,000,000 × .01 = $20,000

31. (a) [B-2] $588,000 × .035 = $20,580

Since $20,580 is the ending credit balance we wish to have in Allowance for Uncollectible Accounts, the adjusting journal entry would have to be made for $19,580 ($20,580 - $1,000 credit balance already in the account).

32. (d) [B-6]

33. (c) [A-4-a] Maturity value is equal to the principal plus the interest on the note.

Principal + Interest = Maturity Value
$10,000 + ($10,000 × .10 × 90/360) = $10,250

34. (d) [A-4-c] The bank discount in this problem is equal to maturity value x bank discount rate x the length of time the bank will hold the note.

Maturity Value × Bank Discount Rate × Time = Bank Discount
$10,250 × .12 × 60/360 = $205

Maturity Value - Bank Discount = Proceeds
$10,250 - 205 = $10,045

35. (b) [A-4-d]

36. (c) [A-4-f] Frank Co. must pay the bank the maturity value of the note plus the protest fee. Frank Co. would then record an account receivable from Alex Co. for the amount paid to the bank.

CHAPTER 10
Debt Equities or Liabilities

OVERVIEW

This chapter is intended to introduce the candidate to the accounting procedures used in recording and reporting liabilities. Many liabilities such as accounts payable and accrued liabilities have been discussed in earlier chapters. The accounting for notes payable and bonds payable is very similar to the accounting for notes and bonds receivable. The candidate may find it useful to review Chapter 6, Accounting for Investments.

The candidate should know the accounting procedures used for interest-bearing and noninterest-bearing notes payable, the calculation of simple and compound interest, the definitions of term and installment notes payable, the treatment of accounts payable, the recording of accrued liabilities, and the accounting for long-term liabilities including notes, mortgages, and bonds.

DEFINITION OF TERMS

BEARER BONDS. Bonds that are not registered in the name of the owner which are assumed to be owned by the individual who possesses the bond (also known as coupon bonds).

BOND SINKING FUND. An investment fund established to ensure that sufficient funds are available to retire the bonds at maturity.

CALLABLE BONDS. Bonds with a provision stating that the issuer may redeem the bonds prior to maturity by payment of a stipulated call price.

COMPOUND INTEREST. When a security earns compound interest, it earns interest on the principal of the security and on any interest which has been earned but not yet paid.

CONVERTIBLE BOND. A bond with a provision allowing the holder to convert the bond into common stock of the issuing company.

DEBENTURE. An unsecured bond backed only by the general credit of the company.

INSTALLMENT NOTE PAYABLE. A note payable that is due in equal periodic payments.

MORTGAGE. A legal agreement that gives the lender the right to be paid from the sale of specific assets that belong to the borrower if the borrower does not repay the loan.

MORTGAGE BOND. A bond secured by specific assets of the issuing company.

REGISTERED BOND. A bond that has the holder's name registered with the issuing company.

SERIAL BONDS. Bonds issued at the same time but coming due at various maturity dates. Issuing serial bonds alleviates some of the cash flow drain which occurs when bonds mature.

SIMPLE INTEREST. Interest which is computed only on the principal of the loan for a single period of time.

TERM BONDS. Bonds which have a single fixed maturity date.

TERM NOTES PAYABLE. A note payable repaid in one lump sum on a specific maturity date.

A. Short-Term Obligations

Short-term obligations are current liabilities which will require payment within the next operating cycle. The following are the basic types of short-term obligations:

1. *Notes Payable:* Notes payable are written documents promising to pay an amount to a creditor on a specific date. Short-term notes payable can be interest bearing or noninterest bearing. Notes payable could be given in exchange for goods or services, for purchase of real estate or equipment, or to a bank in exchange for cash.

    a. *Interest-bearing notes payable:* Interest-bearing notes payable require the payment of principal and interest at their maturity date. Interest-bearing notes payable should be recorded at their face value. If the accounting period ends before the note matures, an adjusting entry should be made to record any accrued interest on the note.

        EXAMPLE: *This example shows the accounting entries for an interest-bearing note payable. Assume that on May 1 Johnson Company issued a $5,000 six-month 12% note payable to Jones*

Company in exchange for merchandise. Johnson Company uses a periodic inventory system. The entry to record the issuance of the note would be:

		dr	cr
May 1	Purchases	5,000	
	Notes Payable		5,000

To record issuance of six-month 12% note in exchange for goods.

Assuming that Johnson Company's year end is December 31, the entry to record payment of the note on November 1 would be:

		dr	cr
Nov. 1	Notes Payable	5,000	
	Interest Expense	300	
	Cash		5,300

Paid six-month note to Jones Co. with interest ($5,000 x .12 x 6/12).

If Johnson Company's year end were August 31, the following adjusting entry would be needed to record the accrued interest expense:

		dr	cr
Aug. 31	Interest Expense	200	
	Accrued Interest Payable		200

To record interest accrued from May 1 through August 31 on Jones Co. note payable ($5,000 x .12 x 4/12).

Assuming Johnson Company's year end was August 31, the entry to record payment of the note on November 1 would be:

		dr	cr
Nov. 1	Notes Payable	5,000	
	Accrued Interest Payable	200	
	Interest Expense	100	
	Cash		5,300

Paid six-month note to Jones Co.

(1) *Simple interest:* Simple interest is calculated for a single period of time and is computed only on the amount of the principal of the note. The formula for calculation of simple interest is:

INTEREST = Principal x Rate of Interest for One Period x Number of Periods or Fraction of a Period

Note: All examples of the calculation of interest made previously in this module are calculations of simple interest.

(2) *Compound or add-on interest:* Compound interest refers to the calculation of interest on the principal and on any interest which is earned but has not yet been paid. Any interest earned during a period earns interest in subsequent periods. Compounding of interest takes place at periodic intervals which may vary in length. For example, many savings accounts compound interest on a daily basis. Interest might also be compounded on a weekly, monthly, quarterly, or yearly basis. The more often interest is compounded, the greater is the total amount of interest earned. Tables are available to aid in solving compound interest problems. The following example shows the calculation of simple and compound interest.

EXAMPLE: Assume that Sara Stein invested $1,000 at 10% interest for five years. The calculation of the total amount she would earn on the investment, assuming simple interest versus compound interest (compounded yearly), would be:

Year	Interest Computation	Simple Interest	Compound Interest
1	Interest on Principal ($1,000 x .10)	$100.00	$100.00
2	Interest on Principal ($1,000 x .10) Interest on Interest ($100 x .10)	100.00	100.00 10.00
3	Interest on Principal ($1,000 x .10) Interest on Interest ($210 x .10)	100.00	100.00 21.00
4	Interest on Principal ($1,000 x .10) Interest on Interest ($331 x .10)	100.00	100.00 33.10
5	Interest on Principal ($1,000 x .10) Interest on Interest ($464.10 x .10)	100.00	100.00 46.41
	Total Interest Earned	$500.00	$610.51

b. *Noninterest-bearing notes payable:* Noninterest-bearing notes payable do not require the payment of interest. Only the payment of the principal amount is required. Since money has a time value, a portion of the payment of the note at maturity is for implied

Debt Equities or Liabilities

interest. Although theoretically all noninterest-bearing notes should be reported at their present value, it is acceptable to treat notes issued for a short period of time (less than one year) as noninterest bearing since any interest included in the face value is normally immaterial.

c. *Discounted note payable:* A company may issue its own noninterest-bearing note payable to a bank in exchange for cash. The bank discounts the note and pays the discounted amount to the borrower. The bank calculates the discount as follows:

$$\frac{\text{Face Value of Note} \times \text{Discount Rate}}{\times \text{Period of Time Note Will Be Outstanding}} = \text{DISCOUNT}$$

The face value of the note less the discount equals the proceeds the borrower will receive. The discount on the note represents interest expense to the borrower.

EXAMPLE: This example shows the accounting entries for a noninterest-bearing note payable discounted with a bank. Robert Corp. discounted its own 90-day note payable for $5,000 at Security National Bank. The bank discount rate is 10%. The proceeds received by Robert Corp. are calculated as follows:

Face Value	5,000
Less: Discount	
($5,000 x .10 x 90/360)	- 125
Proceeds	4,875

The entry to record the loan would be:

	dr	cr
Cash	4,875	
Discount on Notes Payable	125	
Notes Payable		5,000

To record discounting of 90-day note with Security National Bank at 10%.

The entry to record payment of the note when it matures would be:

	dr	cr
Notes Payable	5,000	
Interest Expense	125	
Discount on Notes Payable		125
Cash		5,000

To record payment of loan from Security National Bank.

d. *Term notes payable:* Term notes payable are repaid in a lump sum on a specific date. They have a specified term of life after which the principal, or principal plus interest, must be repaid.

e. *Installment notes payable:* Installment notes payable are repaid through a series of periodic payments. Each payment represents a payment of a portion of the principal plus interest. Purchase of a television set to be paid for in 20 equal monthly installments would represent an installment note payable.

2. *Accounts Payable:* Accounts payable result from the purchase of merchandise or services on open account. Accounts payable are not formal written documents and usually do not require the payment of interest. The accountant must be careful to ensure that all accounts payable are recorded. Cash (or purchase) discounts are often offered for prompt payment of accounts payable. Companies should take advantage of cash discounts whenever possible since substantial cash savings result from doing so.

3. *Accruals:* Accruals are liabilities recorded through year-end (or monthly) adjusting entries. The recording of accrued liabilities is discussed in Chapter 4, Section E. Some examples of accrued liabilities are:

   a. Accrued interest payable.

   b. Accrued salaries payable.

   c. Accrued payroll taxes payable.

B. Long-Term Obligations

Long-term liabilities will not require repayment within the next operating cycle. Long-term liabilities could include mortgages, long-term notes payable, bonds payable, leases, and pensions.

1. *Notes Payable:* Long-term notes payable might be issued when large items such as machinery, equipment, or real estate are purchased. Long-term notes payable are accounted for in the same way as short-term notes payable. Most long-term notes payable are interest bearing, and any applicable interest should be accrued at the end of each accounting period. If a long-term note payable is noninterest bearing, the interest imputed on the note should be recorded as a discount on notes payable. The discount on Notes Payable account is a contra-liability which is shown as a deduction from Notes Payable on the balance sheet. By using a discount account, the note is valued on the balance sheet at its present value. If the discount were not recorded, the cost of the item obtained in exchange for the note would be overstated. Interest should also be

imputed on any long-term notes payable that have unreasonably low rates of interest. The Discount on Notes Payable account is amortized to Interest Expense over the life of the note.

The following example is based on the same information as the example in Chapter 9, Section A-2. Accounting for noninterest-bearing notes payable parallels the accounting for noninterest-bearing notes receivable. The candidate should review both examples together in order to ensure a complete understanding of the concept.

EXAMPLE: Zebo Company issued a $10,000 two-year noninterest-bearing note payable to Moomey Company on January 1, 19XA. The note was given in exchange for merchandise. The interest rate normally charged in this type of transaction is 10 percent. The computation of interest to be imputed is:

$$\frac{\$10,000}{1.21} = \$8,264 \quad \text{[See Chapter 9, Section A-2, for the formula.]}$$

The discount (interest) on the note would be:

$$\$10,000 - 8,264 = \underline{\underline{\$1,736}}$$

The journal entry to record the issuance of the note would be:

		dr	cr
Jan. 1	Purchases	8,264	
	Discount on Notes Payable	1,736	
	Notes Payable		10,000

Issued a two-year noninterest-bearing
note to Moomey Co. Interest was imputed
at 10%.

The journal entry to accrue the first year's interest would be:

		dr	cr
Dec. 31	Interest Expense	826	
	Discount on Notes Payable		826

To record interest accrued on the Moomey
Co. note payable. (Carrying Value x
Interest Rate x Time, or $8,264 x .10 x
1 year)

The journal entry to record the payment of the note on December 31, 19XB, would be:

	dr	cr
Dec. 31 Notes Payable	10,000	
Interest Expense	910	
Discount on Notes Payable		910
Cash		10,000

To record payment of the Moomey Co. note
and to write off the balance in the
discount account.

2. *Mortgages:* Mortgages are legal agreements that protect the lender by giving him or her the right to be paid from the sale of specific assets that belong to the borrower.

   a. *Installment payments:* Mortgages usually require equal monthly installment payments. These payments include a portion for payment of interest and a portion for payment of principal on the loan.

   b. *Security:* Mortgages are usually secured by the asset (often real estate) which has been purchased with the mortgage.

   Mortgages and installment notes are accounted for in the same way. The current portion of any mortgage (that portion which is to be paid within the next operating cycle) should be classified as a current asset.

   EXAMPLE: *This example illustrates typical accounting entries used for mortgages or installment notes. Assume Lloyd Corp. purchases real estate for $100,000 on January 1. The firm pays $25,000 cash and obtains a 4-year 12% mortgage for $75,000. Lloyd Corp. makes the following entry to record the purchase of the real estate:*

	dr	cr
Land	20,000	
Building	80,000	
Cash		25,000
Mortgage Payable		75,000

Purchased real estate using cash and
   a 4-year 12% mortgage.

The monthly mortgage payments are $1,975. The following schedule shows the calculation of the portion of each payment which relates to interest and to principal for three months:

Debt Equities or Liabilities

Payment Date	Monthly Payment	Interest of 12% on Principal Balance	Principal Reduction	Unpaid Principal Balance
1/1				$75,000.00
2/1	$1,975.00	$750.00[a]	$1,225.00	73,775.00
3/1	1,975.00	737.75[b]	1,237.25	72,537.75
4/1	1,975.00	725.38[c]	1,249.62	71,288.13

[a] (75,000.00 x .12 x 1/12)
[b] (73,775.00 x .12 x 1/12)
[c] (72,537.75 x .12 x 1/12)

The entries to record the payments in February and March would be:

		dr	cr
Feb. 1	Interest Expense	750.00	
	Mortgage Payable	1,225.00	
	Cash		1,975.00

Paid monthly mortgage payment.

		dr	cr
Mar. 1	Interest Expense	737.75	
	Mortgage Payable	1,237.25	
	Cash		1,975.00

Paid monthly mortgage payment.

3. *Bonds Payable:* When an accounting entity wishes to raise a large sum of money, long-term bonds payable might be issued. Bonds are usually sold to numerous investors. Bonds normally have a face value of $1,000 each and pay interest semiannually on the face value of the bond. Bonds are usually issued by large corporations or governmental entities.

   a. *Types of bonds payable:* There are many different types of bonds payable. The basic characteristics of some of these types are shown here.

      (1) *Debentures:* Debentures are unsecured bonds payable. Debentures are usually issued by large, financially sound companies.

      (2) *Mortgage bonds:* Mortgage bonds are secured by specific assets.

      (3) *Term bonds:* Term bonds have a single fixed date of maturity.

      (4) *Serial bonds:* Serial bonds have varying maturity dates but are issued at the same time. Issuing serial bonds avoids the cash flow drain which might occur when term bonds mature.

      (5) *Callable bonds:* Callable bonds may be redeemed by the

issuer prior to their maturity date through payment of a stipulated call price. Callable bonds allow the company to take advantage of interest rate changes over time.

(6) *Convertible bonds:* Convertible bonds have a special provision which allows the bond holder to convert the bonds into common stock of the issuing company. Convertible bonds are often issued as inducements to the lender.

(7) *Registered bonds:* Registered bonds have the name of the owner registered with the issuing company. The issuing company mails the interest checks to the registered owner.

(8) *Coupon bonds or bearer bonds:* Bearer bonds are not registered to a specific person. The owner of a bearer bond is assumed to be the person who has possession of the bond. Bearer bonds have coupons attached to them which, when an interest payment is due, the owner sends to the issuing company or to a bank acting as trustee. The issuer then pays the bond interest when the coupon is received.

b. *Sale of bonds:* Bonds are traded regularly on securities exchanges. Bonds may be held to maturity, or they may be sold on the market prior to maturity.

c. *Interest accrued on bonds sold:* When bonds are sold between interest dates, the purchaser must pay the seller for any interest which has accrued on the bonds. When the next interest payment date arrives, the issuer then pays the holder interest for the full six-month period.

EXAMPLE: Assume that Weller Corp. sells $1,000,000 of 10-year 12% bonds payable on March 1, 19XA. Interest is paid on the bonds on January 1 and July 1. The bonds are sold at face value. The entry to record the sale is:

		dr	cr
Mar. 1	Cash	1,020,000	
	Bonds Payable		1,000,000
	Bond Interest Payable		20,000

To record issuance of $1,000,000 of
10-year 12% bonds at face value plus
two months' accrued interest (1,000,000
× .12 × 2/12).

The entry to record the semiannual interest payment on July 1 is:

Debt Equities or Liabilities

		dr	cr
July 1	Interest Expense	40,000	
	Bond Interest Payable	20,000	
	Cash		60,000

Paid semiannual interest on 12% bonds
(1,000,000 × .12 × 2/12).

d. *Recording of bonds payable:* Bonds payable are always recorded in the accounts at face value. However, bonds may be sold at an amount different from their face value. For example, assume that the market rate of interest for bonds of the same grade as those sold by Weller Corp. was 15%. When Weller Corp. attempted to sell their 12% bonds on the market, investors would be unwilling to pay a full $1,000 for the bonds. This is because the bonds pay interest at an amount lower than the market rate of interest. The purchaser would be willing to pay only enough for the bond so that the effective rate of interest on the bond would be equal to market rate of interest. Usually the coupon rate (also called contract or stated rate) is fairly close to the market rate at the time of initial issue.

(1) Bond prices are quoted as a percentage of the bond's stated face value.

EXAMPLES:

A $1,000 stated value bond quoted at 98 is selling at 98% of face value, or $980 ($1,000 × .98).

A bond quoted at 104 is selling at 104% of face value, or $1,040 ($1,000 × 1.04).

(2) When the market rate of interest is higher than the stated rate of interest paid by the bond, the bond will sell at a discount.

EXAMPLE: Onsi Corp. issued $1,000,000 of 20-year 8% bonds on July 1, 19XA. The market rate of interest for bonds of the same grade was higher than 8% so the bonds sold at 97 ($970 for each $1,000 bond). The bonds were sold on an interest payment date. The entry to record issuance of the bonds would be:

		dr	cr
July 1	Cash	970,000	
	Discount on Bonds Payable	30,000	
	Bonds Payable		1,000,000

Issued 1,000 8% bonds at 97.

Note that bonds payable are always recorded at face value, as compared to bonds receivable which are recorded at cost. Discount on Bonds Payable is a contra-liability account and is shown as a deduction from Bonds Payable on the balance sheet.

(3) When the market rate of interest is lower than the stated rate of interest paid by the bond, the bond will sell at a premium.

EXAMPLE: Zeta Corp. issued $1,000,000 of 10-year 15% bonds on January 1, 1982. The market rate of interest for bonds of the same grade was lower than 15% so the bonds sold at 105 ($1,050 for each $1,000 bond). The bonds were sold on an interest payment date. The entry to record issuance of the bonds would be:

		dr	cr
Jan. 1	Cash	1,050,000	
	Premium on Bonds Payable		50,000
	Bonds Payable		1,000,000

Issued 1,000 15% bonds at 105.

Bond Premium is an adjunct account. An adjunct account is related to another account and has a balance which is on the same side of an account as the account to which it is related. Premium on Bonds Payable is added to Bonds Payable on the balance sheet to report book value of the bonds.

(4) Bond Premium or Discount should be amortized to Interest Expense over the life of the bond. There are two methods of bond premium or discount amortization: the straight-line method and the effective-interest method. The purpose of the amortization of bond premium or discount is to reflect the effective rate of interest paid by the issuer on the bonds. The effective-interest method is a more accurate method of adjusting the interest paid to the effective rate.

e. *Bond redemption:* When bonds payable mature, the issuer pays the bond holders the face value of the bonds. At maturity, all of the bond premium or discount has been amortized and the carrying value of the bonds is equal to the face value.

EXAMPLE: Assume that Zeta Corp. redeemed the $1,000,000 of bonds on their maturity date, January 1, 19XA. The entry to record the redemption would be:

	dr	cr
Jan. 1 Bonds Payable	1,000,000	
Cash		1,000,000

Retired 15% bonds at maturity.

(1) *Sinking fund:* Some bonds provide for the establishment of a sinking fund to accumulate sufficient funds to retire the bonds when they mature. The bond issuer makes periodic cash payments into the sinking fund, and the money is invested to earn a return. The sinking fund should cover the cost of retiring the bonds when they mature. Sinking funds are reported as a long-term investment on the balance sheet.

(2) *Redemption prior to maturity date:* Bonds may be redeemed prior to their maturity date, either through payment of the call price or by purchasing the bonds on the market. A gain or loss might be reported on the early redemption of bonds payable. Gains or losses from bond retirements should be reported as extraordinary items.

Chapter 10: Review Questions

PART A: Multiple-Choice Questions

DIRECTIONS: Select the best answer from the four alternatives. Write the letter of your answer in the blank to the left of the number. Assume 360 days per year in all interest calculations.

_____ 1. Interest-bearing notes

 a. require payment of principal and interest at maturity.
 b. are reported at face value on the balance sheet.
 c. necessitate the recording of any accrued interest at year end.
 d. All of the above statements are true.

_____ 2. Which of the following statements is true?

 a. Simple interest is calculated based only on the principal amount of the note.
 b. If two securities with a two-year life are identical in all ways except that one earns simple interest and the other earns compound interest, with monthly compounding, the security earning simple interest will earn the larger amount of interest.
 c. The more often interest is compounded the less the total amount of interest which is earned.
 d. Interest must be imputed on short-term noninterest-bearing notes.

_____ 3. The method of calculating interest in which interest is earned on both principal and previously accumulated interest is called

 a. imputed interest.
 b. accrued interest.
 c. simple interest.
 d. compound interest.

4. A $20,000 two-year noninterest-bearing note payable is issued. What is the amount of the discount on notes payable which should be recorded if the interest rate for comparable transactions is 5 percent? (Round your answer to the nearest dollar.)

   a. $10,141
   b. $ 1,859
   c. $ 9,524
   d. $ 2,000

5. Discount on Notes Payable is

   a. an owners' equity account.
   b. a liability account.
   c. a contra-liability account.
   d. a contra-asset account.

6. Jones Co. discounts their own $10,000 note payable (noninterest-bearing) at the Second Security Bank. The bank discount rate is 9 percent. The note is due in 180 days. The proceeds received by Jones Co. are

   a. $ 9,000.
   b. $ 9,100.
   c. $ 9,550.
   d. $10,000.

7. A legal agreement which gives the lender the right to be paid from the sale of specific assets that belong to the borrower is a/an

   a. installment note.
   b. bond.
   c. debenture.
   d. mortgage.

8. Bonds payable

   a. may be traded on securities exchanges.
   b. may be sold for more or less than their face value depending on the relationship between the current market rate of interest and the contract rate of interest printed on the bond.
   c. normally pay interest semiannually.
   d. are characterized by all of the above statements.

Debt Equities or Liabilities

9. A fund provided to accumulate a sufficient amount to repay bonds when they mature is usually called a/an

   a. bond sinking fund.
   b. bond redemption fund.
   c. bond call fund.
   d. investment fund.

10. Zeb Co. issued $100,000 of 10% (contract rate) bonds on May 1, 19XA. The market rate of interest for similar bonds on May 1, 19XA, was 8 percent. The bonds were sold

    a. at a discount.
    b. at face value.
    c. at a premium.
    d. at an amount that cannot be determined from the information given.

11. When bonds sell for less than face value, the difference between the selling price of the bonds and face value is called

    a. adjunct on bonds payable.
    b. premium on bonds payable.
    c. discount on bonds payable.
    d. contra bonds payable.

12. Bond Premium is

    a. a liability account.
    b. a contra account.
    c. deducted from Bonds Payable on the balance sheet.
    d. added to Bonds Payable on the balance sheet.

13. A bond which is quoted at 103 would sell for

    a. $1,003.
    b. $1,030.
    c. $1,300.
    d. $1,033.

_____   14. The entry to record payment of a $10,000 90-day 9% note payable would include

   a. a credit to Notes Payable for $10,000.
   b. a debit to Notes Payable for $10,225.
   c. a credit to Cash for $10,225.
   d. a debit to Interest Expense for $900.

_____   15. Installment notes payable are repaid through

   a. periodic payments on principal only.
   b. periodic payments on interest only.
   c. periodic payments which include both principal and interest.
   d. a lump sum payment of principal and interest due.

Debt Equities or Liabilities

PART B: Matching Sets

MATCHING SET 1

Match each description (16-22) with the appropriate term relating to bonds (A-H). Write the letter of your answer in the blank to the left of the number.

                BOND TERMS

        A. Debentures
        B. Mortgage Bonds
        C. Term Bonds
        D. Serial Bonds
        E. Convertible Bonds
        F. Callable Bonds
        G. Registered Bonds
        H. Coupon or Bearer Bonds

                DESCRIPTIONS

_____ 16. This type of bond has the name of the owner registered with the company. Interest checks are mailed directly to the owner.

_____ 17. This type of bond issue is issued on one date but comes due at varying maturity dates.

_____ 18. This type of bond is secured by specific assets of the borrower (issuer).

_____ 19. This type of bond may be redeemed by the issuer prior to its maturity date through payment of a stipulated amount.

_____ 20. These bonds are unsecured.

_____ 21. These bonds have a special provision which gives the bondholder the right to convert the bonds to stock of the issuing company at a given rate.

_____ 22. The owner of this type of bond is assumed to be the person who has possession of the bond.

MATCHING SET 2

Match the following statements (23-26) with the term (A-F) which best fits. Write the letter of your answer in the blank to the left of the number.

TERMS

A. Bond
B. Accounts Payable
C. Mortgage
D. Term Note Payable
E. Installment Note Payable
F. Accrual

STATEMENTS

_____ 23. A liability which results from a year-end adjusting entry that records an expense that has been incurred but not yet paid or recorded.

_____ 24. A liability resulting from a purchase made on open account.

_____ 25. A promissory note that requires a series of payments which consist of both interest and a portion of the principal.

_____ 26. A long-term liability, usually issued in $1,000 denominations, that pays interest semiannually and pays the face value at maturity.

Debt Equities or Liabilities 259

PART C: Problem Situations

DIRECTIONS: For each of the questions pertaining to the problem situations that follow, select the best answer from the four alternatives. Write the letter of your answer in the blank to the left of the number. Assume 360 days per year in all interest calculations.

Problem 1

Jack Nimble invested $5,000 at 10 percent for three years.

_____ 27. The total interest for the three-year period, assuming simple interest, is

   a. $ 500.
   b. $5,500.
   c. $1,500.
   d. $6,500.

_____ 28. The total interest for the three-year period, assuming compound interest, is

   a. $1,050.
   b. $1,655.
   c. $1,600.
   d. $6,665.

Problem 2

Jill Sykes Company made the following journal entry to record a two-year, noninterest-bearing note payable:

	dr	cr
Equipment	24,793	
Discount on Notes Payable	5,207	
Notes Payable		30,000

The equipment was purchased on October 1, 19XA, and the interest rate was assumed to be 10 percent. Sykes Company's year-end is December 31.

_____ 29. The amount of interest expense to be recorded on December 31, 19XA, would be (rounded to the nearest dollar)

   a. $ 620.
   b. $2,479.
   c. $ 651.
   d. $ 521.

30. The entry made by Jill Sykes Company to record the accrued interest would include

    a. a debit to Interest Expense and a credit to Interest Payable.
    b. a debit to Interest Receivable and a credit to Interest Income.
    c. a debit to Discount on Notes Payable and a credit to Interest Income.
    d. a debit to Interest Expense and a credit to Discount on Notes Payable.

31. The carrying value of the note on Jill Sykes Company's December 31, 19XA balance sheet would be

    a. $24,793.
    b. $30,000.
    c. $25,413.
    d. $29,479.

Debt Equities or Liabilities 261

Chapter 10: Solutions

PART A: Multiple-Choice Questions

	Answer	Refer to Chapter Section
1.	(d)	[A-1-a]
2.	(a)	[A-1-a(1)]
3.	(d)	[A-1-a(2)]

4. (b)   [B-1]

$$\frac{\$20,000}{(1 + .05)^2} = \frac{\$20,000}{1.1025} = \$18,141 \text{ (present value of note)}$$

Face Value of Note - Present Value of Note = Discount
$20,000 - $18,141 = $1,859

5. (c)   [B-1]

6. (c)   [A-1-c]
Discount = $10,000 x .09 x 180/360 = $450

Proceeds = Face Value - Discount
$9,550 = $10,000 - 450

7. (d)   [B-2]

8. (d)   [B-3]

9. (a)   [B-3-e(1)]

10. (c)   [B-3-d(3)]

11. (c)   [B-3-d(2)]

12. (d)   [B-3-d(3)]

13. (b)   [B-3-d(1)]
$1,000 x 1.03 = $1,030

14. (c)   [A-1-a]

Interest Expense = $10,000 × .09 × 90/360 = $225

The journal entry to record payment of the note would be:

	dr	cr
Notes Payable	10,000	
Interest Expense	225	
Cash		10,225

15. (c)   [A-1-e]

PART B: Matching Sets

MATCHING SET 1

16. (G)   [B-3-a(7)]

17. (D)   [B-3-a(4)]

18. (B)   [B-3-a(2)]

19. (F)   [B-3-a(5)]

20. (A)   [B-3-a(1)]

21. (E)   [B-3-a(6)]

22. (H)   [B-3-a(8)]

MATCHING SET 2

23. (F)   [A-3]

24. (B)   [A-2]

25. (E)   [A-1-e]

26. (A)   [B-3]

PART C: Problem Situations

27. (c)   [A-1-a(1)]
$5,000 × .10 × 3 years = $1,500

Debt Equities or Liabilities

28. (b)   [A-1-a(2)]
Year 1 $5,000   x .10 = $ 500
Year 2 ($5,000 + 500)   x .10 =   550
Year 3 ($5,000 + 500 + 550)   x .10 =   605
Total Interest $1,655

29. (a)   [B-1] Interest expense would be computed as follows:
Carrying Value x Interest Rate x Time = Interest
$24,793^a x .10 x 3/12   = $620

30. (d)   [B-1]

31. (c)   [B-1]
Notes Payable $30,000
- Discount on Notes Payable   - 4,857^b
Carrying Value of the Note $25,413

^{a}Carrying value is equal to the face value of the note less the balance in the Discount on Notes Payable account ($30,000 - $5,207 = $24,793).

^{b}Discount on Notes Payable = $5,207 - $620 = $4,857.

CHAPTER 11
Owners' Equity

OVERVIEW

This chapter covers accounting and reporting for owners' equity. The three forms of business entities were introduced in Chapter 1, Introduction to Accounting, and are elaborated upon further in this chapter. Chapter 3, Basic Financial Statements, introduced the recording of owners' equity on the balance sheet. The candidate might wish to first review the owners' equity section of Chapter 3 which emphasizes accounting for the owners' equity of sole proprietorships, partnerships, and corporations. Accounting for the owners' equity of a corporation is more complex than accounting for the owners' equity of a sole proprietorship or a partnership, so the majority of the material in this chapter relates to corporations.

The candidate should understand the three basic types of business entities and their advantages and disadvantages. The candidate should understand the recording of transactions affecting owners' equity in a sole proprietorship and a partnership. The candidate should also understand the following topics pertaining to corporations: the rights of and accounting for common and preferred stock, accounting for treasury stock, calculation of book value of stock, securities markets, and accounting for unappropriated and appropriated retained earnings.

DEFINITION OF TERMS

APPROPRIATED RETAINED EARNINGS. Retained earnings which have been segregated into a separate account to inform the financial statement reader that a portion of retained earnings is not available for the payment of dividends.

AUTHORIZED SHARES OF CAPITAL STOCK. The number of shares of capital stock which may legally be sold. The authorized amount of capital stock is determined by the corporate charter.

BOOK VALUE. Book value per share of common stock is a numerical measure of the net assets of a corporation as reflected in a single share of common stock.

CALLABLE PREFERRED STOCK. Callable preferred stock may be redeemed by the issuing corporation at a stipulated call price.

CONVERTIBLE PREFERRED STOCK. Convertible preferred stock may be exchanged by the stockholder for a predetermined number of shares of common stock.

CUMULATIVE PREFERRED STOCK. Cumulative preferred stock is cumulative with respect to dividends. This means that any dividends not paid in one period must be made up before any current dividends may be paid to common shareholders.

DIVIDENDS IN ARREARS. Dividends earned on cumulative preferred stock which have not yet been declared.

ISSUED SHARES. Shares which have been issued to shareholders at any time.

LIMITED LIABILITY. Shareholders of a corporation are liable for the debts of the corporation only to the amount of their investment in the corporation.

ORGANIZED STOCK EXCHANGES. Established markets for securities where buy and sell orders are matched at public auction. Examples of organized stock exchanges are the New York Stock Exchange and the American Stock Exchange.

OVER-THE-COUNTER MARKET. All markets for securities except organized stock exchanges.

OUTSTANDING SHARES. The shares which are currently in the hands of stockholders.

PAR VALUE. An arbitrary value placed on a share of stock at the time the corporation seeks authorization of the stock.

PARTICIPATIVE PREFERRED STOCK. Shares of preferred stock which enable the stockholders to receive not only their stated dividend but also to share in dividend distributions of earnings of the corporation.

PRIVATE PLACEMENT. The sale of an entire issue of securities by the issuing corporation directly to one or a few large institutional investors.

TREASURY STOCK. The shares of a corporation's own capital stock reacquired by the corporation.

UNAPPROPRIATED RETAINED EARNINGS. The portion of the retained earnings of a corporation which have not been appropriated for a specific purpose.

UNLIMITED LIABILITY. The liability of sole proprietors and partners for business debts not only from business assets but also from personal assets.

A. Sole Proprietorships and Partnerships

As previously discussed in Chapter 1, Introduction to Accounting, sole proprietorships are businesses owned by one individual. Partnerships are

Owners' Equity

businesses with two or more co-owners who share profits and losses. These forms of business carry with them certain advantages and disadvantages.

1. *Advantages of Sole Proprietorships and Partnerships:* The following advantages are common to both sole proprietorships and partnerships.

    a. *Formation:* Formation is relatively easy. No legal formalities are required to create the business.

    b. *Regulation:* There is less regulation of the business during its existence than that involved in a corporation.

    c. *Tax advantage:* There exists a possible tax advantage. There is no double taxation of the business firm since no tax is assessed at the business level. All taxable income is passed through to the owners. Losses, too, may be passed through. However, the tax laws are extremely complicated so it is best to seek expert advice relating to tax matters before deciding which form of business organization to use.

2. *Disadvantages of Sole Proprietorships and Partnerships:* Both these forms of business enterprises do not create new legal entities, as happens when a corporation is formed. There are several disadvantages that are common to both sole proprietorships and partnerships.

    a. *Limited life:* Because the form of business is not a legal entity, the business terminates on the death or withdrawal of an owner.

    b. *Unlimited liability:* The sole owner in a sole proprietorship and each general partner in a partnership are liable for the debts of the business, not only from business assets but also from personal assets.

    c. *Limited capital-raising ability:* As compared to a corporation, both sole proprietorships and partnerships have far less ability to generate capital from contributors.

3. *Accounting for Owners' Equity:* In sole proprietorships and partnerships, accounting for owners' equity may be handled in the following ways:

    a. *Sole proprietorships:* The accounting for a sole proprietorship is relatively simple (see Chapter 3, Basic Financial Statements). Owner's equity consists of one capital account which records all increases and decreases in owner's equity.

    b. *Partnerships:* The accounting for a partnership was discussed in Chapter 3, Basic Financial Statements. In a partnership, capital accounts for each individual partner record the increases and decreases in the owner's equity for individual partners. Since there is more than one capital account in a partnership, one of the major differences between accounting for a sole proprietorship and a partnership is in the division of profit or loss.

(1) If no agreement is apparent among partners as to the sharing of profits, the division will be made equally, even if time or capital contributions devoted to the business are not equal. Losses will also be shared equally. However, if any agreement has been reached, either oral or written, that agreement will hold for both profits and losses in the same manner unless otherwise specified.

(2) The division of profits and losses can take many forms, depending on the agreement of the partners. Division may be according to a fixed ratio (for example, 3:2:4) or a ratio reflecting capital contributed. Salaries may be allowed as a distribution of profit as well as interest on the capital balances.

Note: If salaries and/or interest are allowed as part of the distribution of income, they are not recorded as salary expense or interest expense.

EXAMPLE: Assume a partnership of P and Q which has a net income for the period of $25,000. The written agreement between P and Q specifies that each partner is to be allowed a salary of $7,000 and interest on invested capital of 10 percent. P has invested $40,000 capital and Q $30,000. The division of profit is to be equal after salaries and interest are accounted for. Division of profits is as follows:

Net Income				$25,000
Salaries: P	$7,000			
Q	7,000	$14,000		
Interest: P	$4,000			
Q	3,000	7,000		(21,000)
Remaining Profit to be Divided:				$ 4,000
To P				$ 2,000
To Q				$ 2,000

Each partner will then receive:

	P	Q
Salaries	$ 7,000	$ 7,000
Interest	4,000	3,000
Remainder	2,000	2,000
Totals	$13,000	$12,000

Owners' Equity

The $25,000 net income has been divided according to the partners' agreement.

The journal entry to record the distribution of income would be:

	dr	cr
Income Summary	25,000	
P, Capital		13,000
Q, Capital		12,000

To record distribution of net income for the period.

B. Corporations

As discussed previously in Chapter 1, Introduction to Accounting, corporations are entities created by state or federal law which are separate and distinct from ownership interests. A corporation can hold and dispose of property, can contract in its own name, can sue and be sued. This type of business entity carries with it certain advantages and disadvantages.

1. *Advantages of the Corporate Form of Ownership:* Corporations have a number of advantages, including limited liability for the shareholders, continuity of existence, capital-raising capacity, and quality of management.

    a. *Limited liability:* The shareholder, or owner, in a corporation risks only the amount of his/her investment. Such a shareholder's personal assets are protected from corporate creditors by the limited liability feature.

    b. *Continuity of life*: Since the corporation is a creature of law, its existence does not depend on continuous ownership by one or a group of individuals. This feature leads to free transferability of ownership interests. Shares in a corporation may be bought and sold freely without the issuing corporation's interference and without affecting the operations of the corporation.

    c. *Capital-raising capacity:* The corporation is efficient as a mechanism for pooling the investments of many individuals. Not only can it raise large amounts of capital, but it also can use several means of raising capital. For example, bonds and several types of capital stock may be issued.

    d. *Quality of management:* Owners need not devote time and energy to managing the entity. Instead, they can employ professional executives to accept the responsibility of management.

2. *Disadvantages of the Corporate Form:* Double taxation and regulation costs are two of the primary disadvantages of the corporate form of business enterprise.

   a. *Double taxation:* Since the corporation is considered a legal entity, it is taxed on its earnings. The distribution of these earnings to the owners in the form of cash dividends is considered to be personal income to the shareholders and is again taxed. (See comments about taxation with respect to the sole proprietor.)

   b. *Regulation costs:* A corporation is regulated by federal and state governments, securities exchanges, and other bodies. The costs of this regulation may be high compared to other types of business entities.

C. **Accounting for Stockholders' Equity of a Corporation**

The ownership of a corporation consists of individuals who hold the shares of capital stock originally issued by the corporation in exchange for contributions of cash, property, or services. The stockholders' equity section of the balance sheet will display this contributed capital. Contributions are not the only source of capital for a corporation. If the business is successful and has income, management may want to retain some of these earnings in the corporation. The stockholders' equity section of the balance sheet allows for the recording of the retention of earnings.

1. *Contributed Capital:* A corporation has flexibility in the amounts and types of capital stock which it offers in exchange for capital. The amount of capital stock which can be offered to individuals is determined by the corporate charter filed with the state of incorporation. This is known as the *authorized amount* and cannot be exceeded. The amount of stock which has actually been issued to investors is known as the *issued amount*. The amount which is in the hands of stockholders is the *outstanding amount*. These three amounts may be identical; however, they need not be the same. (Some authorized shares may not have been issued to investors, and some shares which were issued to investors may have been repurchased by the company and are no longer considered outstanding. When a corporation holds treasury stock, the treasury shares are still classified as issued; but they are no longer considered outstanding since they are not in the hands of shareholders.) Flexibility in the types of capital stock offered to investors exists. There are two major types of capital stock: common stock and preferred stock.

   a. *Common stock:* Common stock is the basic unit of ownership in a corporation. If a corporation has only one class of capital stock, it will be common stock. Common stock carries with it four basic rights which are inherent in its ownership unless specified otherwise by the corporation on issue or waived by the stockholder after issuance. These rights are:

(1) *The right to have a voice in management:* Stockholders elect the board of directors, which is responsible for the overall management of the firm. Stockholders are also able to vote on matters such as the issuance of long-term debt or the amendment of the state charter.

(2) *The right to share in profits on distribution:* Each shareholder is entitled to obtain a proportionate share of the earnings of the corporation in the form of dividends based on the number of shares owned. This right does not commence until and unless dividends are declared by the board of directors.

(3) *The right to maintain percentage ownership in the corporation:* Each shareholder may have the right to purchase additional shares of stock in new issues at market value in order to maintain his/her percentage of ownership in the firm. This is often called the *preemptive right*.

(4) *The right to share in assets upon liquidation:* Common stockholders have a residual claim; that is, in the event of liquidation, common stockholders cannot receive any distributions unless creditors and preferred stockholders, if any, have received their claims. Once these claims have been paid, common shareholders are entitled to the remaining or residual assets in relation to proportional ownership in the firm.

b. *Basic accounting for common stock:*

(1) *Issuance of common stock:* At authorization in the corporate charter, common stock may be given a par value. *Par value* is a fixed amount printed on the face of the stock certificate. In many states, par value represents the minimum legal capital of the corporation. This means that an individual who buys stock from a corporation must give the corporation at least par value for the stock or be liable for the difference. Most states prohibit the issuance of stock at less than par value. Although par value may bear some relationship with the original price, it is often arbitrarily set and should not be confused with market value in any way. On the issuance of par value common stock, the asset Cash is increased with a debit for the total amount received by the corporation. The account Common Stock is increased or credited for par value. The remainder, if any, is a credit and is placed in the account Paid-in Capital in Excess of Par.

EXAMPLE: Zeta Company issues 100 shares of its $10 par value stock for $28 per share. The journal entry to record this transaction is as follows:

	dr	cr
Cash	2,800	
Common Stock		1,000
Paid-in Capital in Excess of Par		1,800

Issued 100 shares of common stock @ $28 per share. ($10 par x 100 shares par value; $2,800 - $1,000 = $1,800 paid-in capital in excess of par).

(a) The issuance of common stock for assets other than cash is recorded in the same manner, with the asset account increased (debited) for market value of the asset and common stock and Paid-in Capital increased (credited) exactly as in the Zeta Company example.

(b) At one time, it was required that all stocks have a par value. Since par value might mislead investors as to the "true value" of a share of stock and sale of stock at less than par value results in a contingent liability, the issuance of stock that does not have a par value (no-par stock) was allowed. The main advantage of no-par stock is that it may be issued at any price. When no-par stock is issued, the asset Cash is debited for the amount received, and the account Common Stock is credited for the total amount received.

Note here that these entries are only for the original issuance of stock by the corporation. Subsequent trading of the stock by investing individuals does not necessitate any entries on the part of the corporation due to the transferability characteristic of corporate stock.

(2) *Dividend payments on common stock:*

(a) *Cash dividends:* Cash dividends on common stock are not an expense of the corporation but are rather a distribution of earnings to the owners. Dividend declarations are at the discretion of the board of directors. Once declared, the cash dividend amount becomes a liability of the corporation until paid.

On declaration, the debit is to Dividends Declared (or Retained Earnings). The credit increases the liability account, Dividends Payable. The date of payment

Owners' Equity

occurs a few weeks later. At this date the liability is removed with a debit, and Cash is decreased with a credit. A cash dividend, then, reduces both assets and stockholders' equity since funds are severed from the business. Dividends Declared is a temporary account which is closed to Retained Earnings.

The entry to record declaration of a $1,000 cash dividend is:

	dr	cr
Dividends Declared	1,000	
Dividends Payable		1,000

The entry to record payment of the $1,000 cash dividend previously declared is:

	dr	cr
Dividends Payable	1,000	
Cash		1,000

(b) *Stock dividends:* A stock dividend of common stock is a distribution of additional shares of common stock to existing common stockholders based on the quantity of shares currently held. A stock dividend is a distribution of earnings just as is a cash dividend. The difference lies in the payment: stock rather than cash.

On declaration, the account Stock Dividends Declared (or Retained Earnings) is debited, and a stockholders' equity account, Stock Dividends to be Distributed, is credited. There is no liability since there is no obligation to pay cash or any other asset. On payment, Stock Dividends to be Distributed is cleared with a debit and Common Stock is credited. Note that the net effect of this event merely reduces one stockholders' equity account (Retained Earnings) and increases another (Common Stock). The total stockholders' equity remains unchanged as well as each stockholder's relative ownership percentage. Stock Dividends Declared is a temporary account which is closed to Retained Earnings.

The entry to record declaration of a $1,000 stock dividend is:

	dr	cr
Stock Dividends Declared	1,000	
Stock Dividends to be Distributed		1,000

The entry to record the distribution of the $1,000 stock dividend declared above is:

	dr	cr
Stock Dividends to be Distributed	1,000	
Common Stock		1,000

c. *Preferred stock:* Preferred stock is a form of contributed capital with features which distinguish it from common stock. Generally, preferred stock will have a preference over common stock with respect to one or more of the rights of common stock (such as dividend payments or receipt of assets if the corporation liquidates) with a sacrifice of another of the rights (voting power or participation in the distribution of earnings past some specified date). The basic accounting for preferred stock involves its issuance, dividend payments, and termination of the preferred status.

(1) *Issuance of preferred stock:* The issuance of preferred stock is similar to the issuance of common stock, except that the par value, if any, is entered into a preferred stock account.

EXAMPLE: *If 10 shares of Beta Company's preferred stock (par value $100) are issued for $105 each, the entry would be:*

	dr	cr
Cash	1,050	
Preferred Stock		1,000
Paid-in Capital in Excess of Par/Preferred Stock		50

Issued 10 shares of preferred stock for $105. ($100 par x 10 shares par value; $1,050 - $1,000 = $50 paid-in capital in excess of par)

(2) *Dividend payments on preferred stock:* Dividend payments on preferred stock are in cash and are stated as a percentage of par value.

EXAMPLE: *If par is $100 on a share of preferred stock and the dividend rate is 9%, the dividend payment would be:*

9% x $100 par = .09 x 100 = $9 per share

This stock may also be referred to as $9 preferred.

(a) *Payment of dividends:* Dividends are payable only at the discretion of the board of directors. Once dividends are declared, preferred dividends normally take precedence over dividends on common stock.

> EXAMPLE: *The Miller Corporation has 100 shares of $9 preferred stock and 1,000 shares of common stock, and the board of directors declares a $2,000 dividend. The distribution will be as follows:*
>
> | | |
> |---|---:|
> | Preferred Stock | $ 900 |
> | ($9 x 100 shares) | |
> | Common Stock | 1,100 |
> | ($2,000 - 900 = $1,100) | |
>
> | Per Share: | |
> |---|---|
> | Preferred Stock | $9.00 |
> | Common Stock | $1.10 |
> | ($1,100/1,000 shares) | |

(b) *Cumulative dividends and participation:* Two features with respect to dividends make preferred stock a more attractive investment. These two features are cumulative dividends and participation.

One reason for investment in preferred stock is the expectation of a regular stream of dividends of a fixed amount. Without a cumulative dividends feature, any dividends not declared in a period will be lost forever. Therefore, most preferred stock is issued with a *cumulative dividends* feature which signifies that any dividends not paid in any one period to the preferred stockholders (called *dividends in arrears*) must be made up before any current dividends to preferred or common stock can be distributed. These dividends in arrears are not a liability since no liability exists until declaration. Dividends in arrears are not recorded in the accounting records.

Normally, preferred stock has no right to share in earnings above the stated rate, even if the corporation has high earnings. One desirable feature of preferred stock is *participation*. Participation means that preferred shareholders may receive not only their stated dividend but also may share in earnings of the corporation when they are high. Participating preferred stock will never receive less than the stated dividend when dividends are declared. Many preferred stock issues contain the cumulative feature, with relatively few participating.

(3) *Termination of the preferred status:* Some preferred stocks carry features which make them terminable at the option of either the issuing corporation or the stockholder.

(a) *Callable preferred stock:* If a preferred stock is callable, the issuing corporation may call, or redeem, the stock at a date after issue for a stipulated price, usually slightly higher than the issue price. Callable preferred stock allows the issuing corporation to raise capital without the loss of control by the existing shareholders. The corporation has the prerogative of redeeming the stock should the funds prove unnecessary in the future.

(b) *Convertible preferred stock:* If a preferred stock is convertible, the stockholder can exchange the preferred stock at his/her option for a predetermined number of shares of common stock. Convertible preferred stock allows the shareholder to participate in periods of high growth by conversion to higher common stock dividends and market value. In this way the former preferred shareholder now has an equity interest in higher earnings which usually translate to higher market value of the stock.

d. *Treasury stock:* The shares of its own capital stock reacquired by a corporation are referred to as *treasury stock*. Treasury stock is reacquired for various purposes (for example, to be used in an employee bonus plan). Treasury stock can be reissued at any time or held in the treasury indefinitely. While in the treasury, the stock carries none of the rights of the other shares in its class (such as cash dividends or voting). On the acquisition of shares for the treasury, the stockholders' equity contra-account, Treasury Stock, is debited to increase the account, and the Cash account is credited for the cost of the treasury stock.

EXAMPLE: *The reacquisition of 10 shares of $100 par common stock originally issued at $115 per share for $1,300 ($130 per share) would be recorded as:*

	dr	cr
Treasury Stock	1,300	
Cash		1,300

To record reacquisition of 10 shares.

Even though it has a debit balance, the Treasury Stock account does not represent an asset. It is deducted from total stockholders' equity on the balance sheet at its reacquisition cost, since the company, in effect, has become smaller.

e. *Book value:* Book value per share of common stock is a numerical measure of the net assets of a corporation as reflected in a single share of common stock. Book value is not market value but rather is computed by referring to the accounting records. Assume stockholders' equity as presented below:

Common Stock (100,000 shares)	$ 200,000
Preferred Stock (2,000 shares)	200,000
Paid-in Capital in Excess of Par	500,000
Retained Earnings	900,000
Total Stockholders' Equity	$1,800,000

Since the common shares have a residual claim, all of the net assets belong to the common stockholders except that which belongs to the preferred shareholders. In this example, book value per common share would be:

Total Stockholders' Equity	$1,800,000
Less: Par Value of Preferred Stock ($100 x 2,000 shares)	- 200,000
Equity Allocated to Common Stock	$1,600,000
Divided by: Number of Common Shares Outstanding	100,000
Book Value Per Share of Common Stock	$16

The number of common shares which is divided into the equity allocated to common stock represents the shares outstanding, which indicates that any unissued or treasury shares would not be included in the computation.

f. *Securities markets:*

(1) *Original issues markets:* The issuing corporation offers its securities in exchange for capital. A new issue of securities may be offered to the public through an investment banker (or underwriter) who is a specialist in marketing securities to investors. Original issues of securities may also be sold through private placement. *Private placement* is the sale of an entire issue of securities by the issuing corporation directly to one or a few large institutional investors. The offering is not open to the public.

(2) *Secondary markets:* Securities are exchanged among the general public in the secondary markets. Organized stock exchanges are markets for securities where buy and sell orders are matched at public auction. Organized exchanges may be national (New York Stock Exchange and American Stock Exchange) or may be regional or local. The over-the-counter market consists of all markets for securities except organized exchanges. In the over-the-counter market, securities dealers maintain inventories of over-the-counter securities and sell these to the public at bid-and-ask prices.

2. *Retained Earnings*: Retained earnings is the portion of stockholders' equity which arises from the retention of earnings in the corporation. The Retained Earnings account is a historical record of all net income (or loss) from the time of incorporation to the present date less any distributions of earnings to stockholders in the form of cash or stock dividends.

   a. *Increases in retained earnings:* The Retained Earnings account has a normal credit balance, but may have a debit balance should accumulated losses be large. In this case, it is presented on the balance sheet as a deficit or negative balance. The Retained Earnings account is increased with a credit entry. Increases result from net income in any period. Increases will also result from releases from the appropriations account.

   b. *Decreases in retained earnings:* The Retained Earnings account is decreased with a debit entry. Decreases will result from a net loss in any period or a transfer to an appropriations account. Decreases will also result from the declaration of cash or stock dividends.

   c. *Appropriated retained earnings:* The division of the Retained Earnings account into two or more separate accounts is achieved by the appropriation of retained earnings. The purpose of this segregation is to inform the financial statement reader that a portion of retained earnings is not available for the payment of dividends. Since the declaration of dividends is at the discretion of the board of directors in all cases, appropriations are not a mandatory accounting procedure. Alternatively, this information may be given in a footnote, which is the most prevalent practice.

   Should an appropriation of retained earnings be desired, the entry will be a debit to reduce Unappropriated Retained Earnings and a credit to establish one or more appropriations accounts:

	dr	cr
Unappropriated Retained Earnings	xx	
Retained Earnings Appropriated		xx

   The total amount of retained earnings remains the same. This appropriation may be voluntary, as in the case of plant expansion, or it may result from contractual or legal obligations such as long-term loan covenants restricting the payment of cash dividends. Note that the appropriation of retained earnings does not provide cash or other assets. It is not a source of funds. Conversely, a lack of an appropriations account does not ensure cash will be available for the declaration of cash dividends. An appropriation of retained earnings is a convention of accounting designed to provide information only. The Retained Earnings account has its own financial statement presentation (refer to Chapter 3, Basic Financial Statements).

Figure 11-1 shows an example of a complete owners' equity section shown in financial statement format, illustrating all of the points discussed in this chapter.

Figure 11-1
Owners' Equity Section/Financial Statement

Stockholders' equity:		
Cumulative 10% preferred stock, $100 par, 9,000 shares authorized and issued	900,000	
Common stock, $1 par, authorized 1,000,000 shares, issued 500,000 shares of which 2,000 shares are held in the treasury	500,000	
Paid-in capital in excess of par value	3,100,000	
Total contributed capital		4,500,000
Retained earnings:		
Appropriated for contingencies	800,000	
Unappropriated retained earnings	2,524,000	3,324,000
Total paid-in capital and retained earnings		7,824,000
Less: Treasury stock 2,000 shares (at cost)		20,000
Total stockholders' equity		7,804,000

Chapter 11: Review Questions

PART A: Multiple-Choice Questions

DIRECTIONS: Select the best answer from the four alternatives. Write the letter of your answer in the blank to the left of the number.

_____ 1. An arbitrary value placed on a share of stock at the time a corporation seeks authorization is called

   a. preferred value.
   b. statutory value.
   c. market value.
   d. par value.

_____ 2. Which of the following statements is false?

   a. Each partner in a general partnership is personally liable for all of the partnership business debts.
   b. A corporation must apply for and receive a charter before it comes into existence.
   c. Formation of a partnership requires the approval of the state.
   d. Corporate stockholders normally have limited liability for debts of the corporation.

_____ 3. In a corporation

   a. dividends in arrears are a liability on the balance sheet.
   b. par value establishes the amount a share of stock will sell for.
   c. declaration of dividends reduces retained earnings.
   d. common stock dividends normally take precedence over dividends on preferred stock.

_____ 4. Which of the following is not normally a right of common stockholders?

   a. The right to share in assets upon liquidation.
   b. The right to maintain their percentage of ownership in the corporation.
   c. The right to share in profits on distribution.
   d. The right to vote on *all* decisions affecting the company.

5. Treasury stock

    a. is an asset account.
    b. should be shown as a reduction from stockholders' equity on the balance sheet.
    c. has the right to receive cash dividends upon declaration.
    d. cannot be reissued by the company.

6. Retained earnings

    a. is a record of cash available for projects which results from earnings kept in the business.
    b. is increased when additional investments are made by owners.
    c. is increased by net income and decreased by net losses.
    d. All of the above statements are true.

7. Joe and Alex own a partnership. They have not signed a partnership agreement as to the division of profits resulting from the business. Which of the following statements is true?

    a. Since Joe contributed twice as much capital as Alex, the ratio for sharing profits is 2:1.
    b. If their agreement is oral, it is invalid.
    c. If there is no oral agreement between the partners regarding the division of profits, both profits and losses will be split equally.
    d. In partnership agreements, profits and losses must be divided in the same manner.

8. Preferred stock

    a. is a class of stock given priority status over common stock with respect to one or more of the rights of common stock, such as dividend payments or receipt of assets upon liquidation.
    b. always carries a feature which signifies that any dividends not paid to the preferred stockholders in any one period must be made up before any current dividends to preferred or common stock can be distributed.
    c. normally has the right to vote.
    d. All of the above statements are true.

9. The right of common stockholders to maintain their proportionate interest in a corporation is called

    a. the preemptive right.
    b. the proportional right.
    c. a proxy.
    d. the participative right.

Owners' Equity

10. On June 30, 19XA, XYZ Corporation declared a dividend of $1.00 per share to the common stockholders of record July 10, 19XA, to be paid July 20, 19XA. XYZ Corporation has 5,000 authorized shares and 3,000 outstanding shares. The journal entry to be made on June 30 would be:

		dr	cr
a.	Dividends Declared	5,000	
	Common Dividends Payable		5,000
b.	Dividends Declared	3,000	
	Common Dividends Payable		3,000
c.	Retained Earnings	3,000	
	Dividends Declared		3,000

d. No journal entry would be made on June 30.

11. Using the information from question 10, the journal entry to be made on July 20 would be:

		dr	cr
a.	Dividends Declared	3,000	
	Cash		3,000
b.	Common Dividends Payable	5,000	
	Cash		5,000
c.	Common Dividends Payable	3,000	
	Cash		3,000

d. No journal entry would be made on July 20.

12. Zeno Corporation issued 10,000 shares of $1.00 par value common stock for $10 per share. The journal entry to record this transaction would include

a. a credit to Common Stock for $100,000.
b. a debit to Cash for $90,000.
c. a credit to Common Stock for $10,000.
d. a debit to Cash for $10,000.

13. Original issues of stock may be sold

a. by private placement to large institutional investors.
b. on the American Stock Exchange.
c. over the counter.
d. through all of the above means.

14. The account Paid-in Capital in Excess of Par

    a. is shown as part of the contributed capital section of stockholders' equity on the income statement.
    b. is credited for the excess of market price over par value on the original issuance of stock.
    c. is only used when stock is sold for cash.
    d. is described by all of the above.

15. Failure to record the declaration and distribution of a stock dividend (dividend issued in stock) would

    a. cause assets to be overstated.
    b. cause total stockholders' equity to be overstated.
    c. cause total stockholders' equity to be understated.
    d. have no effect on total stockholders' equity.

16. An appropriation of retained earnings

    a. reduces the total retained earnings of the company.
    b. is used to inform the financial statement readers that a portion of retained earnings is not available for the payment of dividends.
    c. is a mandatory procedure when all of the retained earnings of the company are not available for dividend payment.
    d. is characterized by all of the above.

Owners' Equity

PART B: Matching Sets

MATCHING SET 1

Match the following characteristics (17-22) with the appropriate form/s of business entity (A-C). More than one letter may apply to a characteristic. Write the letter(s) of your answer in the blank to the left of the number.

TYPES OF BUSINESS ENTITIES

A. Sole Proprietorship
B. Partnership
C. Corporation

CHARACTERISTICS

_____ 17. The owner or owners have limited liability.

_____ 18. The business is a separate legal entity.

_____ 19. The owner or owners have unlimited liability.

_____ 20. The business has a limited life.

_____ 21. The profits of the business are taxed at two different levels (double taxation).

_____ 22. The business has free transferability of ownership interests.

MATCHING SET 2

Match each of the definitions (23-31) with the appropriate accounting terms (A-K). Write the letter of your answer in the blank to the left of the number.

ACCOUNTING TERMS

A. Appropriated Retained Earnings
B. Authorized Shares of Capital Stock
C. Book Value per Share of Common Stock
D. Callable Preferred Stock
E. Convertible Preferred Stock
F. Cumulative Preferred Stock
G. Dividends in Arrears
H. Outstanding Shares of Capital Stock
I. Participative Preferred Stock
J. Treasury Stock
K. Unappropriated Retained Earnings

DEFINITIONS

_____ 23. A numerical measure of net assets of a corporation as reflected in a single share of common stock.

_____ 24. Shares of stock which are currently in the hands of stockholders.

_____ 25. Preferred stock which may be exchanged by the stockholder for a predetermined number of shares of common stock.

_____ 26. The number of shares of capital stock which may be legally sold as determined by the corporate charter.

_____ 27. Any dividends not paid on this form of stock must be made up before any current dividend may be paid to stockholders.

_____ 28. Retained earnings which have been segregated into a separate account to inform the financial statement reader that a portion of retained earnings is not available for the payment of dividends.

Owners' Equity

_____ 29. The shares of its own capital stock reacquired by a corporation on the open market.

_____ 30. This form of preferred stock may be redeemed by the issuing corporation at a stipulated price.

_____ 31. The portion of retained earnings of a corporation which has not been segregated for a specific purpose.

PART C: Problem Situations

DIRECTIONS: For each of the questions relating to the following problem situations, select the best answer from the four alternatives. Write the letter of your answer in the blank to the left of the number.

Problem 1

Bob and Sally own a partnership. The written agreement between Bob and Sally specifies that each partner is to be allowed a salary of $10,000 and interest on invested capital of 12 percent. Sally has invested $60,000 in the partnership, and Bob has invested $20,000. The division of profit after salaries and interest have been accounted for is to be made equally.

_____ 32. Assuming that the partnership has net income of $40,000 for the period, the amount allocated to Bob would be

a. $20,000.
b. $22,400.
c. $17,600.
d. none of the above.

_____ 33. Assuming that the partnership has net income of $20,000 for the period, the amount allocated to Sally would be

a. $12,400.
b. $ 7,600.
c. $22,000.
d. ($ 4,800).

_____ 34. Assuming that the partnership has net income of $20,000, the journal entry to record the distribution of earnings would include

a. a debit to each partner's Capital account and a credit to Income Summary.
b. a debit to Income Summary and a credit to each partner's Capital account.
c. a debit to Salaries Expense, a debit to Interest Expense, a debit to Income Summary, and a credit to each partner's Capital account.
d. a debit to Cash and a credit to each partner's Capital account.

Problem 2

The stockholders' equity of Martin Corporation is as follows:

Preferred Stock	$100 par value 100 shares outstanding	$100,000
Common Stock	$10 par value 10,000 shares outstanding	100,000
Paid-in Capital in Excess of Par--Common		100,000
Retained Earnings		500,000
		$800,000
Less Treasury Stock (2,000 shares)		- 150,000
Total Stockholders' Equity		$650,000

35. What is the book value per common share?

    a. $25.00
    b. $87.50
    c. $75.00
    d. $68.75

Problem 3

Morgan Corporation has 100 shares of $100 par 10% cumulative preferred stock outstanding. Two years' dividends are in arrears on the preferred stock. (No dividends were paid in 19XA and 19XB.) There are 10,000 shares of common stock outstanding. Morgan Corporation declares a $10,000 cash dividend at the end of 19XC.

36. The total amount of the $10,000 dividend which will be paid to the preferred shareholders is

    a. $3,000.
    b. $1,000.
    c. $2,000.
    d. $ 100.

37. The amount that common stockholders will receive per share is

    a. $1.00.
    b. $ .70.
    c. $ .80.
    d. $ .99.

Owners' Equity

Chapter 11: Solutions

PART A: Multiple-Choice Questions

	Answer	Refer to Chapter Section
1.	(d)	[C-1-b(1)]
2.	(c)	[A-1-a]
3.	(c)	[C-1-b(2)]
4.	(d)	[C-1-a]
5.	(b)	[C-1-d]
6.	(c)	[C-2]
7.	(c)	[A-3-b]
8.	(a)	[C-1-c]
9.	(a)	[C-1-a(3)]
10.	(b)	[C-1-b(2)(a)] Dividends are paid to outstanding shares (3,000 shares x $1.00 per share).
11.	(c)	[C-1-b(2)(a)]
12.	(c)	[C-1-b(1)] The journal entry to record this transaction would be:

```
Cash                              100,000[a]
    Common Stock (at par)                    10,000[b]
    Paid-in Capital in
        Excess of Par                        90,000[c]
```

13.	(a)	[C-1-f(1)]
14.	(b)	[C-1-b(1)]

[a]10,000 shares x $10.00 per share = $100,000.
[b]10,000 shares x $1.00 per share = $10,000.
[c]Cash paid - par value = $100,000 - $10,000 = $90,000.

15. (d) [C-1-b(2)(b)] A stock dividend results in a transfer from retained earnings to contributed capital. If this entry were omitted, total stockholders' equity would be correct, but the components of stockholders' equity would be misstated.

16. (b) [C-2-c]

PART B: Matching Sets

MATCHING SET 1

17. (C) [B-1-a]

18. (C) [B]

19. (A, B) [A-2-b]

20. (A, B) [A-2-a]

21. (C) [B-2-a]

22. (C) [B-1-b]

MATCHING SET 2

23. (C) [C-1-e]

24. (H) [C-1]

25. (E) [C-1-c(3)(b)]

26. (B) [C-1]

27. (F) [C-1-c(2)(b)]

28. (A) [C-2-c]

29. (J) [C-1-d]

30. (D) [C-1-c(3)(a)]

31. (K) [C-2-c]

Owners' Equity

PART C: Problem Situations

32. (c)   [A-3-b] The allocation of income would be:

	Sally	Bob	Total
Income to be split			$40,000
Salary	$10,000	$10,000	(20,000)
Interest	7,200	2,400	(9,600)
Balance to be			$10,400
split equally	5,200	5,200	(10,400)
	$22,400	$17,600	0

33. (a)   [A-3-b] The allocation of income would be:

	Sally	Bob	Total
Income to be split			$20,000
Salary	$10,000	$10,000	(20,000)
Interest	7,200	2,400	(9,600)
Balance to be			9,600
split equally	(4,800)	(4,800)	9,600
	$12,400	$ 7,600	0

34. (b)   [A-3-b]

35. (d)   [C-1-e]

Total Stockholders' Equity $650,000
Less: Par Value of Preferred Stock   (100,000)
Equity Available to Common Shares $550,000

$$\frac{\text{Equity Available to Common Shares}}{\text{Common Shares Outstanding}} =$$

$$\frac{\$550,000}{8,000^d} = \$68.75$$

36. (a)   [C-1-c(2)(b)]

Dividends in Arrears 19XA $1,000
  (100 × $100 × .10)
Dividends in Arrears 19XB   1,000
Current Dividend   19XC   1,000
Total Preferred Dividend $3,000

37. (b)   [C-1-b(2)(a)]
$7,000^e/ 10,000 shares = $.70/share

---

[d] 10,000 - 2,000 = 8,000.
[e] $10,000 total dividend - $3,000 allocable to preferred stock.

CHAPTER 12
Income Statement Accounts

OVERVIEW

This chapter covers accounting for revenues and expenses. (The general accounting for revenue and expense accounts is covered in Chapter 2, Theory and Classification of Accounts. The candidate should review this material if necessary. Chapter 12 emphasizes accounting for payroll, payroll-related expenses, and accounting for individual federal income taxes. In studying the material related to payroll and income taxes, the candidate should focus review on definitions and methods of recording rather than tax rates or amounts of exclusions since these amounts are subject to frequent change by the federal government.

The candidate should understand the recording of revenues and expenses in general; the specific treatment of payroll, payroll taxes, and payroll fringe benefits; and the treatment of individual federal income taxes.

DEFINITION OF TERMS

CAPITAL ASSETS. Any property a taxpayer holds which is not listed in Section 1221 of the U. S. Internal Revenue Code. Section 1221 property includes inventory, accounts receivable, and depreciable property or real estate used in a business. Examples of capital assets are investments in stocks, bonds, or real estate which are not used in a trade or business.

CAPITAL GAIN. A gain resulting from the disposition of a capital asset.

CAPITAL LOSS. A loss resulting from the disposition of a capital asset.

FICA TAX. The Federal Insurance Contributions Act (FICA) tax; commonly called social security tax.

LONG-TERM CAPITAL GAIN OR LOSS. A gain or loss resulting from the disposition of a capital asset held for more than one year.

SHORT-TERM CAPITAL GAIN OR LOSS. A gain or loss resulting from the sale of a capital asset held for one year or less.

A. **Revenues**

Revenues are earnings resulting from the receipt of cash or other assets (or the reduction of a liability) in exchange for goods sold by an entity or services performed by an entity. (A complete discussion of revenues is presented in Chapter 2, Theory and Classification of Accounts.)

B. **Expenses**

Expenses are the cost of goods and services consumed (used up) by an entity as a result of earning revenue. (A complete discussion of expenses is presented in Chapter 2, Theory and Classification of Accounts.)

1. *Operating Expenses:* Operating expenses are those expenses related to the normal operations of a business. They include selling expenses and general or administrative expenses.

    EXAMPLES OF OPERATING EXPENSES: Salaries, payroll taxes, sales commissions, advertising, state and local taxes, telephone, legal fees, insurance, depreciation, and bad debt expense.

    a. *Payroll accounting:* Accounting for payroll expenses includes more than just recording the cash paid out for salaries. Companies must also account for health insurance (if provided), employees' income tax which is withheld, social security (FICA) taxes, union dues (if applicable), pension plans, savings bond purchases, and employer payroll taxes.

        (1) *Income tax withheld:* Employers are required to withhold a portion of their employees' gross wages for payment of federal income taxes. They are also required to keep records of the tax withheld. These taxes must be remitted to the federal government periodically. State and local income taxes might also be required to be withheld from the employees' pay. The amount withheld for federal income tax purposes is based upon withholding tax tables provided by the government. These tables are based upon the amount of

the employees' earnings, the frequency of pay periods, and the number of exemptions to which each employee is entitled.

(2) *FICA tax:* Federal Insurance Contributions Act (social security) tax must also be withheld from each employee's pay. Employers withhold a specific percentage of each employee's earnings until a maximum limit is reached. The employer must also pay a tax at the same rate as the employee. The rate used to calculate FICA tax and the base salary (maximum amount which will be taxed) have changed frequently in recent years. The rate in effect in 1990 was 7.65 percent on the first $51,300 of gross income. For simplicity, it is assumed in this module that the rate is 7 percent on the first $50,000 of income.

EXAMPLE: Assume that Chase Co. has two employees, Harlan Howe and George Peters. Harlan Howe earned $2,000 for the month of May. Harlan's gross pay for the year as of May 1 was $10,000. George Peters earned $12,000 for the month of May. George's gross pay for the year as of May 1 was $47,000. Chase Co. would withhold $140 of Harlan's earnings for payment of FICA taxes ($2,000 x .07 = $140). Chase Co. would withhold $210 of George's earnings for payment of FICA taxes ($3,000 x .07 = $210). Only $3,000 of George's May earnings are subject to FICA tax since George reached the $50,000 limit in May. Chase Co. will have to match the amount paid by the employees, so they must remit a total of $700 to the federal government for FICA taxes related to payroll in May.

(3) *Voluntary deductions from employees' pay:* The employee might also have other amounts withheld from pay such as insurance premiums, pension plan payments, and purchase of savings bonds. The employer must keep records of all voluntary deductions.

Note: Amounts withheld from employees' pay are part of salary expense to the company. The amount withheld represents a liability for the company since employees' earnings are held until payment is remitted to the appropriate party.

(4) *Employer payroll expenses:*

(a) *FICA tax:* The employer's portion of the FICA tax is an employer payroll expense.

(b) *Federal unemployment insurance tax:* Employers must

pay an amount for Federal Unemployment Insurance Tax. This tax is levied only on the employer, and no portion is deducted from the employee's pay. Like FICA taxes, the rates used to calculate federal unemployment tax change periodically. The rate in effect in 1990 was 6.2 percent on the first $7,000 paid to an employee. The employer is allowed to take a maximum credit of 5.4 percent for contributions to state unemployment programs. For most companies, the net federal tax is .8 percent on the first $7,000.

(c) *State unemployment tax:* The states administer distribution of unemployment insurance payments and also collect a state unemployment tax. Most states only tax the employer for unemployment tax, but a few states also tax the employee. Many states use 5.4 percent on the first $7,000 as the basic rate for unemployment taxes. Most states assign a merit rating based on the employment history of the company. A company that has a favorable merit rating will normally have its state unemployment tax rate reduced.

(d) *Employee fringe benefits:* The employer might also provide fringe benefits such as paid vacations, health insurance (the employer might pay all or a portion of the premiums), retirement plans, paid holidays. These fringe benefits are a substantial amount for most companies.

EXAMPLE: This example illustrates the recording of payroll and related expenses for one payroll period. Nelson Company's employees earned gross pay of $10,000 for the week ending August 31, 19XA. The net cash paid out to employees was $7,000. The following amounts were withheld from the employees' gross pay:

Federal income tax	$2,000
State income tax	200
FICA tax	700
Health insurance premiums	100

The employer payroll taxes were $700 for FICA, $60 for federal unemployment tax, and $180 for state unemployment tax. The employer expenses for fringe benefits were $750 for the retirement plan and $200 for health insurance. The entries to record the payroll and related expenditures were:

Income Statement Accounts

		dr	cr
Aug. 31	Salary Expense	10,000	
	Federal Income Tax Withholding Payable		2,000
	State Income Tax Withholding Payable		200
	FICA Tax Withholding Payable		700
	Insurance Withholding Payable		100
	Salaries Payable		7,000

To record salaries for the week of August 31.

Aug. 31	Salaries Payable	7,000	
	Cash		7,000

To record payment of August 31 salaries.

Aug. 31	Payroll Taxes Expense	940	
	FICA Tax Payable		700
	State Unemployment Tax Payable		60
	Federal Unemployment Tax Payable		180

To record employer payroll taxes for salaries for the week of August 31.

		dr	cr
Aug. 31	Payroll Benefits Expense	950	
	Retirement Plan Payable		750
	Health Insurance Payable		200

To record expenses for benefits associated with August 31 payroll.

(5) *Accrual of payroll-related taxes and expenses:* When payroll is accrued at the end of the accounting period, all of the payroll-related taxes and expenses should also be accrued. This results in proper matching of revenues and expenses. Payroll taxes are not a legal liability until the salaries are paid. Therefore, some businesses do not accrue payroll taxes.

(6) *Payroll liabilities:* Liabilities related to payroll are recorded as current liabilities.

(7) *Filing of quarterly reports:* A business must file quarterly reports with the government showing the amounts withheld from employees' earnings for federal income taxes and FICA

taxes. Payroll taxes must be accounted for on a calendar-year basis in reporting to the government. Amounts withheld from employees must be deposited periodically. The frequency of deposit depends upon the amount of taxes withheld. If the total amount is very small, it may be remitted with the quarterly tax returns. If the amounts withheld are significant, they must be deposited with a Federal Reserve Bank or a designated commercial bank on a frequent basis.

2. *Federal Individual Income Taxes:* Individuals must pay federal income tax on the amount of taxable income they earn. Taxable income is calculated as follows:

    Income
    <u>Less: Adjustments to Income</u>
    Adjusted Gross Income (AGI)
    <u>Less: Personal and Dependency Exemptions
               Itemized Deductions or Standard Deductions
               (whichever is greater)</u>
    = Taxable Income

    a. *Income:* Some of the common items included in income are: wages, salaries, tips, taxable interest income, dividend income, taxable refunds of state and local income tax, alimony received, business income, capital gains, rents, bonuses, and royalties. Some of the common items excluded from gross income include: accident insurance proceeds, child support payments, cost-of-living allowances (for military), damages for personal injury or sickness, gifts, disability benefits, life insurance paid on death, a limited amount of social security benefits, certain scholarship grants, and inheritances.

    b. *Gains and losses from property transactions:* When property is disposed of, a gain or loss may result. Gains are generally recognizable for income tax purposes. Losses from the disposition of property held for personal use (not for investment or used in a trade or business) are not recognizable for tax purposes. In order to determine the appropriate tax treatment of a recognizable gain or loss, the amount of the gain or loss must be classified as *ordinary* or *capital*. Usually ordinary gains and losses result from the disposition of assets not classified as capital items.

    c. *Capital gains and losses:* Capital gains and losses result from the disposition of capital assets. The U. S. Internal Revenue Code defines capital assets as any property a taxpayer holds which is not listed in Section 1221. Section 1221 property includes inventory, accounts receivable, and depreciable property or real estate used in a business.

EXAMPLE: Individual capital assets include property held for personal use, such as a house or a car, and assets held for investment purposes, such as securities.

Capital gains must be classified as short term or long term in nature in order to determine the appropriate tax treatment.

(1) *Short-term capital gains or losses:* Short-term capital gains or losses result from dispositions of capital assets held for one year or less. Short-term gains and losses must initially be offset to determine net short-term capital gain or loss.

(2) *Long-term capital gains or losses:* Long-term capital gains or losses result from dispositions of capital assets held for more than one year. Long-term capital losses are used to offset long-term capital gains.

(3) *Net short-term capital gains or losses:* Next, any net short-term capital losses are offset against any net long-term capital gains. If the taxpayer has net long-term capital losses and net short-term capital gains, they are also offset.

(4) *Taxing of net capital gains:* Net capital gains (short-term or long-term) are currently taxed as ordinary income. Prior to 1988, net long-term capital gains were afforded special beneficial tax treatment.

(5) *Deduction of net capital losses:* Net capital losses are deductible (as a deduction from adjusted gross income) to a maximum of $3,000 per year. Any unused amount of net capital loss may be carried forward indefinitely.

d. *Deductions (business/personal):* Deductions allowed to individual taxpayers include deductions from gross income to arrive at adjusted gross income and deductions from adjusted gross income.

(1) *Adjusted gross income:* Some of the deductions from gross income to arrive at adjusted gross income are:

(a) Ordinary and necessary expenses incurred in a trade or business

(b) Employee business expenses which are reimbursed by the employer

(c) Penalties on early withdrawal of savings

(d) Alimony paid

(e) Capital loss deduction

(f) Some IRA payments

(g) Certain retirement plan contributions

(2) *Itemized deductions:* Certain personal expenses are allowed as itemized deductions from adjusted gross income (AGI). Some of the items which may be included as itemized deductions are:

(a) Medical expenses that exceed 7.5 percent of adjusted gross income (AGI)

(b) Real estate taxes

(c) Personal property taxes

(d) Interest on a home mortgage

(e) Charitable contributions

(f) Casualty and theft losses which exceed 10 percent of AGI

(g) Moving expenses

(h) Job expenses and other miscellaneous deductions (only the total amount which exceeds 2 percent of AGI is deductible):

· Union dues
· Professional dues and subscriptions
· Job education
· Job travel (with limitations)
· Tax return preparation fees
· Investment counsel fees
· Safety deposit box fees

Note: Items which are allowed as a deduction from gross income to arrive at adjusted gross income provide a greater potential benefit for the taxpayer than itemized deductions from AGI. This is because the taxpayer will always benefit from the deduction for AGI. Itemized deductions will only benefit the taxpayer if the total amount of itemized deductions exceeds the amount of the standard deduction allowed for the taxpayer. The amount of the standard deduction is specified by Congress and depends on the filing status of the taxpayer.

Chapter 12: Review Questions

PART A: Multiple-Choice Questions

DIRECTIONS: Select the best answer from the four alternatives. Write the letter of your answer in the blank to the left of the number.

_____ 1. Which of the following is legally required to be withheld from employees' pay?

    a. Federal unemployment taxes
    b. FICA taxes
    c. Insurance premiums
    d. IRA deductions

_____ 2. Which of the following items would be recorded in the Payroll Taxes Expense account?

    a. Federal income tax withheld
    b. Company pension plan contributions
    c. Federal Unemployment Tax Act payments
    d. State income tax withheld

_____ 3. Which of the following items deducted from employees' pay *must* be matched by an equal contribution by the employer?

    a. Insurance premiums
    b. Company pension plan contributions
    c. Federal income tax withheld
    d. FICA tax

_____ 4. Items withheld from employees' pay should be classified by the employer as

    a. current liabilities.
    b. long-term liabilities.
    c. expenses.
    d. current assets.

5. When a company records payroll, Salaries or Wages Expense should be

   a. debited for the amount of net pay.
   b. debited for the amount of gross pay.
   c. credited for the amount of net pay.
   d. credited for the amount of gross pay.

6. Which of the following statements about payroll is false?

   a. Employers are allowed to take a credit on their federal unemployment taxes for contributions made to their state unemployment programs.
   b. FICA tax is subject to a maximum earnings limit. (Taxes are no longer paid once the employee has reached that maximum limit.)
   c. Employees may choose to have amounts voluntarily withheld from their pay.
   d. State unemployment taxes are normally levied only on the employee.

7. Short-term capital gains

   a. could result from sales of any asset held for one year or less.
   b. could result from the sale of capital assets held for two years or less.
   c. could result from the disposition of a capital asset held for one year or less.
   d. may be carried forward indefinitely.

8. In the United States, long-term capital gains

   a. are currently given preferential tax treatment.
   b. may be carried forward indefinitely.
   c. could result from the sale of Section 1221 property.
   d. could result from the sale of investments held by an individual for more than one year.

9. Which of the following items would not be included in gross income for individual income tax purposes?

   a. Wages
   b. Tips
   c. Life insurance proceeds paid upon death of insured
   d. Alimony received

Income Statement Accounts 305

_____ 10. Which of the following statements about capital gains and losses is false?

   a. Net capital losses are deductible to a maximum of $3,000 per year.
   b. Net capital gains are currently taxed as ordinary income.
   c. Since capital gains are no longer afforded preferential tax treatment, there is no need to net capital gains and losses.
   d. The sale of inventory would not result in a capital gain or loss.

_____ 11. The sale of a personal automobile at a loss

   a. could be used to offset any capital gains earned by the owner during the year.
   b. would not be recognizable for tax purposes.
   c. would be deductible as an ordinary expense item.
   d. would be deductible only if the loss was long term in nature.

_____ 12. Operating expenses normally include all of the following except

   a. sales commissions.
   b. payroll taxes.
   c. advertising.
   d. interest.

PART B: Matching Sets

MATCHING SET 1

Match each of the items (13-19) with the appropriate tax classification (A-B). Write the letter of your answer in the blank to the left of the number.

U. S. TAX CLASSIFICATIONS

A. Capital Asset
B. Section 1221 Property

ITEMS

_____ 13. Building used as a business sales office

_____ 14. Personal automobile

_____ 15. Machinery used in a business

_____ 16. Personal home

_____ 17. Inventory

_____ 18. Investment in stocks of ABC Company

_____ 19. Accounts receivable

Income Statement Accounts 307

MATCHING SET 2

Match each of the deductions (20-29) with the appropriate placement on the tax return (A-B). Write the letter of your answer in the blank to the left of the number.

U. S. TAX RETURN PLACEMENT

A. Deduction from Gross Income to arrive at Adjusted Gross Income
B. Itemized Deduction from Adjusted Gross Income

U. S. DEDUCTION ITEMS

_____ 20. Real estate taxes

_____ 21. Penalties on early withdrawal of savings

_____ 22. Charitable contributions

_____ 23. Ordinary and necessary expenses incurred in a trade or business

_____ 24. Union dues

_____ 25. Alimony paid

_____ 26. Employee business expenses which are reimbursed by the employer

_____ 27. Capital loss deduction

_____ 28. Medical expenses that exceed the required limit

_____ 29. Individual investment counsel fees

PART C: Problem Situations

DIRECTIONS: For each of the questions relating to the following problem situation, select the best answer from the four alternatives. Write the letter of your answer in the blank to the left of the number.

Problem 1

Young Company has an employee named Charles Wiley. During the past week Charles earned gross pay of $1,500. Charles' federal income tax withholding based on the federal tax tables is $200 and his state income tax withholding is $20. Charles has requested that a $10 insurance premium and $2 in union dues be withheld from his check each week. Assume that the FICA rate is 7% on the first $50,000, the federal unemployment tax rate is .8% on the first $7,000, and the state unemployment tax rate is 2% on the first $7,000. Charles' gross pay to date for this year is $6,000.

_____ 30. Charles Wiley's take home pay (net pay) would be

 a. $1,268.
 b. $1,500.
 c. $1,175.
 d. $1,163.

_____ 31. Young Company's total payroll tax expense related to Charles' earnings for the week would be

 a. $133.
 b. $105.
 c. $147.
 d. $353.

Chapter 12: Solutions

PART A: Multiple-Choice Questions

	Answer	Refer to Chapter Section
1.	(b)	[B-1-a(2)]
2.	(c)	[B-1-a(4)]
3.	(d)	[B-1-a(2)]
4.	(a)	[B-1-a(6)]
5.	(b)	[B-1-a(4)(d)]
6.	(d)	[B-1-a(4)(c)]
7.	(c)	[B-2-c(1)]
8.	(d)	[B-2-c(2)]
9.	(c)	[B-2-a]
10.	(c)	[B-2-c(4)]
11.	(b)	[B-2-b] Losses from the sale of assets held for personal use are not recognizable for tax purposes.
12.	(d)	[Chapter 3, B-5-a(2)]

PART B: Matching Sets

MATCHING SET 1

13.	(B)	[B-2-c]
14.	(A)	[B-2-c]
15.	(B)	[B-2-c]
16.	(A)	[B-2-c]
17.	(B)	[B-2-c]

18. (A)   [B-2-c]

19. (B)   [B-2-c]

MATCHING SET 2

20. (B)   [B-2-d(2)]

21. (A)   [B-2-d(1)]

22. (B)   [B-2-d(2)]

23. (A)   [B-2-d(1)]

24. (B)   [B-2-d(2)]

25. (A)   [B-2-d(1)]

26. (A)   [B-2-d(1)]

27. (A)   [B-2-d(1)]

28. (B)   [B-2-d(2)]

29. (B)   [B-2-d(2)]

PART C: Problem Situations

30. (d)   [B-1-a]

Gross Pay		$1,500
Less:		
Federal income tax withheld	$200	
State income tax withheld	20	
Insurance withheld	10	
Union dues withheld	2	
FICA withheld ($1,500 × .07)	105	337
Net Pay or Take Home Pay		$1,163

31. (a)   [B-1-a(4)]

FICA ($1,500 × .07)	$ 105
Federal Unemployment Tax ($1,000 × .008)	8
State Unemployment Tax ($1,000 × .02)	20
Total Payroll Tax Expense	$ 133

CHAPTER 13
Analysis and Interpretation of Financial Statements

OVERVIEW

Users of financial statements have developed techniques in order to evaluate the financial data contained in published statements. To a skilled reader, the statements themselves show a wealth of information. A balance sheet can give a good indication of the amount and composition of a firm's assets and liabilities. The income statement displays the results of operations. Finally, the Statement of Cash Flows indicates from where a firm is obtaining cash and how it is being used. Comparative statements, if prepared on a consistent basis, allow trend analysis, that is, how a firm is progressing through time. Ratio analysis is another widely used technique for evaluating a firm's activities.

The balance sheet, income statement, and statement of retained earnings were discussed in Chapter 3, Basic Financial Statements. The candidate should review those particular topics at this time.

DEFINITION OF TERMS

CASH FLOW STATEMENT. A cash flow statement accounts for the increase or decrease in a company's cash during a period by showing where the company got cash and how it was used.

COMPARATIVE FINANCIAL STATEMENTS. Financial statements which show financial data for a series of years in adjacent columns.

FINANCING ACTIVITIES. Transactions with the company's owners and long-term creditors.

INVESTING ACTIVITIES. Transactions that involve the investment of a company's cash.

OPERATING ACTIVITIES. Transactions that relate to the calculation of net income. These items are usually related to the production and sale of goods and services.

RATIO. The relationship of one amount to another.

SOURCE OF WORKING CAPITAL. Any transaction which results in an increase in working capital.

USE OF WORKING CAPITAL. Any transaction which results in a decrease in working capital.

WORKING CAPITAL. Current assets minus current liabilities.

A. Statement of Changes in Financial Position

The balance sheet provides a picture of the status of the firm at a particular time. Comparative balance sheets give an indication of change over time in the composition of the firm's assets and liabilities. Prior to 1988, the Statement of Changes in Financial Position was a required financial statement which incorporated input from comparative balance sheets and the income statement to show formally the changes in the balance sheet. This was often done by showing the sources and uses of working capital for the firm.

In November, 1987, the Financial Accounting Standards Board (FASB) issued Statement of Financial Accounting Standards No. 75, "Statement of Cash Flows," which requires the presentation of a Statement of Cash Flows in place of the Statement of Changes in Financial Position.

Note: The material covering the Statement of Changes in Financial Position was left in this module because the CPS Study Outline still includes this topic. Concepts used in developing a Statement of Changes in Financial Position on a working-capital basis should also aid the candidate in understanding and interpreting financial statements.

1. *Working Capital:* Working capital is defined as current assets minus current liabilities. Working capital is employed as a basis for preparing the Statement of Changes in Financial Position. The statement shows the sources and uses of working capital during a period.

    a. *Source of working capital:*

        (1) *Resources provided by operations:* If a firm is operating profitably, working capital will increase. The actual net income figure as reported in the income statement must be adjusted for items which are included in the calculation of net

income that do not affect working capital.

(a) *Additions to net income:* Certain expenses must be added back to net income in arriving at resources provided by operations. For example, the entry to record depreciation expense would be:

	dr	cr
Depreciation Expense	xx	
Accumulated Depreciation		xx

The Depreciation Expense account is closed to the income statement, and the Accumulated Depreciation account remains on the balance sheet as a contra-asset until the depreciable asset is disposed of. No working capital account is affected; yet, net income is reduced by the appropriate amount. Therefore, in order to determine resources (working capital) provided by operations, the amount of depreciation expense must be added back to net income. Other income statement items which must be added back include amortization of goodwill, amortization of bond discount, and losses on disposal of assets.

(b) *Subtractions from net income:* Similarly, certain items are added to net income, yet provide no working capital. These items must be subtracted from net income to arrive at income provided by operations. Examples include: amortization of bond premium and gains on disposal of assets.

EXAMPLE OF WORKING CAPITAL:

Resources Provided by Operations:

Net Income		xx
Add: Expenses not affecting working capital:		
Depreciation	xx	
Amortization of Bond Discount	xx	
Loss on Sale of Assets	xx	
Less: Items not affecting working capital:		
Amortization of Bond Premium	(xx)	
Gain on Sale of Assets	(xx)	xx
Working Capital Provided by Operations		<u>XXX</u>

(2) *Sale of noncurrent assets:* When noncurrent assets are sold for cash, working capital is increased. The amount provided to resources of the firm is irrespective of any gain or loss on the disposition. For example, if land with a book value of $10,000 is sold for $12,000, the entry is:

	dr	cr
Cash	12,000	
Land		10,000
Gain		2,000

In the Statement of Changes in Financial Position, the $12,000 is recorded as a source of working capital.

(3) *Borrowing through the use of long-term debt:* When a firm issues long-term debt for cash, working capital is increased. If bonds are sold at a discount or premium, it is the amount of cash received, not the face value of the bonds, which is shown as a source of funds.

(4) *Sale of capital stock:* When a firm sells additional shares of capital stock, working capital is increased.

b. *Uses of working capital:*

(1) *Net loss:* An adjusted net loss decreases a firm's working capital. A failure to operate profitably is thus a use of working capital.

(2) *Purchase of noncurrent assets:* When noncurrent assets are purchased, working capital is decreased. Each acquisition or class of acquisitions is usually shown separately. Note that purchase of inventory is not a use of working capital since inventory is a current asset.

(3) *Declaration of cash dividends:* When cash dividends are declared, working capital decreases. The declaration of a cash dividend creates a current liability, Dividends Payable. The payment of a cash dividend which has already been declared does not affect working capital.

(4) *Repayment of long-term debt:* Payment of long-term debt which is outstanding reduces the amount of working capital available.

(5) *Repurchase of common stock:* The repurchase of outstanding common stock reduces the amount of working capital available.

Analysis and Interpretation of Financial Statements

c. *All-financial-resources concept:* Some transactions which do not affect working capital are also shown on the Statement of Changes in Financial Position. If common stock is exchanged for a noncurrent asset, there is no change in working capital. In order to better present the sources and uses of resources, such transactions are treated as if two transactions had occurred. The common stock is shown as a source of working capital, and the acquisition is shown as a use of working capital. This procedure was referred to as the all-financial-resources concept, and its use was required by generally accepted accounting principles prior to the issuance of FASB Statement 75.

d. *Reading the statement of changes in financial position:* To the trained reader, the Statement of Changes in Financial Position provides a wealth of information. Management's performance can be evaluated in terms of how resources were obtained and utilized. A set of comparative balance sheets will show only the net change in the accounts whereas the Statement of Changes in Financial Position will show each change in the accounts. For example, if land with a historical cost of $10,000 is sold for book value and land costing $12,000 is bought, comparative balance sheets will show a net change of $2,000 while the Statement of Changes in Financial Position will show a source of working capital of $10,000 and a use of $12,000. The additional information is intended to help users of financial statements make a more effective evaluation for their purposes.

Figure 13-1 shows an example of the Statement of Changes in Financial Position.

B. **Statement of Cash Flows**

The Statement of Cash Flows explains the differences between the beginning and ending balances of cash (including cash equivalents). Cash equivalents are generally short-term temporary investments which are readily convertible to a known amount of cash *and* sufficiently close to their maturity date so that their market value is relatively insensitive to changes in interest rates. Generally, only investments purchased within three months of their maturity dates meet these two criteria. Short-term investments in Treasury bills, investments in money market funds, and some investments in commercial paper would normally qualify as cash equivalents. The Statement of Cash Flows presents information about cash flows from operating, investing, and financing activities.

1. *Operating Activities:* Operating activities generally include transactions that relate to the calculation of net income. These items are usually related to the production and sale of goods and services.

Figure 13-1
Statement of Changes in Financial Position
Lee Company

Sources of working capital		
Resources provided by operations		
Net income	50,000	
Add: Expenses not requiring use of working capital		
Depreciation	20,000	
Loss on sale of assets	5,000	
Total working capital provided by operations		75,000
Sale of bonds		50,000
Sale of long-term assets		10,000
Sale of capital stock		50,000
Total sources of working capital		185,000
Uses of working capital		
Purchase of equipment		60,000
Retirement of bonds payable		70,000
Declaration of cash dividends		30,000
Total uses of working capital		160,000
Increase in working capital		25,000

  a. *Operating cash inflows:* Typical operating cash inflows include:

    (1) Cash sales to customers.

    (2) Cash collections from credit sales.

    (3) Cash dividends received from stock investments.

    (4) Interest payments received.

    (5) Refunds from suppliers.

  b. *Operating cash outflows:* Typical operating cash outflows include:

    (1) Payments for salaries and wages.

    (2) Payments made for goods and services used by the company.

Analysis and Interpretation of Financial Statements

      (3)   Interest payments.

      (4)   Payments to the government for taxes.

      (5)   Payments for other normal business expenses.

2. *Investing Activities:* Investing activities include transactions that involve the investment of a company's cash.

   a. *Investing cash inflows:* Typical investing cash inflows include:

      (1)   Cash received from sale of investments (stocks or bonds of other firms).

      (2)   Cash received from the sale of property, plant, and equipment.

      (3)   Cash received from repayment of loans made by the company to other entities.

      (4)   Cash received from the sale (discounting) of loans made by the company to other entities.

   b. *Investing cash outflows:* Typical investing cash outflows include:

      (1)   Payments made to buy property, plant, and equipment.

      (2)   Payments made in purchasing stocks of other entities as an investment.

      (3)   Payments made to purchase debt securities of other entities as an investment (excluding cash equivalents).

      (4)   Payments made in making loans to other entities.

3. *Financing Activities:* Financing activities include transactions with the company's owners and long-term creditors.

   a. *Financing cash inflows:* Typical financing cash inflows include:

      (1)   Cash received from sale of stock.

      (2)   Cash received from the issuance of bonds or nonoperating notes payable.

   b. *Financing cash outflows:* Typical financing cash outflows include:

      (1)   Payment of dividends to owners.

(2) Payments of the principal amount on nonoperating loans or bonds payable.

(3) Payments made to acquire treasury stock.

4. *Noncash Investing and Financing Activities:* Some important investing and financing transactions do not involve cash. For example, a company might purchase equipment and issue a long-term note payable to the seller. This transaction does not involve an inflow or an outflow of cash, but both financing and investing activities are involved. Since the Statement of Cash Flows would omit significant financing and investing activities if noncash financing and investing transactions were excluded, the FASB requires that noncash investing and financing transactions be disclosed in a separate schedule on the Statement of Cash Flows. Examples of noncash investing and financing activities which must be disclosed are:

· Conversion of bonds payable to stock
· Conversion of preferred stock to common stock
· Exchange of one noncash asset for another noncash asset
· Purchase of long-term assets through the issuance of a note payable to the seller
· Purchase of a building by securing a mortgage loan
· Purchase of noncash assets in exchange for stock
· Leasing of assets in a transaction that involves a lease classified as a capital lease

5. *Presentation of a Statement of Cash Flows:* An example of a Statement of Cash Flows is presented in Figure 13-2a. The cash flows from operating activities may be presented in either a direct or an indirect fashion.

   a. *Direct method:* The direct method involves the calculation and presentation of individual operating cash inflows and outflows (examples are cash received from customers and cash paid to suppliers). Figure 13-2a shows a Statement of Cash Flows using the direct method. The FASB recommends that the direct method be used in presenting the Statement of Cash Flows. When the direct method is used, a reconciliation of net income to net cash provided (or used) by operating activities must be presented. This reconciliation shows the same information as the indirect method in the same format.

   b. *Indirect method:* Although the direct method is preferred by the FASB, the presentation of a Statement of Cash Flows using the indirect method is allowed. Because the indirect method is required to be shown as a reconciliation when the direct method is used, most companies use the indirect method. When the indirect method is used, net income must be adjusted for items included in net income which do not affect cash.

EXAMPLES: Depreciation expense, amortization expense, losses on the sale of long-term assets, and changes in current asset and current liability accounts.

Figure 13-2a
Schmaus Company
Statement of Cash Flows
For the Year Ended December 31, 19XA

Cash Flows from Operating Activities:		
Cash received from customers	$220,000	
Dividends received	9,000	
Cash inflows from operating activities		$229,000
Less cash paid for:		
Payments for merchandise	$ 98,000	
Payments for salaries and wages	64,000	
Payments for taxes	9,250	
Payment of interest	2,300	
Cash disbursed for operating activities		173,550
Net cash provided by operating activities		$ 55,450
Cash Flows from Investing Activities:		
Proceeds from sale of equipment	$ 20,000	
Proceeds from sale of investments	40,000	
Purchase of building	(55,000)	
Purchase of land	(40,000)	
Net cash used by investing activities		(35,000)
Cash Flows from Financing Activities:		
Proceeds from bond issue	$ 50,000	
Payment of long-term note	(30,000)	
Payment of dividends	(6,000)	
Net cash provided by financing activities		14,000
Net increase (decrease) in cash		$ 34,450
Cash balance, January 1, 19XA		40,250
Cash balance, December 31, 19XA		$ 74,700
Schedule of Noncash Investing/Financing Activities		
Purchase of equipment through the issuance of a long-term note payable		$100,000

The procedures for adjusting net income to cash flow are beyond the scope of this module.

Figure 13-2b
Schmaus Company
Partial Statement of Cash Flows
For the Year Ended December 31, 19XA
(Indirect Method)

Cash Flows from Operating Activities:

Net income		$50,750
Adjustments to reconcile net income to net cash flow from operating activities:		
Depreciation expense	$ 5,000	
Gain on sale of equipment	(4,000)	
Loss on sale of investments	3,300	
Decrease in accounts receivable	6,000	
Increase in merchandise inventory	(4,500)	
Increase in accounts payable	1,500	
Decrease in salaries payable	(2,600)	
Total adjustments		4,700
Net cash provided by operating activities		$55,450

Figure 13-2b shows an example of the cash flows from the operating activities section presented on an indirect basis. The remainder of the Statement of Cash Flows on an indirect basis would be the same as shown in Figure 13-2a.

C. **Comparative Statements**

Firms often present financial data for several years in annual statements to allow comparison of current performance to previous performance. In order to allow such comparison, it is important that the statements be prepared on a consistent basis. Any consistency exceptions are prominently noted in the auditor's report and the financial statements themselves. A common practice is to show percent increases or decreases in selected items. Financial analysts often get a better idea of the progress of a firm by such reports.

D. **Ratio Analysis**

Ratio analysis essentially studies the relationships between various amounts on financial statements. A ratio for a given firm can be compared to others in the same industry. Such ratios are printed regularly by publishing services. Ratios from the current year are often compared to the same ratio in preceding years in order to provide information about changes within the company.

1. *Liquidity Ratios:* Liquidity ratios are concerned with a firm's ability to meet current obligations. For purposes of short-term financing, these ratios are very important. Creditors are often interested in liquidity ratios.

    a. *Current ratio:* The current ratio is expressed as:

    $$\frac{\text{Current Assets}}{\text{Current Liabilities}}$$

    b. *Acid-test ratio or quick ratio:* Since inventories and prepaid expenses may be difficult to liquidate quickly, the acid-test ratio is often computed as a supplement to the current ratio. The acid-test ratio compares only the highly liquid assets of cash, marketable securities, and receivables with current liabilities.

    $$\frac{\text{Cash + Marketable Securities + Receivables}}{\text{Current Liabilities}}$$

    c. *Receivables turnover:* This ratio shows how often, or how quickly, a firm's receivables are collected. Too large a ratio may indicate too lenient a credit policy. This is important as receivables are often interest free. A firm may be giving credit to customers at no charge for extended periods while paying interest on its own short-term debt to finance the receivables. The ratio is:

    $$\frac{\text{Credit Sales}}{\text{Average Receivables}}$$

    If credit sales are not available, net sales may be used. Average receivables is a better number to use than year-end receivables as the average allows for the effects of seasonal business.

    d. *Inventory turnover:* Inventory turnover is identical in concept to the receivables turnover. A low ratio may indicate overstocking of inventory or the presence of obsolete inventory, usually financed with short-term debt. The inventory turnover ratio is:

    $$\frac{\text{Cost of Goods Sold}}{\text{Average Inventory}}$$

    Note that cost of goods sold, rather than sales, is comparable to inventory cost.

2. *Debt Ratios:* Debt ratios are more concerned with a firm's policy on long-term debt. The capital structure of a corporation is composed of

both debt and owners' equity. A firm which is primarily financed by debt must be able to service that debt in a timely manner in order to maintain its credit standing.

    a. *Debt-to-equity ratio:* The debt-to-equity ratio measures the balance between the portion of assets provided by stockholders and the portion provided by creditors.

$$\frac{\text{Total Liabilities}}{\text{Total Stockholders' Equity}}$$

This ratio often is expressed as long-term debt over equity.

    b. *Debt-to-total-assets ratio:* The debt-to-total assets ratio is similar to the debt-to-equity ratio. This ratio shows the percentage of assets financed by debt.

$$\frac{\text{Total Liabilities}}{\text{Total Assets}}$$

    c. *Times-interest-earned ratio:* This ratio relates to a firm's ability to service debt from earnings. Obviously a firm which is barely able to generate sufficient earnings to make interest payments is a suspect investment. The ratio may be calculated in different ways. In general, a good representation of the ratio is:

$$\frac{\text{Earnings Before Interest Expense and Income Taxes}}{\text{Interest Expense}}$$

A weakness of the ratio is that principal must also be repaid, as well as the fact that payments are made from cash rather than earnings. Nevertheless, if there aren't sufficient earnings, there will not be enough cash generation in the long run.

3. *Profitability Ratios:* Profitability ratios are designed to measure a firm's efficiency in generating profits in relation to sales and in relation to investment. Investors are generally interested in profitability ratios.

    a. *Earnings per share:* This is one of the most common ratios. This ratio relates to shares of common stock only. If preferred stock exists, the earnings must be adjusted for the dividends. The ratio is:

$$\frac{\text{Net Income Less Preferred Stock Dividend}}{\text{Average Shares of Common Stock Outstanding}}$$

Treasury stock is not included in the denominator. Average shares of common stock are calculated using a weighted average. For example, if 750 shares of common stock are outstanding on January 1, 19XA, and 500 shares are issued on June 30, 19XA, average shares at the end of the year can be calculated as:

$$750 \times 12 \text{ months} = 9,000$$
$$500 \times 6 \text{ months} = 3,000$$
$$\text{Total Shares} \quad 12,000$$

$$\frac{12,000}{12 \text{ months}} = 1,000 \text{ average shares outstanding}$$

Such computations as primary earnings per share and fully diluted earnings per share are also calculated for firms with complex capital structures.

b. *Dividend yield:* Yield is an investor's tool for comparing the cash return by means of dividends in relation to the market value of the stock. The ratio is:

$$\frac{\text{Dividend per Share}}{\text{Market Value per Share}}$$

c. *Price-earnings ratio:* An investor might use the price-earnings ratio to determine whether the price of the stock is suitable for his/her purposes, considering the earnings of the stock. The price-earnings ratio compares the market price of the stock with the earnings per share of the stock:

$$\frac{\text{Market Price per Share}}{\text{Earnings per Share}}$$

d. *Gross profit margin:* The gross profit margin is an indicator of a firm's efficiency at producing goods and pricing them for sale. The ratio is calculated as:

$$\frac{\text{Sales - Cost of Goods Sold}}{\text{Sales}}$$

A net profit margin may also be calculated by:

$$\frac{\text{Net Income}}{\text{Sales}}$$

Two firms may produce the same product and sell it at the same price, yet have different profit margins.

e. *Return on investment:* There are many different ways to calculate return on investment. The easiest method is simply:

$$\frac{\text{Net Income}}{\text{Tangible Assets}}$$

Intangible assets are usually subtracted from total assets in arriving at this figure. For purposes of evaluating management performance, the DuPont method is often employed as follows:

$$\frac{\text{Sales}}{\text{Tangible Assets}} \times \frac{\text{Net Income}}{\text{Sales}}$$

f. *Book value:* Book value per share is a marginally useful number which is computed in this way:

$$\frac{\text{Owners' Equity - Par Value of Preferred Stock}}{\text{Number of Shares Common Stock Outstanding}}$$

The reason book value per share is not particularly useful is the reliance on historical cost in preparation of financial statements.

The ratios discussed in this module represent many of the most common ratios used in analyzing financial statements. Numerous other ratios might be used as well.

Figure 13-3c shows the calculation of the ratios presented in this module. The calculations are based on the financial statements for the XYZ Company shown in Figures 13-3a and 13-3b.

Figure 13-3a
Consolidated Balance Sheet

XYZ Company
Consolidated Balance Sheet
December 31, 19XB

Assets	19XB		19XA		Liabilities and Stockholders' Equity	19XB		19XA	
Current Assets:					Current Liabilities:				
Cash		20,000		15,000	Accounts Payable		125,000		100,000
Marketable Securities		100,000		80,000	Notes Payable		220,000		200,000
Accounts Receivable		300,000		280,000	Accrued Liabilities		100,000		80,000
Inventories		280,000		260,000					
Total Current Assets		700,000		635,000	Total Current Liabilities		445,000		380,000
Investments		250,000		200,000	Long-Term Debts:				
Fixed Assets:					Bonds Payable		700,000		700,000
Plant and Equipment	2,150,000		1,800,000		Notes Payable		25,000		50,000
Less: Accumulated Depreciation	(800,000)		(600,000)		Total Long-Term Debts		725,000		750,000
Total Fixed Assets		1,350,000		1,200,000	Total Liabilities		1,170,000		1,130,000
Total Assets		2,300,000		2,035,000	Stockholders' Equity:				
					Common Stock		150,000		150,000
					Additional Paid-in Capital		600,000		600,000
					Retained Earnings		380,000		155,000
					Total Stockholders' Equity		1,130,000		905,000
					Total Liabilities and Stockholders' Equity		2,300,000		2,035,000

325

Figure 13-3b
Statement of Income

XYZ Company
Statement of Income
For the Year Ended December 31, 19XB

	19XB	19XA
Revenues:		
Net Sales	1,500,000	1,300,000
Interest Income	5,000	10,000
Other Income	20,000	35,000
Total Revenue	1,525,000	1,345,000
Expenses:		
Cost of Goods Sold	750,000	670,000
Depreciation Expense	200,000	160,000
Selling and Administrative Expenses	145,000	115,000
Interest Expense	72,500	75,000
Total Expenses	1,167,500	1,020,000
Net Income Before Income Taxes	357,500	325,000
Less: Income Tax Expense	82,500	75,000
Net Income After Taxes	275,000	250,000
Earnings Per Share	$5.50	$5.00

Additional Information:

    50,000 shares of common stock were outstanding during 19XA and 19XB.
    Cash dividends were $50,000 or $1.00 per share.
    All sales were made on credit.
    Market price of XYZ's stock at the end of 19XB was $50 per share.

Analysis and Interpretation of Financial Statements

Figure 13-3c
Summary of Financial Ratios

Ratio	Calculation	Example
1. Liquidity Ratios		
a. Current Ratio	$\dfrac{\text{Current Assets}}{\text{Current Liabilities}}$	$\dfrac{700{,}000}{445{,}000} = 1.57$ times or 1.57 to 1
b. Acid-test Ratio	$\dfrac{\text{Cash + Marketable Securities + Receivables}}{\text{Current Liabilities}}$	$\dfrac{20{,}000 + 100{,}000 + 300{,}000}{445{,}000} = .94$ times or .94 to 1
c. Receivables Turnover	$\dfrac{\text{Credit Sales}}{\text{Average Receivables}}$	$\dfrac{1{,}500{,}000}{290{,}000} = 5.17$ times
d. Inventory Turnover	$\dfrac{\text{Cost of Goods Sold}}{\text{Average Inventory}}$	$\dfrac{750{,}000}{270{,}000} = 2.78$ times
2. Debt Ratios		
a. Debt-to-Equity Ratio	$\dfrac{\text{Total Liabilities}}{\text{Total Stockholders' Equity}}$	$\dfrac{1{,}615{,}000}{1{,}130{,}000} = 1.43$ or 143%
b. Debt-to-Total Assets Ratio	$\dfrac{\text{Total Liabilities}}{\text{Total Assets}}$	$\dfrac{1{,}615{,}000}{2{,}300{,}000} = 70.22\%$
c. Times-Interest-Earned Ratio	$\dfrac{\text{Earnings Before Interest Expense and Income Taxes}}{\text{Interest Expense}}$	$\dfrac{430{,}000^a}{72{,}500} = 5.93$ times

[a] Net income before income taxes plus interest expense = (357,500 + 72,500) = 430,000.

3. Profitability Ratios

a. Earnings per Share

$$\frac{\text{Net Income} - \text{Preferred Dividends}}{\text{Average Shares of Common Stock Outstanding}} = \frac{275{,}000}{50{,}000} = \$5.50$$

b. Dividend Yield

$$\frac{\text{Dividend per Share}}{\text{Market Value per Share}} = \frac{\$1.00}{\$50.00} = 2\%$$

c. Price-Earnings Ratio

$$\frac{\text{Market Price per Share}}{\text{Earnings per Share}} = \frac{\$50.00}{\$5.50} = \$9.09$$

d. Gross Profit Margin

$$\frac{\text{Sales} - \text{Cost of Goods Sold}}{\text{Sales}} = \frac{1{,}500{,}000 - 750{,}000}{1{,}500{,}000} = 50\%$$

e. Return on Investment

$$\frac{\text{Net Income}}{\text{Tangible Assets}} = \frac{275{,}000}{2{,}300{,}000} = 11.96\%$$

f. Book Value

$$\frac{\text{Owners' Equity less Par Value of Preferred Stock}}{\text{Number of Shares of Common Stock Outstanding}} = \frac{1{,}310{,}000}{50{,}000} = \$22.60$$

Analysis and Interpretation of Financial Statements 329

Chapter 13: Review Questions

PART A: Multiple-Choice Questions

DIRECTIONS: Select the best answer from the four alternatives. Write the letter of your answer in the blank to the left of the number.

_____ 1. The financial statement which shows the differences between the beginning and ending balances of cash including cash equivalents is called the

    a. Statement of Changes in Financial Position Working Capital Basis.
    b. Statement of Cash Flows.
    c. Income Statement.
    d. Balance Sheet.

_____ 2. Comparative financial statements

    a. need not be prepared on a consistent basis.
    b. are not useful in determining trends affecting a business.
    c. allow financial statement users to make comparisons between current performance and past performance.
    d. are characterized by all of the above.

_____ 3. Which of the following transactions will result in a reduction of Y Company's current 2:1 ratio?

    a. Borrowing money from the bank in exchange for a note payable due in five months.
    b. Selling a fixed asset for a loss.
    c. Collection of an account receivable.
    d. Sale of common stock.

_____ 4. Which of the following ratios would normally be used to analyze a firm's ability to pay its short-term obligations?

    a. Price-earnings ratio
    b. Return on investment
    c. Earnings per share
    d. Acid-test ratio

5. If a building were acquired by signing a mortgage note payable, the transaction would be reported on the Statement of Cash Flows in the

   a. operating activities section.
   b. investing activities section.
   c. schedule of noncash investing/financing activities.
   d. financing activities section.

6. Which of the following methods does the FASB recommend be used in preparing a Statement of Cash Flows?

   a. The indirect method
   b. The direct method
   c. The working-capital method
   d. The accrual method

7. Current assets minus current liabilities is called

   a. working capital.
   b. the current ratio.
   c. the acid-test ratio.
   d. changes in financial position.

8. Which of the following is a source of working capital?

   a. Purchase of equipment
   b. Declaration of cash dividends on capital stock
   c. Repurchase of common stock
   d. Sale of equipment used in the business

9. Which of the following items would not be included in the schedule of noncash investing/financing activities?

   a. Purchase of merchandise on account
   b. Conversion of bonds to common stock
   c. Exchange of common stock for land
   d. Conversion of preferred stock to common stock

10. The term used to describe the ratio between cost of goods sold and merchandise inventory is

    a. accounts receivable turnover.
    b. debt-to-equity ratio.
    c. return on investment.
    d. merchandise inventory turnover.

Analysis and Interpretation of Financial Statements

_____ 11. Which of the following is considered to be a liquidity ratio?

   a. Times-interest-earned ratio
   b. Earnings per share
   c. Current ratio
   d. Dividend yield

PART B: Matching Sets

MATCHING SET 1

Match each of the following transactions (12-22) with the appropriate classification on the Statement of Cash Flows (A-C). Write the letter of your answer in the blank to the left of the number.

CASH FLOW CLASSIFICATIONS

A. Operating Activity
B. Investing Activity
C. Financing Activity

TRANSACTIONS

_____ 12. Interest payments received.

_____ 13. Cash received from the issuance of bonds payable.

_____ 14. Cash received from sale of an investment in bonds of XYZ Co.

_____ 15. Cash dividends paid.

_____ 16. Cash collections from credit sales.

_____ 17. Payments for income taxes.

_____ 18. Cash dividends received.

_____ 19. Payments made to purchase stock in XYZ Company.

_____ 20. Payments to creditors of the principal amount on loans.

_____ 21. Cash received from repayment of long-term note receivable from ABC Co.

_____ 22. Payments for salaries and wages.

MATCHING SET 2

Match each of the following formulas (23-30) with the appropriate ratio (A-J). Write the letter of your answer in the blank to the left of the number.

RATIOS

A. Current Ratio
B. Acid-Test Ratio
C. Receivables Turnover
D. Inventory Turnover
E. Debt-to-Equity Ratio
F. Debt-to-Total-Assets Ratio
G. Dividend Yield
H. Price-Earnings Ratio
I. Gross Profit Margin
J. Return on Investment

FORMULAS

_____ 23. Total Liabilities / Total Stockholders' Equity

_____ 24. Credit Sales / Average Receivables

_____ 25. Net Income / Tangible Assets

_____ 26. Current Assets / Current Liabilities

_____ 27. (Cash + Marketable Securities + Receivables) / Current Liabilities

_____ 28. (Sales - Cost of Goods Sold) / Sales

_____ 29. Dividend per Share / Market Value per Share

_____ 30. Total Liabilities / Total Assets

PART C: Problem Situations

DIRECTIONS: For each of the questions relating to the following problem situation, select the best answer from the four alternatives. Write the letter of your answer in the blank to the left of the number.

Problem 1

The following financial information for the years 19XA and 19XB is available for the ABC Company:

Current Assets	19XA	19XB
Cash	20,000	30,000
Accounts Receivable	90,000	85,000
Inventory	90,000	98,000
Prepaid Expenses	5,000	6,000
Total Current Assets	205,000	219,000

Current Liabilities	19XA	19XB
Accounts Payable	10,000	12,000
Notes Payable	40,000	30,000
Accrued Liabilities	12,000	11,000
Total Current Liabilities	62,000	53,000

_____ 31. What is the current ratio for 19XB? (Round your answer to two decimal places.)

    a. 4.13
    b. 3.31
    c. .26
    d. 2.00

32. If credit sales are equal to $890,000, what is receivables turnover for 19XB? (Round your answer to two decimal places.)

   a. 10.47
   b. 9.89
   c. 10.17
   d. 12.45

33. What is the acid-test ratio for 19XA? (Round your answer to two decimal places.)

   a. 3.23
   b. 1.85
   c. 1.77
   d. 2.20

34. Cargo Company had net income of $20,000, which was 10 percent of net sales. Cost of goods sold was 60 percent of sales. The dollar amount of gross profit (or gross margin) for the company was

   a. $200,000.
   b. $120,000.
   c. $ 60,000.
   d. $ 80,000.

Chapter 13: Solutions

PART A: Multiple-Choice Questions

	Answer	Refer to Chapter Section
1.	(b)	[B]
2.	(c)	[C]
3.	(a)	[D-1-a] Borrowing money on a short-term basis would increase current assets and current liabilities by an equal amount. Since current assets were greater than current liabilities before the loan was taken out, the ratio of current assets to current liabilities would decrease.
4.	(d)	[D-1-b]
5.	(c)	[B-4]
6.	(b)	[B-5-a]
7.	(a)	[A-1]
8.	(d)	[A-1-a(2)]
9.	(a)	[B-4]
10.	(d)	[D-1-d]
11.	(c)	[D-1]

PART B: Matching Sets

MATCHING SET 1

12.	(A)	[B-1]
13.	(C)	[B-3]
14.	(B)	[B-2]
15.	(C)	[B-3]

16. (A)   [B-1]

17. (A)   [B-1]

18. (A)   [B-1]

19. (B)   [B-2]

20. (C)   [B-3]

21. (B)   [B-2]

22. (A)   [B-1]

MATCHING SET 2

23. (E)   [D-2-a]

24. (C)   [D-1-c]

25. (J)   [D-3-e]

26. (A)   [D-1-a]

27. (B)   [D-1-b]

28. (I)   [D-3-d]

29. (G)   [D-3-b]

30. (F)   [D-2-b]

PART C: Problem Situations

31. (a)   [D-1-a]
   Current Assets / Current Liabilities
   $219,000 / $53,000 = 4.13

32. (c)   [D-1-c]
   Credit Sales / Average Receivables
   $890,000 / $87,500[a] = 10.17

33. (c)   [D-1-b]
   (Cash + Marketable Securities + Accounts Receivable)
   / Current Liabilities
   ($20,000 + 0 + $90,000) / $62,000 = 1.77

[a] ($90,000 + $85,000) / 2

34. (d) [D-3-d] The solution is calculated as follows:

Sales	$200,000[b]	100%
- Cost of Goods Sold	-120,000	60%
Gross Profit	$ 80,000	40%

[b]Net Income = .10 x Sales
$20,000 = .10 x Sales
$200,000 = Sales

CHAPTER 14
Managerial Accounting

OVERVIEW

Managerial accounting is concerned with aiding managers in planning and controlling the operations of a business. The candidate should be familiar with basic techniques used in managerial accounting.

The candidate needs to understand the difference between fixed and variable costs and the effects of different costs on the decision-making process (cost-volume profit analysis). The candidate needs to understand the differences between accounting for a merchandising firm and accounting for a manufacturing firm.

Another topic that the candidate needs to understand is the budgeting process. The candidate may already be familiar with budgeting from the standpoint of preparing a personal budget. Budgeting for a business firm is more complex, but the same basic task is being performed. A plan (budget) is prepared and used to aid in making decisions during the period. At the end of the period, actual results should be compared to the plan to see how well the business met its objectives.

DEFINITION OF TERMS

BREAKEVEN POINT. The point where a company has zero profit or loss (total revenue for the company is equal to total costs).

BUDGET. A detailed plan which shows acquisitions and uses of financial resources for a period of time.

CONTRIBUTION MARGIN. Contribution margin is equal to sales minus variable expenses.

COST BEHAVIOR. Cost behavior refers to changes in a cost when changes in the level of activity occur.

DIRECT LABOR. All labor performed by employees directly involved in production.

DIRECT MATERIALS. Raw materials which become a part of the company's end product and can be traced easily to that end product.

FIXED COSTS. Costs which remain constant in total in spite of changes in the volume of output of a company.

FORECASTING. The prediction of a value of a variable in the future.

JOB ORDER COSTING. The form of product costing used most often by firms which produce a number of products; these products can be easily divided into separate projects or batches.

MANUFACTURING OVERHEAD. Overhead which includes all costs of production except direct materials and direct labor.

MIXED COST. A cost which is composed of both variable and fixed elements.

PREDETERMINED OVERHEAD RATE. A rate which is determined in advance and used to allocate manufacturing overhead costs to the jobs in work-in-process inventory and to the jobs completed during the period. The predetermined overhead rate is calculated as follows:

$$\frac{\text{Estimated Total Manufacturing Overhead Costs}}{\text{Estimated Total Units in the Application Base}}$$

PROCESS COSTING. The method of product costing most often used by firms which produce a homogeneous product using a continuous manufacturing process.

PROFORMA FINANCIAL STATEMENT. A forecasted (or budgeted) financial statement.

RELEVANT RANGE. The range over which assumptions made about the nature of cost behavior (that is, fixed or variable) are valid.

STANDARD COST. The cost which should be incurred when producing a product or performing an operation efficiently.

VARIABLE COST. A cost which varies in total in direct proportion to changes in the level of activity.

VARIANCE. The difference between the amount budgeted for an item and the amount which actually results for that item at the end of the period.

A. Cost Analysis

Costs are analyzed in various ways in managerial accounting. One of the most important ways in which costs are classified in managerial accounting is by cost behavior. Cost behavior refers to changes in a cost when changes in the output of goods or services occur.

1. *Determining Unit Costs:* The per unit cost of an item is calculated as follows:

$$\frac{\text{Total Cost of the Item}}{\text{Total Number of Units of Output}}$$

   EXAMPLE: Assume Quik-Copy, Inc. produced 10,000 copies during the month of June. The total cost of copying fluid for the month was $10. The per unit cost of copying fluid would be $.001 ($10/$10,000).

2. *Variable and Fixed Costs:*

   a. *Variable costs:* Variable costs vary in total directly with the level of output. As production increases, the total amount of a variable cost will increase proportionately while the per unit cost will remain the same. Raw materials are an example of a variable cost.

   EXAMPLE: Assume Quik-Copy, Inc. pays $.01 for each sheet of paper it uses in making copies. If 10 copies are made, the total cost is 10 x $.01 = $.10. If 10,000 copies are made, the total cost is 10,000 x $.01 = $100. The per unit cost remains at $.01 regardless of the level of activity.

   b. *Fixed costs:* Fixed costs remain constant in total in spite of changes in the volume of output. The per unit amount of a fixed cost varies as the level of activity changes. For example, if Quik-Copy, Inc. rents a building for $500 per month, the $500 rental expense will be incurred whether Quik-Copy produces 0 copies, 100 copies, or 10,000 copies. Depreciation, insurance, and advertising are other examples of fixed costs.

   EXAMPLE: Assume Quik-Copy, Inc. has $200 per month in insurance expense which is a fixed cost. If Quik-Copy produced 10 copies in a month, the total cost of insurance expense would be $200 and the per unit cost would be $20 ($200/10 copies). If Quik-Copy produced 10,000 copies in a month, the total cost of insurance would be $200 and the per unit cost would be $.02 ($200/10,000).

   c. *Mixed or semivariable costs:* Mixed costs vary with level of activity but by less than a proportionate amount. A common example of a mixed cost is electricity. The cost of electricity is not constant or fixed; yet, it does not vary directly with production. The cost of electricity could be separated into fixed and variable portions. This might be done by various methods such as regression analysis, simultaneous equations, or the high-low method.

EXAMPLE: Assume Quik-Copy, Inc. is able to separate the mixed cost of maintenance into the following components: $100 per month plus $.001 per copy. If Quik-Copy produced 10,000 copies, the cost of maintenance would be $110 [$100 + (10,000 x $.001)]. If Quik-Copy produced 100,000 copies, the cost of maintenance would be $200 [$100 + (100,000 x $.001)].

    d. *Relevant range:* Fixed and variable costs retain their characteristics within a certain relevant range. Outside of the relevant range, the assumptions made about cost behavior are not valid.

3. *Cost-Volume Profit Analysis:* Cost-volume profit analysis, also called breakeven analysis, is a powerful management tool used for budgeting, forecasting, pricing, and decision making.

    a. *Contribution margin:* In managerial accounting, the income statement is often classified in the following manner:

$$
\begin{array}{l}
\text{Sales} \\
\underline{\text{- Variable Costs}} \\
\text{Contribution Margin} \\
\underline{\text{- Fixed Costs}} \\
\text{Net Income}
\end{array}
$$

    b. *Breakeven analysis:* The central concept of breakeven analysis rests on the equation:

$$\text{Sales} = \text{Fixed Costs} + \text{Variable Costs} + \text{Profit}$$

The breakeven point is the point where total revenues are equal to total expenses and net income is equal to zero. Thus, the breakeven point is where:

$$\text{Sales Revenue} = \text{Variable Expenses} + \text{Fixed Expenses}$$

This equation may be rewritten as:

$$SP\,(SQ) = VC\,(SQ) + \text{Fixed Expenses}$$

where SP is selling price, VC is variable cost per unit, and SQ is sales quantity.

EXAMPLE: Quik-Copy wants to know its breakeven point in number of copies if it sells copies for $.05 each. Costs are as follows:

Fixed Costs:
Rent	$500
Electricity	150
Depreciation	100
Total Fixed Costs	$750

Variable Costs:
Materials	$.01/copy
Labor	.01/copy
Total Variable Cost per Copy	$.02/copy

The breakeven point is then calculated:

$$\text{Sales} = \text{Variable Expenses} + \text{Fixed Expenses}$$
$$(\$.05)(SQ) = (\$.02)(SQ) + \$750$$

Simplifying the equation, we get:

$$(\$.03)(SQ) = \$750$$
$$SQ = 25{,}000$$

The breakeven number of copies is 25,000. The breakeven amount in sales dollars is equal to:
25,000 copies × $.05/copy = $1,250.

c. *Contribution margin approach to breakeven analysis:* The contribution margin ratio is equal to:

$$\frac{\text{Sales (in dollars)} - \text{Variable Expenses (in dollars)}}{\text{Sales (in dollars)}}$$

The breakeven point (BEP) in sales dollars is equal to:

$$\text{Breakeven Point (BEP)} = \frac{\text{Fixed Expenses}}{\text{Contribution Margin Ratio}}$$

EXAMPLE: *The Quik-Copy breakeven problem could be solved using the contribution margin approach as follows:*

The contribution margin ratio is:

$$(.05 - .02)/.05 = .60$$
$$\text{Breakeven Point (BEP)} = \$750/.60 = \$1{,}250$$

d. *Cost-volume profit analysis for planning:* If a company wishes to use cost-volume profit analysis for planning purposes, various quantities may be inserted into the cost-volume profit equation.

EXAMPLE: *To determine profit when 60,000 units are sold, multiply the unit prices by 60,000.*

Sales = Variable Expenses + Fixed Expenses + Profit

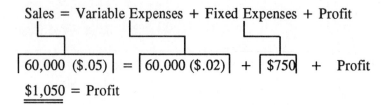

$1,050 = Profit

By changing the variables for sales price, fixed expenses, and variable expenses, the effects of such changes on profitability can be forecast.

e. *Graphical analysis:* The cost-volume-profit relationships may be shown in a graphical manner as shown in Figure 14-1. Fixed costs are shown as a straight horizontal line. Since the costs do not change with an increase in volume, the slope of this line is 0. The total cost line is equal to fixed costs at zero volume and increases with volume with a slope equal to variable costs per unit. The revenue line is equal to zero at zero volume and increases with volume with a slope equal to sales price. The breakeven point is where total costs intersect total revenue. Note that volume refers to sales quantity, not to quantity produced.

Using data for Quik-Copy, Inc., the graph shown in Figure 14-2 can be prepared. The fixed cost line is drawn at $750. Since total costs are fixed costs at zero volume, only one other point must be calculated to draw the total cost line. At 40,000 copies, total costs are $750 + 40,000 (.02) = $1,550. Total revenue is zero at zero volume, so one other point is needed to draw a revenue line. At 40,000 copies, revenue is equal to 40,000 (.05) = $2,000. The intersection of the total revenue and total expense lines is the breakeven point. The distance between the lines at any given volume is the amount of profit or loss associated with sales at the volume given, assuming that all other relationships remain the same.

4. *Reporting for a Manufacturing Concern:*

   a. *Balance sheet:* The balance sheet of a manufacturing company is the same as that of a merchandising company except that three inventory accounts are shown. A manufacturing company maintains the following three inventory accounts:

      (1) Raw materials inventory.

      (2) Work-in-process inventory.

      (3) Finished goods inventory.

Figure 14-1
Breakeven Point

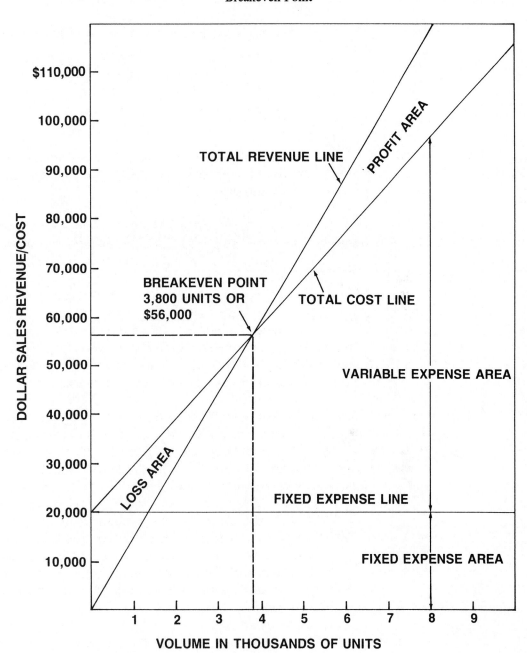

b. *Income statement:* In order to prepare an income statement for a manufacturing company, costs must be classified as product or period costs.

(1) *Product costs:* Product costs include direct materials, direct labor, and all manufacturing overhead costs.

Figure 14-2
Dollar Revenue Breakeven Point

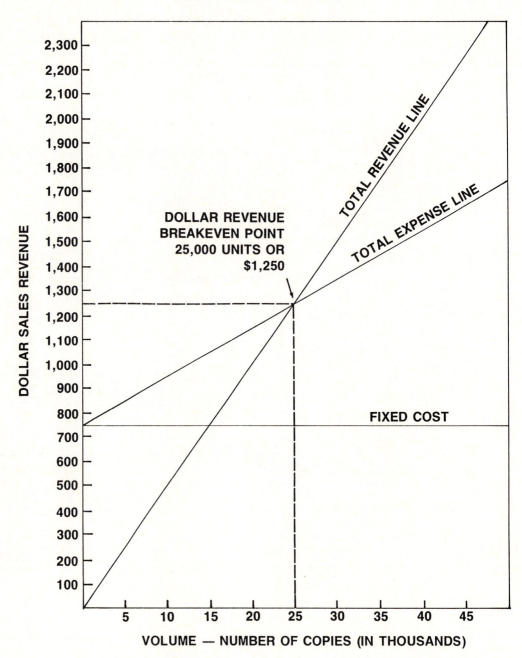

(2) *Period costs:* Period costs include those costs which are not related to the manufacturing of a unit of product.

Period costs are accounted for in the same manner for both manufacturing and merchandising companies. Most period costs are treated as part of operating expenses. Product costs are summarized in a cost of goods manufactured statement and Cost of Goods Manufactured replaces Purchases in the income statement for a manufacturing company. (See Figure 14-3.)

Figure 14-3
Partial Income Statement with
Statement of Cost of Goods Manufactured

**Jones Manufacturing Co.
Partial Income Statement
For the Period Ending December 31, 19XA**

Sales		200,000
Cost of Goods Sold:		
Beginning Finished Goods Inventory	10,000	
Cost of Goods Manufactured*	120,000	
Goods Available for Sale	130,000	
Less: Ending Finished Goods Inventory	20,000	
Cost of Goods Sold		110,000
Gross Profit		90,000

**Jones Manufacturing Co.
Statement of Cost of Goods Manufactured*
For the Period Ending December 31, 19XA**

Beginning Work-in-Process Inventory			30,000
Direct Materials		50,000	
Direct Labor		50,000	
Manufacturing Overhead:			
Indirect Materials	2,000		
Indirect Labor	10,000		
Depreciation — Factory	20,000		
Utilities — Factory	5,000		
Maintenance	5,000		
Insurance	5,000	47,000	
Total Manufacturing Costs			147,000
Total Cost of Work-in-Process During the Period			177,000
Less: Ending Work-in-Process Inventory			57,000
Cost of Goods Manufactured			120,000

5. *Cost Accounting:* Costs for a unit of product must be determined in order to satisfy legal and reporting requirements of the firm and to fulfill management's need for information. There are many possible methods

of accumulating costs. The two most common methods, job order costing and process costing, will be discussed in this module.

  a. *Job order costing:* Job order costing is used by firms with production which is easily divided into separate projects or batches. For example, a construction firm would accumulate all costs for each building on a separate job card. Costs are separated into direct labor, direct materials, and manufacturing overhead. The combination of direct labor and direct materials is known as *prime costs*. Direct labor and manufacturing overhead together are called *conversion costs*.

    (1) *Direct labor:* Direct labor is all labor performed by personnel directly involved in production. A machine operator's wage is direct labor. Salaries of production supervisors, inspectors, and maintenance personnel are not direct labor. These are not directly related to the production of a product. These costs are accumulated as indirect labor in the manufacturing overhead account. Officers' and secretaries' salaries are considered to be administrative expenses and are not considered to be part of the cost of production. They are treated as operating expenses.

    (2) *Direct materials:* Direct materials are raw materials which are readily identified with an individual product. In the production of furniture, wood and cloth would be direct materials. Other items such as the glue and nails which are either difficult to measure or of such small value that accurate measurement is not worthwhile are classified as *indirect materials*. Indirect materials are part of the manufacturing overhead account.

    (3) *Manufacturing overhead:* Manufacturing overhead contains all other costs of production. The unique aspect of manufacturing overhead is that while direct labor and direct materials are variable costs, manufacturing overhead is composed of both fixed and variable costs. Fixed costs could include salaries, rent, and depreciation, while variable costs could include electricity, indirect materials, or any other expense which varies with volume. Manufacturing overhead is a control account in which numerous expenses are accumulated.

    (4) *Cost flows in job order costing:* In job order costing, each project has a job card on which costs are accumulated. The job cards are subsidiary records of the costs which are recorded in the work-in-process inventory account. The flow of costs in job order costing is as follows:

(a) When raw materials are purchased, the Raw Materials Inventory account is debited and Accounts Payable is credited.

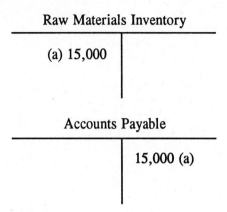

(b) When materials are requisitioned by the production department, the Raw Materials Inventory account is credited for the total amount requisitioned; the Work-in-Process inventory account is debited for the portion of the materials requisitioned which are direct materials (DM) and the Manufacturing Overhead account is debited for the indirect materials (IM) portion.

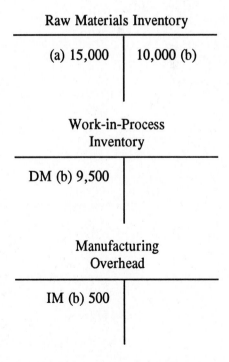

The amount of direct materials used on each individual job is also recorded on the individual job cost sheets.

(c) When employees perform work on the product, the Wages Payable account is credited for the total labor cost which is related to the product; the Work-in-Process Inventory account is debited for the direct labor cost (DL) and the Manufacturing Overhead account is debited for the indirect labor cost (IL).

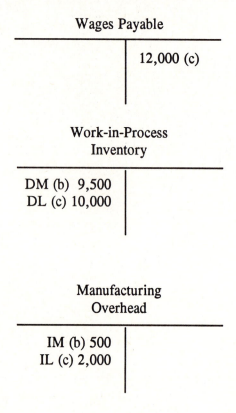

Wages Payable	
	12,000 (c)

Work-in-Process Inventory	
DM (b) 9,500	
DL (c) 10,000	

Manufacturing Overhead	
IM (b) 500	
IL (c) 2,000	

The amount of direct labor incurred on each individual job is also recorded on the individual job cost sheets.

(d) As items of manufacturing overhead other than indirect materials and indirect labor are incurred, the Manufacturing Overhead account is debited and the related payable account (or Cash) is credited.

Manufacturing Overhead	
IM (b) 500	
IL (c) 2,000	
Electricity (d) 1,000	
Rent (d) 5,000	

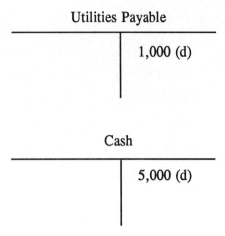

(e) Manufacturing overhead is applied to individual jobs based upon a predetermined overhead rate. The predetermined overhead rate is used to allocate manufacturing overhead costs to the jobs included in the work-in-process inventory and to the jobs completed during the period. A predetermined overhead rate is used to avoid charging individual jobs with different overhead amounts due to seasonal variations in production volume.

In order to calculate the predetermined overhead rate, total overhead costs are estimated for the period and the total overhead application base for the period is estimated. The overhead application base chosen should be common to all jobs worked on during the period, and it should reflect each job's utilization of the manufacturing overhead incurred. Direct labor hours, direct labor cost, and machine hours are examples of commonly used overhead application bases. The formula for calculating the predetermined overhead rate is:

$$\text{Predetermined Overhead Rate} = \frac{\text{Estimated Total Manufacturing Overhead Costs}}{\text{Estimated Total Units in the Application Base}}$$

EXAMPLE: Assume total manufacturing overhead costs were estimated to be $9,000 for the period and overhead is to be applied on the basis of direct labor hours. Assume the total direct labor hours for the period are estimated to be 6,000 hours. The predetermined overhead rate would be $9,000/6,000 hours, which is $1.50 *per direct labor hour. Assume that 5,800 direct labor hours were worked during the period and all jobs worked on are still in work-in-process inventory, that is, no jobs have been completed and transferred to finished goods inventory during the period. The company would apply $8,700 (5,800 direct labor hours worked x $1.50 per direct labor hour) of Manufacturing Overhead to the Work-in-Process Inventory account. The entry to record the application of manufacturing overhead would be a debit to Work-in-Process Inventory and a credit to Manufacturing Overhead.*

```
              Work-in-Process
                 Inventory
    ─────────────────────────────────
    DM (b) 9,500  │
    DL (c)10,000  │
    ManOH (e) 8,700 │
```

```
              Manufacturing
                 Overhead
    ─────────────────────────────────
           IM (b) 500  │  8,700 (e) Mfg.
           IL (c) 2,000 │      Overhead
    Electricity (d) 1,000 │      Applied
          Rent (d) 5,000 │
                        │
                        │  200 Overapplied
                        │      Mfg. Overhead
```

Based on the predetermined overhead rate, $8,700 of manufacturing overhead was applied to work-in-process inventory, but only $8,500 of actual manufacturing overhead was incurred during the period. Since more overhead was applied than was incurred, there is a $200 credit balance in the Manufacturing Overhead account which is called *overapplied manufacturing overhead*. If more manufacturing overhead was incurred than was applied during a period, the Manufacturing Overhead account would have a debit balance which would be called Underapplied Manufacturing Overhead.

Overapplied or Underapplied Manufacturing Overhead is normally closed to Cost of Goods Sold at the end of the period. Overhead applied to individual jobs is recorded on the individual job cost sheet. If 200 direct labor hours have been worked on Job C, $300 of manufacturing overhead would be applied to Job C (200 direct labor hours x $1.50 per direct labor hour).

(f) As individual jobs are completed, the costs of producing the units within the job are transferred from the Work-in-Process Inventory account to the Finished Goods Inventory account. Assume Job C has been completed, using $400 of direct materials, $450 of direct labor, and $300 of manufacturing overhead. The total cost of the job is $1,150 which would be transferred to finished goods by debiting Finished Goods Inventory for $1,150 and crediting Work-in-Process Inventory for $1,150. If 50 widgets were produced in Job C, the per unit cost of an individual widget would be $23 per unit ($1,150/50 units).

(g) The cost of any units sold during the period is transferred from Finished Goods Inventory to Cost of Goods Sold. If 20 widgets from Job C were sold, Cost of Goods Sold would be debited for $460 (20 units x $23 per unit) and Finished Goods Inventory would be credited for $460.

b. *Process costing:* Process costing is a method of product costing used to cost products in companies which employ a continuous manufacturing process to produce a homogeneous product. The same accounts are utilized as in job order costing: direct labor, direct materials, and manufacturing overhead. When work is in process at the end of a period, costs may be allocated to the ending inventory on a weighted average or a FIFO basis. The inventory pricing is based on equivalent units of production. The actual technique is complicated and can be found in any cost accounting text.

B. Budgets

A *budget* is a detailed plan which shows proposed acquisitions of financial resources and uses of financial resources during a period of time. Budgets are a powerful planning and control tool of management. Their uses are many, including cash management, inventory planning, production scheduling, profit planning, and performance evaluation. The budgeting process is sequential, beginning with the sales budget; there is great interdependence between budgets. Normally a firm will make only the quantity of goods which it intends to sell and purchase only the required raw materials for the quantity which it intends to make. This is the key to the planning function of budgeting.

After the fact, budgets may also be used to compare actual results with planned objectives and evaluate the firm's and management's performance.

1. *Types of Budgets:*

    a. *Sales budget:* The sales budget is the foundation for all other budgets. Various scientific and not-so-scientific methods of preparing a sales budget exist. This is essentially a marketing function and is passed on to management and accounting when completed. The sales budget must include the *quantity* and *timing of sales*. More sophisticated budgets also include the place where a sale is to occur.

    EXAMPLE:

	Jan	Feb	Mar	Apr
Sales (in thousands)	20	24	32	50
Sales Price	.05	.05	.05	.05
Total Sales	$1,000	$1,200	$1,600	$2,500

    Another schedule related to the sales budget is the cash collection schedule. If sales are made on an account, there may be a time lag between delivery of the product and collection of cash. Usually, depending on a firm's credit policy, a certain amount will prove to be uncollectible. These data are critical for cash planning.

    EXAMPLE: *Assuming 25 percent of sales are made on account and are collected in the next month, a cash collection schedule would show:*

	Jan	Feb	Mar	Apr
Current Sales (Cash) (75% of Current Sales)	$750	$900	$1,200	$1,875
Collections on Account (25% of Previous Month's Sales)	0	250	300	400
Total	$750	$1,150	$1,500	$2,275

    b. *Production budget:* The production budget is prepared next. The production budget shows the quantity and timing of units required to be produced during the period in order to meet sales and inventory requirements. Usually there is a time lag between production and sales. Orders might be produced in advance, and some standard items might be kept in stock. If 20 percent of orders can be produced in advance, the production budget would appear as follows:

EXAMPLE:

	Jan	Feb	Mar	Apr	
Current Req.	20,000	24,000	32,000	50,000	Current Sales
End Inventory	4,800	6,400	10,000	?	20% of Next Month's Sales
Totals	24,800	30,400	42,000		Total Production Needs
Less Beg. Inv.	0	4,800	6,400		Amount Already Produced
To Be Produced	24,800	25,600	35,600		

c. *Raw materials budget:* The timing and quantity of materials purchases can now be planned in the raw materials budget. This is important as many materials must be ordered in advance. A shortage of raw materials will cause delays in production and sales losses in the short run and potential long-term customer dissatisfaction. The process is identical to the production budget in terms of planning ending inventory and purchases to accommodate the firm's needs.

d. *Labor budget:* The labor budget shows the quantity of labor expected to be needed during the period. The labor budget is identical to the above production and materials budgets except that labor cannot be stored in inventory. Management can plan to have sufficiently trained labor available and plan the necessary cash needed to pay them in a timely fashion. Management might plan to start with two employees and add one employee in March. If each employee earns $600 per month, the labor budget is:

	Jan	Feb	Mar	Apr
Salary	600	600	600	600
No. of Employees	2	2	3	3
	1,200	1,200	1,800	1,800

Another aspect, which is omitted for simplicity, is the timing and amount of withholding payments and employment taxes usually paid no later than the following month. Large firms often must make deposits every few days.

e. *Manufacturing overhead budget:* Overhead includes both fixed and variable components. A budget is prepared for each aspect. The fixed portion is constant for any volume by definition, whereas the variable portion is largely dependent on the production schedule. Some of the costs are discretionary as to timing and even as to incurrence. Machine maintenance costs may be higher in slack periods and lower in peak periods due to management policy.

f. *Selling expense budget:* Selling expenses, like manufacturing overhead, are composed of fixed and variable elements. The fixed elements remain constant, though some may be discretionary, such as advertising. The variable elements will vary with sales volume, not production volume as manufacturing overhead does.

g. *Administrative expense budget:* The administrative expense budget, like the manufacturing overhead and selling expense budgets, has fixed and variable components. Administrative expenses are dependent on management policy for amount and timing of expenditures.

h. *Cash budget:* The cash budget is very important to the success of a firm. The timing and quantity of cash inflows and outflows need to be estimated to the best of management's ability in order to provide sufficient funds to continue operations. With many firms, the seasonal nature of sales will result in a cash surplus in some months and a cash deficiency in other months. In times of surplus, excess funds are invested in such a manner as to maximize returns while maintaining liquidity.

i. *Master budget:* After all of the individual sales, production, and expense budgets are prepared, they are combined into a master budget which is approved by the board of directors and becomes the plan or objective for the period. Master budgets are usually prepared on a quarterly or annual basis. The master budget serves as the financial and operating plan for the period.

j. *Capital budget:* A capital budget is a long-range budget which includes plans for addition of new product lines or purchase of any new plant or equipment items. A capital budget might cover a period as long as five to ten years.

2. *Factors Considered in Budget Preparation:*

a. *Participative budgeting:* Budgets are used as a motivational tool to help managers understand and meet the company's goals and objectives. When the individuals responsible for implementing the budget provide input into the budgeting process, it is called *participative budgeting.* When individuals help to draft a plan or budget, it is assumed that they will want to try to meet the budget goals. Participative budgeting is used to aid in getting employees to accept the budget as their goal and improve motivation within the company.

b. *Zero-base budgeting:* Zero-base budgeting is a method of budgeting where managers are required to start at zero budget levels each year. They must justify all costs as if they were first-time costs.

Frequently, traditional budgets are prepared by starting with last year's budget and adding to it or subtracting from it. With zero-base budgeting every expenditure is reviewed, not just taken for granted.

c. *Continuous budgeting:* When continuous budgeting is followed, the budget is continually updated and reviewed each month. At any time, a continuous budget covers a 12-month period since it is updated every month.

d. *Using budgets as control tools:* In order to use budgeting effectively, a company must use budgets not only as planning tools but also as control tools. Control involves the methods through which management assures that the company is operating in such a way as to attain the goals set out in the plan. One part of the control process is budget variation and analysis.

3. *Budget Variation and Analysis:* After a period for which a budget had been prepared has ended, the performance of the firm and responsible personnel can be evaluated by comparing budgeted items to actual results. Any difference between the two is known as a *variance*. A favorable variance occurs when an actual expense is less than a budgeted expense or an actual revenue is greater than a budgeted revenue. An unfavorable variance occurs when an actual expense is greater than a budgeted expense or an actual revenue is less than a budgeted revenue.

Actual Expense > Budgeted Expense }
Actual Revenue < Budgeted Revenue } Unfavorable Variance

Actual Expense < Budgeted Expense }
Actual Revenue > Budgeted Revenue } Favorable Variance

If actual results are compared to budgeted items for only one level of activity, the budget is known as a *static* budget. A better means of evaluating performance is by means of a *flexible* budget. Flexible budgets have varying amounts budgeted for different levels of activity. Variable costs are budgeted at an appropriate amount for the attained output. Static or fixed budgets are a good planning tool but are less meaningful for control or evaluation purposes.

EXAMPLE: *Assume the following information is budgeted for ABC Company:*

Fixed Costs	$750
Variable Manufacturing Costs	.02/unit
Variable Selling Costs	.01/unit
Sales Price	.05/unit

Assume a static budget for 60,000 units was prepared and compared to the actual results.

	Static Budget	Actual Results
Sales	60,000 x .05 = 3,000	65,000 x .05 = 3,250
Variable Mfg. Cost	60,000 x .02 = 1,200	65,000 x .025 = 1,625
Variable Selling Cost	60,000 x .01 = 600	65,000 x .009 = 585
Fixed Costs	= 750	= 750
Profit	450	290

Analysis of the static budget as compared to the actual results gives the following variances.

Sales Variance	$250	Favorable	(3,000-3,250)
Variable Mfg. Variance	(425)	Unfavorable	(1,200-1,625)
Variable Selling Variance	15	Favorable	(600- 585)
Total Variance	(160)		

a. *Static budget:* When a static budget is compared to actual results line by line, the variances computed may have little meaning. This is because efficiency, level of sales quantity, and changes in prices are lumped into one amount. For example, we would expect that the actual variable manufacturing cost for ABC Co. would be greater than the budgeted cost per the static budget because ABC Co. produced more units than they anticipated. The variance does not provide information about whether the 65,000 units were produced efficiently. Variances which provide information about cost efficiency are based on a flexible budget related to the actual level of activity. Two variances are often calculated using the master or static budget: the sales price variance and the sales volume variance.

(1) *Sales price variance:* The sales price variance is computed by multiplying the difference between budgeted selling price and actual selling price per unit by the number of units sold.

(2) *Sales volume variance:* The sales volume variance is determined by multiplying the difference between actual sales and budgeted sales (in units) by the budgeted contribution margin per unit. The sales volume variance is considered to be a measure of the effectiveness of management for a given period.

EXAMPLE: *Using the static budget and actual results from the previous ABC Company example, the sales price and sales volume variance would be calculated as follows:*

Sales Price Variance = Actual Units Sold (ASP - BSP) where BSP is the budgeted selling price per unit and ASP is the actual selling price per unit.

Sales Price Variance = 65,000 (.05-.05) = 0 per unit. This variance is zero since budgeted selling price and actual selling price were equal.

Sales Volume Variance = Budgeted CM (ASU - BSU) where CM is the contribution margin per unit, ASU is the actual number of units sold, and BSU is the budgeted number of units expected to be sold.

Sales Volume Variance = .02 (65,000-60,000) = 100 Favorable. The budgeted contribution margin is (.05-.03) = .02.

b. *Flexible budget:* A flexible budget is a budget which is prepared for different levels of activity. After actual production for the period is known, a flexible budget can be prepared which shows budgeted production costs for the actual level of activity.

EXAMPLE: Now, assume that a flexible budget for three different levels of activity was prepared as follows:

	Level of Activity		
	50,000 Units	*60,000 Units*	*70,000 Units*
Sales	$2,500	$3,000	$3,500
Variable Mfg. Costs	1,000	1,200	1,400
Variable Selling Costs	500	600	700
Fixed Costs	750	750	750
Profit	$ 250	$ 450	$ 650

This is very similar to cost-volume-profit analysis in providing expectations of revenues and expenditures at varying levels of activity. Actual results are not compared to budgeted allowances for the actual activity level.

	Flexible Budget	*Actual results*
Sales	65,000 x .05 = 3,250	65,000 x .05 = 3,250
Variable Mfg. Cost	65,000 x .02 = 1,300	65,000 x .025 = 1,625
Variable Selling Cost	65,000 x .01 = 650	65,000 x .009 = 585
Fixed Costs	= 750	= 750
Profit	550	290

Analysis of Results

Sales Variance	$ 0	
Variable Mfg. Variance	(325)	Unfavorable
Variable Selling Variance	65	Favorable
Total Variance	(260)	Unfavorable

The flexible budget variances may be split into price and efficiency variances. (See Section C-2 of this chapter.)

C. **Standard Costing and Variance Analysis**

A standard cost is a predetermined estimate of the cost per unit for materials, labor, and manufacturing overhead. A *standard cost* is the cost which should be incurred to produce a product or perform an operation efficiently. When a standard costing system is used, managers compare actual results with the predetermined standard goal to determine whether performance was satisfactory.

1. *Management by Exception:* A standard costing system allows managers to direct their attention to those areas which require corrective action. This is called *management by exception.* When a standard costing system is used, managers do not spend time reviewing areas which do not differ significantly from standard cost.

2. *Variance:* The difference between standard cost and actual cost is called the *variance.* A *favorable variance* occurs when actual cost is less than standard cost. An *unfavorable variance* occurs when actual cost is more than standard cost. The following example shows the calculation of the most common standard costing variances.

EXAMPLE: *Assume that Hamsmith Co. has established the following cost standards for its product Snac:*

Material (1 pound per unit @ $5 per lb.)	$ 5.00
Direct Labor (1 hour per unit @ $10 per hour)	10.00
Overhead ($5 per standard direct labor hour)	5.00
Total standard cost of one Snac	$20.00

Direct Material Variances

Hamsmith Co. produced 1,000 units of Snac. They used 1,100 pounds of raw materials which cost $4.95 per pound to produce the 1,000 Snacs.

Actual Cost (1,100 lbs. @ $4.95) =	$5,445
- Standard Cost (1,000 lbs. @ $5.00) =	5,000
Total Direct Material Variance (unfavorable)	-$ 445

The total direct material variance (flexible budget variance) may be divided into price and efficiency components as follows:

Price Variance

Actual units used x actual price:	
1,100 lbs. x $4.95 =	$5,445
- Actual units used x standard price:	
1,100 lbs. x $5.00 =	5,500
Direct Material Price Variance (favorable)	+$ 55

Efficiency Variance (also called Quantity Variance)

Actual units x standard price:	
1,100 lbs. x $5.00 =	$5,500
- Standard units allowed x standard price:	
1,000 lbs. x $5.00 =	5,000
Direct Material Efficiency Variance (unfavorable)	-$ 500

Direct Material Price Variance	+$ 55	(favorable)
+ Direct Material Efficiency Variance	- 500	(unfavorable)
= Total Direct Material Variance	-$445	(unfavorable)

Direct Labor Variances

Hamsmith Co. used 1,110 hours costing $10.10 per hour to produce the 1,000 units of Snac.

Actual Labor Cost:	
1,110 hours x $10.10 =	$11,211
- Standard Labor Cost:	
1,000 hours x $10.00 =	10,000
Total Direct Labor Variance (unfavorable)	-$ 1,211

The total direct labor variance (flexible budget variance) may be divided into price and efficiency components as follows:

Direct Labor Price Variance

Actual hours used x actual price:	
1,110 x $10.10 =	$11,211
- Actual hours used x standard price:	
1,110 x $10.00 =	11,100
= Direct Labor Price Variance (unfavorable)	-$ 111

Direct Labor Efficiency Variance

Actual hours used x standard price:	
1,110 x $10.00 =	$11,100
- Standard hours allowed x standard price:	
1,000 x $10.00 =	10,000
= Direct Labor Efficiency Variance (unfavorable)	$ 1,100
Direct Labor Price Variance (unfavorable)	-$ 111
Direct Labor Efficiency Variance (unfavorable)	- 1,100
Total Direct Labor Variance (unfavorable)	-$ 1,211

Overhead variances may be computed in several ways. When standard costs are used, overhead is applied to production on the basis of a predetermined standard overhead rate. The calculation of overhead variances is beyond the scope of this module. The candidate should refer to an elementary managerial accounting text for further discussion of this topic.

D. Forecasting

Forecasting is the prediction of a value of a variable in the future. This prediction may be based on past values of the variable, values of related variables, or expert judgment. Forecasts are needed in business in order to plan for the future development of the company.

1. *Types of Forecasts:* Forecasts may be short term, medium term, or long term in nature. Short-term forecasts cover a period of only a few months. Medium-term forecasts cover the period from about three months to two years in the future. Long-term forecasts cover periods beyond two years into the future. Forecasts which cover a shorter time frame are generally more accurate than long-term forecasts.

    a. *Sales forecast:* A sales forecast is generally the first step in preparing a budget. After sales are forecast, production needs can be estimated based upon the forecasted level of sales.

    b. *Capital expenditures forecast:* A company also needs to forecast what its capital expenditure requirements will be in the future. Advance planning is necessary in order to ensure that sufficient funds are available to purchase additional capital equipment.

    c. *Product demand forecast:* Forecasts of demand for company's products are useful in preparing sales forecasts and in determining where new products should be introduced and old product lines dropped.

    d. *Other forecasts:* The different types of items which might be forecast are endless. Any item of information which would aid management in meeting goals and objectives of the company might be forecast.

2. *Factors Considered in Preparation of Forecasts:* A number of different methods can be used to prepare a forecast.

    a. *Forecasting methods:* These methods may be quantitative or qualitative in nature.

        (1) Quantitative forecasts are based on past data. It is assumed that the trends observed in the past will continue in the future. Time series models base the forecast on past values of the variable. Regression models assume that the variable to be forecast exhibits a cause-and-effect relationship with another variable or variables.

        (2) Qualitative forecasts are not based on past data but on intuitive thinking, judgment, and expert knowledge.

    The type of method which should be used depends upon the individual situation. In making forecasts pertaining to new products, there may be no relevant past data. Many firms use a combination of methods to forecast.

    b. *Accuracy of forecast:* A forecast is usually inaccurate. It might be useful to provide more than one value for a forecasted item. For example, pessimistic, most likely, and optimistic values of the forecast might be provided or a range might be provided (that is, $\$10,000 \pm 15\%$).

    c. *Monitoring actual performance:* After a forecast is prepared, actual performance of the variable should be monitored in order to determine the accuracy of the forecast and to aid in preparing future forecasts.

3. *Proforma Statements:* Proforma statements are forecasted financial statements. After the budgeting process is complete, a forecasted balance sheet and income statement can be prepared. These are called proforma financial statements and are used for planning and evaluation purposes.

Managerial Accounting

Chapter 14: Review Questions

PART A: Multiple-Choice Questions

DIRECTIONS: Select the best answer from the four alternatives. Write the letter of your answer in the blank to the left of the number.

_____ 1. A variable cost

   a. will not be affected by changes in activity from period to period.
   b. will remain constant in total as the level of activity changes.
   c. increases or decreases proportionately (in total) with changes in the level of activity.
   d. will increase on a per unit basis as the level of activity increases.

_____ 2. Which of the following costs is variable?

   a. Straight-line depreciation on machinery
   b. Direct labor
   c. The salary of the controller
   d. Rent on the sales building

_____ 3. As the number of units produced by a manufacturing company decreases

   a. the variable cost per unit increases.
   b. fixed costs per unit remain the same.
   c. fixed costs in total remain the same.
   d. the variable cost in total increases.

_____ 4. Which of the following costs is fixed?

   a. Direct materials
   b. Property taxes on the factory land and buildings
   c. Wages of maintenance employees
   d. Freight-out on goods sold

5. When a company's actual sales for a period are equal to its breakeven sales

   a. total contribution margin for the company will be equal to total fixed expenses for the period.
   b. total revenues will be equal to total expenses.
   c. net income for the period will be zero.
   d. All of the above conditions will occur.

6. Janet Company produces a game that sells for $20 per game. Variable costs are $12 per game, and fixed costs total $172,000 annually. The breakeven point in units is (rounded to the nearest unit)

   a. 19,111 units.
   b. 10,118 units.
   c. 21,500 units.
   d. 24,000 units.

7. Karl Company produces dolls. Each doll sells for $15 per unit and has a contribution margin ratio of 60 percent. Total annual fixed expenses are $240,000. If Karl Company wishes to earn $30,000 of net income, how many dolls must be sold?

   a. 28,667 dolls
   b. 30,000 dolls
   c. 18,000 dolls
   d. 45,000 dolls

8. In a job order cost system, the entry to record the requisition of direct materials for use in production would include

   a. a debit to the Direct Materials account.
   b. a credit to the Manufacturing Overhead account.
   c. a debit to the Work-in-Process Inventory account.
   d. a credit to Accounts Payable.

9. In a job order cost system, the entry to record the wages paid to factory maintenance workers would include

   a. a debit to the Work-in-Process Inventory account.
   b. a credit to the Manufacturing Overhead account.
   c. a debit to the Direct Labor account.
   d. a debit to the Manufacturing Overhead account.

10. In a job order cost system, the entry to record the application of overhead to a job would include

   a. a debit to the Manufacturing Overhead account.
   b. a debit to the Work-in-Process Inventory account.
   c. a credit to the Work-in-Process Inventory account.
   d. a credit to the Cost of Goods Sold account.

11. Assume XYZ Company applies overhead to production on the basis of a predetermined overhead rate. A debit balance in the Manufacturing Overhead account at the end of the period means

   a. the overhead cost which was actually incurred was greater than the amount applied to production.
   b. the overhead cost which was actually incurred was less than the amount applied to production.
   c. the amount of manufacturing overhead incurred was equal to the manufacturing overhead applied during the period.
   d. more hours were actually worked during the period than were predicted in calculating the predetermined overhead rate.

12. Which of the following companies would be most likely to use process costing?

   a. A custom home builder
   b. A manufacturer of specialized machine tools
   c. A contractor building bridges
   d. A company which manufactures tint base for paint

13. Electricity is a mixed cost for ABC Company. ABC Company estimates that the fixed portion of the monthly electrical cost is $500 and the variable portion is $.10 per machine hour. If ABC Company used 10,000 machine hours in April, their estimate of total electrical cost for the month would be

   a. $ 600.
   b. $1,500.
   c. $1,000.
   d. $ 500.

14. The fixed cost per unit for rent is $.50 at a production level of 100,000 units. If 125,000 units are produced, the total fixed cost for rent would be

   a. $ 65,500.
   b. $100,000.
   c. $ 50,000.
   d. $125,000.

15. Kilo Company applies overhead to units of product based on machine hours. At the beginning of the period Kilo Company estimated that total manufacturing overhead would be $500,000 and that the number of machine hours used during the period would be 200,000. Kilo Company actually used 210,000 machine hours during the period. The total amount of overhead applied for this period was

   a. $500,000.
   b. $ 84,000.
   c. $210,000.
   d. $525,000.

16. Budgets can be used for

   a. production scheduling.
   b. cash management.
   c. inventory planning.
   d. all of the above.

17. When the individuals responsible for implementing the budget are involved in preparing the budget, it is called

   a. participative budgeting.
   b. collective budgeting.
   c. zero-base budgeting.
   d. employee budgeting.

18. The budget which is used to plan for long-range purchases of new plant and equipment is called the

   a. cash budget.
   b. continuous budget.
   c. capital budget.
   d. production budget.

19. Farley Enterprises has budgeted sales in units of:
   May   5,000 units
   June   6,000 units
   July   4,000 units
   Farley Enterprises desires to have an ending inventory equal to 25 percent of next month's sales needs. The beginning inventory on May 1 was 1,250 units. The total units to be produced in May are
   a. 5,000.
   b. 5,250.
   c. 5,500.
   d. 4,750.

20. An unfavorable variance results when

    a. actual revenue is greater than budgeted revenue.
    b. actual expense is less than budgeted expense.
    c. actual revenue is greater than actual expense.
    d. actual expense is greater than budgeted expense.

21. A method of budgeting where managers are expected to justify all costs as if they were first-time expenditures is called

    a. capital budgeting.
    b. participative budgeting.
    c. continuous budgeting.
    d. zero-base budgeting.

22. A predetermined estimate of the cost per unit for materials, labor, or manufacturing overhead is called

    a. a standard cost.
    b. management by exception.
    c. unit cost.
    d. variance cost.

23. Which of the following statements about forecasts is false?

    a. A forecast is a prediction of the future.
    b. Forecasts can be based on past data.
    c. Forecasts are based only on quantitative information.
    d. Pessimistic, most likely, and optimistic estimates can be prepared for a given forecast.

24. Forecasted financial statements are called

    a. estimated financial statements.
    b. proforma financial statements.
    c. futuristic financial statements.
    d. flexible financial statements.

PART B: Matching Sets

MATCHING SET 1

Match each of the following definitions (25-29) with the appropriate accounting term (A-F). Write the letter of your answer in the blank to the left of the number.

        ACCOUNTING TERMS

    A. Breakeven Point
    B. Contribution Margin
    C. Job Order Costing
    D. Process Costing
    E. Relevant Range
    F. Predetermined Overhead Rate

        DEFINITIONS

_____ 25. The range over which assumptions made about the nature of cost behavior are valid.

_____ 26. The point where total revenue for a company is equal to total expenses (where net income = zero).

_____ 27. Sales minus variable expenses.

_____ 28. A rate which is determined in advance and is used to allocate manufacturing overhead to jobs.

_____ 29. The method of product costing most often used by firms which produce a homogeneous product using a continuous manufacturing process.

MATCHING SET 2

Determine the appropriate classification (A-D) for each of the following cost items (30-35) associated with the manufacture and sale of chairs. Write the letter of your answer in the blank to the left of the number.

CLASSIFICATIONS

A. Direct Materials
B. Direct Labor
C. Manufacturing Overhead
D. Selling and Administrative Cost

COST ITEMS

_____ 30. Wood used in making the chairs.

_____ 31. The salary of the factory supervisor.

_____ 32. Sales commissions.

_____ 33. Wages of the worker who varnishes the chairs.

_____ 34. Salary of the vice-president for finance.

_____ 35. Cost of cleaning materials used by factory maintenance workers.

PART C: Problem Situations

DIRECTIONS: For each of the questions pertaining to the following problem situations, select the best answer from the four alternatives. Write the letter of your answer in the blank to the left of the number.

Problem 1

The following financial information pertains to the sales activities of the 4R Corporation for the year 19XA:

Selling Price per Unit	$ 20
Variable Production Cost per Unit	12
Fixed Production Cost	3,000
Selling Commission per Unit	2
Fixed Selling Expenses	2,400
Number of Units Sold in 19XA	6,000

_____ 36. The total contribution margin generated in 19XA was (rounded to the nearest dollar)

   a. $36,000.
   b. $48,000.
   c. $45,000.
   d. $30,600.

_____ 37. The breakeven point in dollars is (rounded to the nearest dollar)

   a. $89,400.
   b. $13,500.
   c. $18,000.
   d. $75,000.

_____ 38. Assuming that the cost information does not change, how many units would the company have to sell in 19XB to earn a $50,000 profit (rounded to the nearest unit)?

   a. 10,000
   b. 3,400
   c. 1,870
   d. 9,233

Managerial Accounting

Problem 2

Jones Company budgeted to sell 10,000 units at $10 per unit. Variable manufacturing costs at $5 per unit were included in the budget. Jones Company actually sold 9,000 units at a price of $11.00 per unit. Their actual variable manufacturing costs were $5.50 per unit.
(F = Favorable; U = Unfavorable)

_____ 39. The sales price variance would be

  a. $ 9,000 F.
  b. $ 9,000 U.
  c. $10,000 F.
  d. $10,000 U.

_____ 40. The sales volume variance would be

  a. $ 5,000 U.
  b. $ 5,500 F.
  c. $10,000 U.
  d. $ 500 U.

Problem 3

The standard costs for a unit of finished product are as follows:

	Standard Quantity	Standard Price
Direct Materials	10 feet	$ 2.00 per foot
Direct Labor	2 hours	$15.00 per hour

The company actually produced 10,000 units. The actual quantity used was 105,000 feet; the actual cost of materials was $199,500. The company actually used 18,000 direct labor hours at a cost of $279,000.

_____ 41. The direct material price variance would be

  a. $ 500 F.
  b. $10,000 F.
  c. $10,500 F.
  d. none of the above.

_____ 42. The direct material quantity variance would be

  a. $10,000 U.
  b. $ 950 U.
  c. $10,000 F.
  d. none of the above.

43. The flexible budget variance for direct materials would be

    a. $ 500 F.
    b. $ 500 U.
    c. $10,000 F.
    d. none of the above.

44. The direct labor rate (price) variance would be

    a. $21,000 F.
    b. $ 9,000 U.
    c. $10,000 U.
    d. none of the above.

45. The direct labor efficiency variance would be

    a. $30,000 F.
    b. $30,000 U.
    c. $21,000 F.
    d. $27,000 F.

Managerial Accounting

Chapter 14: Solutions

PART A: Multiple-Choice Questions

	Answer	Refer to Chapter Section
1.	(c)	[A-2-a]
2.	(b)	[A-2-a]
3.	(c)	[A-2-b]
4.	(b)	[A-2-b]
5.	(d)	[A-3-b]
6.	(c)	[A-3-b]

$$\frac{\text{Fixed Expenses}}{\text{Contribution Margin/Unit}} = \text{Breakeven Point in Units}$$

$$\frac{\$172,000}{\$20 - 12} = 21,500 \text{ Units}$$

7. (b)   [A-3] The formula to solve this question is:

$$\frac{\text{Fixed Expenses + Desired Net Income}}{\text{Contribution Margin per Unit}} = \text{Breakeven Point in Units}$$

$$\frac{\$240,000 + \$30,000}{\$9 \text{ per Unit}} = 30,000 \text{ Dolls}$$

If the selling price per unit is $15 and the contribution margin ratio is 60 percent, the per unit contribution margin is $9.

Selling Price	$15	100%
- Variable Cost	- 6	40%
Contribution Margin	$ 9	60%

8. (c)   [A-5-a(4)(b)]

9. (d)   [A-5-a(4)(c)]

10. (b)   [A-5-a(4)(e)]

11. (a)   [A-5-a(4)(e)]

12. (d)   [A-5-b]

13. (b)   [A-2-c]
          Total Cost = Variable Cost + Fixed Cost
          $1,500   = $.10(10,000) + $500

14. (c)   [A-2-b]
          100,000 x $.50 = $50,000
          Since fixed cost remains constant in total regardless of the level of activity (within the relevant range), the total fixed cost would be the same whether 100,000 units or 125,000 units were produced.

15. (d)   [A-5-a(4)(e)]

$$\text{Predetermined Overhead Rate} = \frac{\text{Estimated Total Overhead}}{\text{Estimated Quantity of the Application Base}}$$

$$\$2.50 \text{ per machine hour} = \frac{\$500,000}{200,000 \text{ hours}}$$

          $525,000 = 210,000 machine hours x $2.50/machine hour

16. (d)   [B]

17. (a)   [B-2-a]

18. (c)   [B-1-j]

19. (b)   [B-1-b]

          Sales   5,000
          + Desired Ending Inventory   1,500   (6,000 x .25)
                                         6,500
          - Beginning Inventory
            already available   -1,250
          Units to be Produced   5,250

20. (d)   [B-3]

Managerial Accounting

21. (d) [B-2-b]

22. (a) [C]

23. (c) [D-2]

24. (b) [D-3]

PART B: Matching Sets

MATCHING SET 1

25. (E) [A-2-d]

26. (A) [A-3-b]

27. (B) [A-3-a]

28. (F) [A-5-a(4)(e)]

29. (D) [A-5-b]

MATCHING SET 2

30. (A) [A-5-a(2)]

31. (C) [A-5-a(3)]

32. (D) [A-4-b]

33. (B) [A-5-a(1)]

34. (D) [A-4-b]

35. (C) [A-5-a(3)]

PART C: Problem Situations

36. (a) [A-3-a]
Sales - Variable Expenses = Contribution Margin

Sales ($20.00 x 6,000)		$120,000
- Variable Expenses:		
Variable Production		
$12.00 x 6,000 =	$72,000	
Variable Selling		
$2.00 x 6,000) =	12,000	84,000
Contribution Margin		$ 36,000

37. (c)   [A-3-c]

$$\frac{\text{Fixed Expenses}}{\text{Contribution Margin Ratio}} = \text{Breakeven Point in \$}$$

$$\frac{\$5,400}{.30} = \$18,000$$

Contribution Margin Ratio = $36,000/$120,000 = .30

38. (d)   [A-3-d]

$$\frac{\text{Fixed Expenses + Desired Net Income}}{\text{Contribution Margin per Unit}} = \text{BEP in Units}$$

$$\frac{\$5,400 + \$50,000}{\$6/\text{Unit}} = 9,233$$

Contribution Margin per Unit = $20 - 14 = $6

39. (a)   [B-3-a]
Sales Price Variance = Actual Units Sold (ASP-BSP) where ASP = Actual Selling Price and BSP = Budgeted Selling Price.

$$\$9,000 = 9,000 \text{ Units Sold } (11.00 - 10.00)$$

The variance is favorable because the actual selling price was greater than the budgeted selling price. When actual revenue > budgeted revenue, the variance is favorable.

40. (a)   [B-3-a]
Sales Volume Variance = Budgeted CM (ASU-BSU) where CM = Contribution Margin, ASU = Actual Sales in Units, and BSU = Budgeted Sales in Units.

$$-\$5,000 = \$5.00 \, (9,000 - 10,000)$$

Budgeted Contribution Margin = $10.00 - 5.00 = $5.00

This variance is unfavorable because actual cost exceeded budgeted cost.

41. (c)   [C-2] The direct material price variance is equal to:
AQ (AP) - AQ (SP)
where AQ = Actual Quantity of Units Used, AP = Actual Price of Units Purchased, and SP = Standard Price per Unit of Material.

The actual price of the units was $1.90 ($199,500/105,000).

105,000 ($1.90) - 105,000 ($2.00) = $10,500

This variance is favorable because the actual price paid was less than the standard price allowed.

Note: It is also possible to base the material price variance on units purchased rather than units used.

42. (a) [C-2] The direct material quantity variance is equal to:
AQ (SP) - SQ (SP)
where AQ = Actual Quantity of Units Used, SP = Standard Price Per Unit of Material, and SQ = Standard Units Allowed.

Standard units allowed is equal to units produced times the standard quantity of material allowed per finished unit.

SQ = 10,000 units x 10 feet = 100,000 feet

DM Quantity Variance = 105,000 ($2.00) - 100,000 ($2.00).
DM Quantity Variance = $10,000.

This variance is unfavorable because the actual quantity of feet used was greater than the standard quantity of feet allowed.

43. (a) [C-2] The flexible budget variance is the difference between the actual cost for materials and the standard cost allowed for materials. It is also equal to the sum of the DM price variance and the DM quantity variance.

Actual Cost	$199,500
- Standard Cost Allowed	-200,000
= Flexible Budget Variance	$ 500

Standard cost allowed is equal to the standard quantity allowed times the standard price (100,000 x $2.00).

This variance is favorable because actual cost was less than standard cost.

44. (b) [C-2] The direct labor rate (price) variance is equal to:
AH (AP) - AH (SP)
where AH = Actual Hours Used, AP = Actual Price Paid Per Hour, and SP = Standard Price Allowed per Hour.

18,000 hours ($15.50) - 18,000 hours ($15.00) = $9,000.

Actual price paid is equal to $270,000/18,000 hours = $15.50/hour.

This variance is unfavorable because the actual rate paid was greater than the standard rate allowed.

45. (a) [C-2] The direct labor efficiency variance is equal to:
AH (SP) - SH (SP)
where AH = Actual Hours Used, SP = Standard Price Allowed per Hour, and SH = Standard Hours Allowed.

Standard hours allowed is equal to the number of units produced times the standard number of hours allowed per finished unit.

SH = 10,000 units x 2 hours/unit = 20,000 hours

DL Efficiency Variance = 18,000 ($15.00) - 20,000 ($15.00).
DL Efficiency Variance = $30,000.

This variance is favorable because the actual number of hours used was less than the standard number of hours allowed.

Glossary

ACCELERATED DEPRECIATION METHOD. A depreciation method which assigns more depreciation expense to the earlier years of an asset's useful life than to its later years of useful life. (8)[1]

ACCOUNT. A device used to collect and summarize information. (2)

ACCOUNT BALANCE. The difference between the total debits and total credits recorded in an account. (2)

ACCOUNTING. The process of recording, measuring, summarizing, analyzing, and interpreting financial information and communicating this information to various users. (1)

ACCOUNTING CYCLE. All of the procedures performed during an accounting period, including analyzing and journalizing of transactions, posting, taking a trial balance, preparing a worksheet, preparing financial statements, journalizing and posting adjusting entries, closing the temporary accounts, and taking a post-closing trial balance. (4)

ACCOUNTING ENTITY. Any business, individual, or not-for-profit organization whose financial affairs can be viewed as being distinct from those of any other entity or unit. (1)

ACCOUNTING EQUATION. Assets = Liabilities + Owners' Equity or, stated another way, Assets - Liabilities = Owners' Equity. (2)

ACCOUNTS RECEIVABLE. The account used to record the right a company has to receive payment for sales made on open account. (2)

ACCRUAL. The concept which states that revenues should be reported when earned rather than when received and expenses should be reported when incurred rather than when paid. (2)

ADJUSTING ENTRIES. A journal entry made at the end of an accounting period to bring an account balance to the correct amount. (4)

AGING OF ACCOUNTS RECEIVABLE. A method of estimating the amount of the allowance for uncollectible accounts and bad debt expense. This method groups the individual accounts according to the length of time they have been outstanding. The amount of uncollectible accounts is then estimated for each group. (9)

ALLOWANCE FOR UNCOLLECTIBLE ACCOUNTS. Contra-account to the accounts receivable account used for reporting accounts receivable at the amount which is expected to be received. (3)

AMORTIZATION. The systematic writing off as an expense of the balance in an account over a period of time. Amortization is usually associated with intangible asset accounts. (9)

APPROPRIATED RETAINED EARNINGS. Retained earnings which have been segregated into a separate account to inform the financial statement reader that a portion of retained earnings is not available for the payment of dividends. (11)

ASSETS. Economic resources from which an entity can expect to receive benefits now or in the future; a thing of value owned. (1) (2)

AUDIT (INDEPENDENT EXTERNAL). An examination of the financial statements of an entity by an independent accountant in order to determine the fairness of the financial statements. The accounting records are referred to in assessing the fairness of the financial statements. (1)

AUTHORIZED SHARES OF CAPITAL STOCK. The number of shares of capital stock which may legally be sold. The authorized amount of capital stock is determined by the corporate charter. (11)

---

[1]The number in parentheses after each entry indicates the chapter location in the text.

BALANCE SHEET. A financial statement which shows the financial position of an entity as of a specific time. Although *balance sheet* is the common term for this financial statement, the formal title is the *statement of financial position*. (3)

BANK RECONCILIATION. A report which explains the difference between the balance per the bank statement and the balance per the general ledger cash account. (5)

BEARER BONDS. Bonds that are not registered in the name of the owner are assumed to be owned by the individual who possesses the bond (also known as coupon bonds). (10)

BOND. A debt security issued in stated dollar denominations with a stated interest rate and maturity date. The most commonly stated dollar value is $1,000. (6)

BOND DISCOUNT. The difference between the face value of a bond and the amount it sells for when the bond sells for less than its face value. (6)

BOND PREMIUM. The difference between the face value of a bond and the amount it sells for when the bond sells for more than its face value. (6)

BOND SINKING FUND. An investment fund established to ensure that sufficient funds are available to retire the bonds at maturity. (10)

BONDS PAYABLE. Long-term liabilities consisting of securities normally issued in stated denominations with a stated interest rate and maturity date. There are numerous types of bonds. (3)

BOOK VALUE OR CARRYING VALUE. The carrying value of an asset on the books, which is the original cost less any accumulated depreciation related to that asset. (3) Book value per share of common stock is a numerical measure of the net assets of a corporation as reflected in a single share of common stock. (11)

BOOKKEEPING. The record-keeping phase of accounting. (1)

BREAKEVEN POINT. The point where a company has zero profit or loss (total revenue for the company is equal to total costs). (14)

BUDGET. A detailed plan which shows acquisitions and uses of financial resources for a period of time. (14)

CALLABLE BONDS. Bonds with a provision stating that the issuer may redeem the bonds prior to maturity by payment of a stipulated call price. (10)

CALLABLE PREFERRED STOCK. Callable preferred stock may be redeemed by the issuing corporation at a stipulated call price. (11)

CAPITAL ASSETS. Any property a taxpayer holds which is not listed in Section 1221 of the U. S. Internal Revenue Code. Section 1221 property includes inventory, accounts receivable, and depreciable property or real estate used in a business. Examples of capital assets are investments in stocks, bonds, or real estate which are not used in a trade or business. (12)

CAPITAL GAIN. A gain resulting from the disposition of a capital asset. (12)

CAPITAL LOSS. A loss resulting from the disposition of a capital asset. (12)

CAPITAL STOCK. Ownership of a corporation is evidenced by shares of capital stock. Capital stock is also the title of the account used to record the total investment in shares of stock of a corporation. (2)

CASH. Coins, paper money, checks, money orders, and money on deposit in banks. (5)

CASH DISBURSEMENTS JOURNAL. A special journal used to record all disbursements of cash. (5)

CASH DISCOUNT. A reduction in the total amount due on an invoice offered if the invoice is paid within a designated period of time. (5)

CASH FLOW STATEMENT. A cash flow statement accounts for the increase or decrease in a company's cash during a period by showing where the company got cash and how it was used. (13)

CASH RECEIPTS JOURNAL. A special journal used to record receipts of cash. (5)

CASUALTY INSURANCE. Insurance coverage which is primarily for the liability of a party which results from negligent acts or omissions resulting in bodily injury and/or property damage to another party. (9)

CERTIFIED CHECK. A check which is guaranteed by the depositor's bank. (5)

CHECK REGISTER. The form of the cash disbursements journal used in conjunction with a voucher system. (5)

CLOSING ENTRY. A journal entry made at the end of an accounting period, which transfers the balance of a temporary account to the owners' equity or retained earnings account. (4)

CO-INSURANCE. A provision in some insurance contracts which requires the insured party to insure property for at least a specified minimum percentage of its fair market value, or to share the loss proportionately with the insurance company. (9)

COMMON STOCK. A classification of capital stock which has no preferences relative to the corporation's other classes of stock. Common stockholders have the right to all residual assets left after the claims of creditors and preferred stockholders have been met. (3)

COMPARATIVE FINANCIAL STATEMENTS. Financial statements which show financial data for a

Glossary

series of years in adjacent columns. (13)

COMPOUND INTEREST. When a security earns compound interest, it earns interest on the principal of the security and on any interest which has been earned but not yet paid. (10)

CONSERVATISM. The principle that requires that the accounting method which is least likely to overstate income and financial position be used. (1)

CONSISTENCY. The principle which requires that once an accounting or reporting method is selected it should be used from one period to another. (1)

CONSOLIDATED STATEMENTS. The combination of two or more accounting entities into one entity for financial reporting purposes. This is done when one entity possesses a controlling interest over the other entity or entities. (6)

CONTINGENT LIABILITY. A potential liability that could become an actual liability only if certain events occur. (9)

CONTRA-ASSET ACCOUNT. An account which is related to a specific asset account and has a credit balance. Contra-assets are reported as deductions from the related asset on the balance sheet. Allowance for uncollectible accounts and accumulated depreciation are examples of contra-asset accounts. (3)

CONTRIBUTION MARGIN. Contribution margin is equal to sales minus variable expenses. (14)

CONTROL ACCOUNT. An account with a balance representing the total of all of the account balances of a related subsidiary ledger. (5)

CONVERTIBLE BOND. A bond with a provision allowing the holder to convert the bond into common stock of the issuing company. (10)

CONVERTIBLE PREFERRED STOCK. Convertible preferred stock may be exchanged by the stockholder for a predetermined number of shares of common stock. (11)

CORPORATION. A business entity which is created by state or federal law and has a separate legal existence from that of its owners. (1)

COST BEHAVIOR. Cost behavior refers to changes in a cost when changes in the level of activity occur. (14)

COST OF GOODS SOLD. The cost of merchandise sold to customers, which is shown as a deduction from sales on the income statement to arrive at gross margin (gross profit). (3)

CREDIT. An entry recorded on the right-hand side of an account. (2)

CUMULATIVE PREFERRED STOCK. Cumulative preferred stock is cumulative with respect to dividends. This means that any dividends not paid in one period must be made up before any current dividends may be paid to common shareholders. (11)

CURRENT ASSETS. Those assets which are expected to be used in operations of the business within the operating cycle of the business or one year, whichever is longer. (3)

CURRENT LIABILITIES. Obligations of a business that are to be repaid during the next operating cycle or one year, whichever is longer. (3)

DEBENTURE. An unsecured bond backed only by the general credit of the company. (10)

DEBIT. An entry recorded on the left-hand side of an account. (2)

DEPLETION. The amount a natural resource is reduced due to usage; for example, cutting timber, mining ore, or pumping oil. (8)

DEPOSITS IN TRANSIT. Bank deposits that have been recorded on the books of a company but have not yet been received and recorded by the bank. (5)

DEPRECIATION. A systematic and rational allocation of the cost of an asset over its useful life. (3)

DIRECT LABOR. All labor performed by employees directly involved in production. (14)

DIRECT MATERIALS. Raw materials which become a part of the company's end product and can be traced easily to that end product. (14)

DIRECT WRITE-OFF METHOD. A method of recording bad debt expense which does not use an allowance for uncollectible accounts or attempt to match bad debt expense with related revenue. When the direct write-off method is used, worthless accounts are written off as a debit to Bad Debt Expense and a credit to Accounts Receivable. This method does not conform to GAAP. (9)

DISCOUNTING OF A NOTE RECEIVABLE. When a note receivable is discounted, it is sold to a bank for cash. The seller remains contingently liable for payment of the note if the maker defaults. (9)

DIVIDEND. A distribution of assets by a corporation to its owners. (2)

DIVIDENDS IN ARREARS. Dividends earned on cumulative preferred stock which have not yet been declared. (11)

DOUBLE-DECLINING-BALANCE DEPRECIATION (DDB). An accelerated depreciation method which uses a depreciation rate which is twice the straight-line rate. (8)

DOUBLE ENTRY ACCOUNTING. In double entry accounting, an equal dollar amount of debits and credits must be recorded in the accounts whenever an accounting transaction is recorded. This is also called the duality principle. (2)

EARNINGS PER SHARE. The amount of net income earned per share of common stock during an accounting period. (3)

EQUITY METHOD. A method used to account for investments in common stock where the investor has significant control over the operations of the investee. (6)

ESTIMATION. Much of what is included in financial reports is the result of an estimate. (1)

EXPENSES. The costs of goods and services consumed (used up) by an entity in order to earn revenues. (2)

EXTERNAL FINANCIAL REPORTS. The standard financial reports issued by entities primarily for the use of decision makers other than the management of the entity (the Balance Sheet, the Income Statement, and the Statement of Cash Flows). (1)

EXTERNAL USERS. Users of accounting information who are not part of the management of the company (examples: bankers, creditors, investors). (1)

EXTRAORDINARY REPAIRS. Repairs which either prolong the useful life of the asset or change the quality of service provided by the asset. (8)

FICA TAX. The Federal Insurance Contributions Act (FICA) tax; commonly called social security tax. (12)

FIDELITY BOND. Insurance that guarantees that the insurance company will pay for losses of money or property that result from the dishonest acts of bonded employees. (9)

FIFO. The *first-in, first-out* method of valuing inventory which assumes that the earliest units purchased are sold first and that ending inventory is made up of the latest purchases. (7)

FINANCING ACTIVITIES. Transactions with the company's owners and long-term creditors. (13)

FIXED ASSETS. Long-lived assets used in the operation of the business. (3)

FIXED COSTS. Costs which remain constant in total in spite of changes in the volume of output of a company. (14)

FORECASTING. The prediction of a value of a variable in the future. (14)

FULL DISCLOSURE. The accounting principle that requires all information which may be relevant to decision makers to be included in the financial statements. (1)

GAINS. Revenues generated from an activity that is not part of the normal operations of the business. (3)

GENERALLY ACCEPTED ACCOUNTING PRINCIPLES (GAAP). The standards governing the recording and reporting of information published in external financial statements. (1)

GOING CONCERN. The assumption that an entity will exist for an indefinite period of time. (1)

GROSS MARGIN (or GROSS PROFIT). The amount that remains after deducting the cost of goods sold from net sales. (3)

GROSS PROFIT METHOD. A method of inventory estimation which is based on the use of the past gross profit percentage experienced by the company. (7)

HISTORICAL COST. The concept that assets should be recorded at their original purchase cost. (1)

INCOME STATEMENT. A financial statement which summarizes the operations of a business showing revenues, expenses, gains, and losses over an accounting period. (3)

INFLATION. A general increase in the prices which must be paid for goods and services. (8)

INSTALLMENT NOTE PAYABLE. A note payable that is due in equal periodic payments. (10)

INTANGIBLE ASSETS. Long-lived assets that do not have any tangible existence. Examples are patents, copyrights, goodwill, and trademarks. (3)

INTEREST-BEARING NOTE RECEIVABLE. A note receivable which requires payment of the principal of the note plus a stated amount of interest on the maturity date. (9)

INTERNAL CONTROLS. The methods and procedures adopted by a business to control its operations and protect its assets from waste, fraud, and theft. (5)

INTERNAL FINANCIAL REPORTS. Reports issued for use by managers of an entity that are usually more detailed than external reports. These reports are also called managerial accounting reports. (1)

INTERNAL USERS. The managers of an entity who use accounting information. (1)

INVENTORY. An asset account which is comprised of goods or merchandise held for future sale. (2)

INVESTING ACTIVITIES. Transactions that involve the investment of a company's cash. (13)

INVESTMENT. Long-term asset which is not used in the operations of the business but is held in the hope of earning a return on the amount invested. (3) (6)

ISSUED SHARES. Shares which have been issued to shareholders at any time. (11)

JOB ORDER COSTING. The form of product costing used most often by firms which produce a number of products; these products can be easily divided into separate projects or batches. (14)

JOURNAL. An accounting record where business transactions are recorded in chronological order. The journal is also known as the book of original entry. (2)

LEDGER. A collection of all of the accounts of a business. Information contained in the journal(s) is posted to the ledger. (2)

LIABILITY. An obligation or debt of an entity owed to another party. (2)

LIFE AND HEALTH INSURANCE. Business life and health coverage provides funds for normal maintenance of a business in the event of a loss of a key person. (9)

LIFO. The *last-in, first-out* method of valuing inventory which assumes that the latest units purchased are sold first and that ending inventory is made up of the earliest units purchased. (7)

LIMITED LIABILITY. Shareholders of a corporation are liable for the debts of the corporation only to the amount of their investment in the corporation. (11)

LIQUIDITY. The more easily an asset can be converted to cash, the higher is its liquidity. (3)

LONG-TERM CAPITAL GAIN OR LOSS. A gain or loss resulting from the disposition of a capital asset held for more than one year. (12)

LONG-TERM LIABILITIES. Obligations of an entity that will not come due during the next year or operating cycle. (3)

LOSSES. Expenses or decreases in owners' equity which do not result from normal operations of the business. (3)

LOWER OF COST OR MARKET. The rule that requires certain assets (such as inventory and temporary investments) be recorded at market value if their market value is below their cost. (7)

MANUFACTURING OVERHEAD. Overhead which includes all costs of production except direct materials and direct labor. (14)

MATCHING. The principle which states that expenses incurred in earning revenues should be matched with those revenues in order to determine net income. (2)

MATERIALITY. The accounting principle which states that insignificant items need not be accounted for in the same manner as more relevant or significant items. (1)

MATURITY DATE OF A NOTE. The date on which a note and any interest are due and payable. (9)

MIXED COST. A cost which is composed of both variable and fixed elements. (14)

MODIFIED ACCELERATED COST RECOVERY SYSTEM (MACRS). An accelerated method of depreciation required for income tax purposes in the United States. (8)

MONEY MEASUREMENT. A common unit of measure (money) used to record all information in the accounting records. (1)

MORTGAGE. A long-term obligation which is normally secured by real estate and is normally repaid in installments. (3) A legal agreement that gives the lender the right to be paid from the sale of specific assets that belong to the borrower if the borrower does not repay the loan. (10)

MORTGAGE BOND. A bond secured by specific assets of the issuing company. (10)

NET INCOME. Revenues - Expenses = Net Income [or Net Loss if Revenues < Expenses]. (2)

NONINTEREST-BEARING NOTE RECEIVABLE. A note in which no provision is included for the payment of interest; only the payment of principal is required. (9)

NOTES PAYABLE. Obligations of an entity consisting of signed documents which promise to pay specific amounts of money plus interest on specific future dates. (3)

NOTES RECEIVABLE. Signed documents given to an entity by a customer promising to pay a specific amount of money plus interest on a specific future date. (3)

NSF CHECK. A check that has been written on a bank account in which there are insufficient funds deposited to cover the amount of the check; commonly called a "bad check." (5)

OBJECTIVITY. The accounting principle which requires that financial information be factual, verifiable, and unbiased. (1)

OPERATING ACTIVITIES. Transactions that relate to the calculation of net income. These items are usually related to the production and sale of goods and services. (13)

OPERATING CYCLE. The period of time it takes for a firm to buy merchandise, sell the merchandise, collect the accounts receivable resulting from the sale of the merchandise, and pay the accounts payable of the firm. (3)

ORGANIZED STOCK EXCHANGES. Established markets for securities where buy and sell orders are matched at public auction. Examples of organized stock exchanges are the New York Stock Exchange and the American Stock Exchange. (11)

OTHER ASSETS. The balance sheet classification used for assets which do not fit under the normal balance sheet classifications of current assets, investments, fixed assets, or intangible assets. (3)

OTHER LIABILITIES. The balance sheet classification used for liabilities which do not fit under the normal balance sheet classifications of current liabilities or long-term liabilities. (3)

OUTSTANDING CHECKS. Checks issued by a company which have not yet been presented to the bank for payment. (5)

OUTSTANDING SHARES. The shares which are currently in the hands of stockholders. (11)

OVER-THE-COUNTER MARKET. All markets for securities except organized stock exchanges. (11)

OWNERS' EQUITY. The resources invested in the business by owners plus profits from successful operations which have been retained in the business. Owners' equity may also be called capital, net worth, or proprietorship. (2)

PAR VALUE. An arbitrary value placed on a share of stock at the time the corporation seeks authorization of the stock. (11)

PARENT COMPANY. A company that owns the majority of the voting stock of another company. (6)

PARTICIPATIVE PREFERRED STOCK. Shares of preferred stock which enable the stockholders to receive not only their stated dividend but also to share in dividend distributions of earnings of the corporation. (11)

PARTNERSHIP. A business with two or more owners who have agreed to operate the business as co-owners. (1)

PERIODIC INVENTORY SYSTEM. A system of accounting for inventory which requires the use of a physical count of inventory at the end of the accounting period in order to determine ending inventory and to calculate cost of goods sold. (7)

PERIODICITY. The concept in accounting which requires that the life of a business be broken down into specific time periods for periodic reporting purposes. The normal accounting period is one year. (1)

PERMANENT ACCOUNTS. Asset, liability, and owners' equity accounts (balance sheet accounts). These may also be called real accounts. (2)

PERPETUAL INVENTORY SYSTEM. A system of accounting for inventory which maintains a continuous record of all inventory transactions. (7)

PETTY CASH FUND. A fund established to pay for small expenditures which would be inconvenient to pay by check. (5)

POSTING. The process of transferring the information contained in the journal to the ledger accounts. (2)

PREDETERMINED OVERHEAD RATE. The rate which is determined in advance and used to allocate manufacturing overhead costs to the jobs in work-in-process inventory and to the jobs completed during the period. The predetermined overhead rate is calculated by dividing estimated total manufacturing overhead costs by estimated total units in the application base. (14)

PREFERRED STOCK. A form of capital stock of a corporation which entitles its owners to certain preferences, such as receipt of a guaranteed amount of annual dividends before common shareholders may receive dividends. (3)

PREPAID EXPENSES. Expenses that consist of the cost of goods or services bought for use in the business which are not used up at the end of the accounting period. (3)

PRICE INDEX. A measure of the changes in prices of a particular group of goods and services. (8)

PRIVATE PLACEMENT. The sale of an entire issue of securities by the issuing corporation directly to one or a few large institutional investors. (11)

PROCESS COSTING. The method of product costing most often used by firms which produce a homogeneous product using a continuous manufacturing process. (14)

PROFORMA FINANCIAL STATEMENT. A forecasted (or budgeted) financial statement. (14)

PROPERTY INSURANCE. Insurance protection of the property (assets) of the company from damage or destruction by fire, smoke, or vandalism. (9)

PURCHASES JOURNAL. A special journal used by record purchases of inventory on account. The purchases journal may also include purchases of supplies on credit. (5)

RATIO. The relationship of one amount to another. (13)

REGISTERED BOND. A bond that has the holder's name registered with the issuing company. (10)

RELEVANT RANGE. The range over which assumptions made about the nature of cost behavior (that is, fixed or variable) are valid. (14)

RETAINED EARNINGS. The portion of the stockholders' equity consisting of earnings of the corporation which have been retained in the corporation rather than paid out as dividends. (2)

REVENUE. Earnings resulting from the receipt of cash or other assets in exchange for goods sold by the entity or services performed by the entity. (2)

REVENUE REALIZATION. The principle which states that revenue is usually recognized only after an exchange has taken place or a service has been performed. (2)

SALES JOURNAL. A special journal used to record sales of merchandise on account. (5)

SALVAGE VALUE. The residual value an asset is expected to have when its useful life is over. (8)

SERIAL BONDS. Bonds issued at the same time but coming due at various maturity dates. Issuing serial bonds alleviates some of the cash flow drain which occurs when bonds mature. (10)

SHORT-TERM CAPITAL GAIN OR LOSS. A gain or loss resulting from the sale of a capital asset held for one year or less. (12)

SIMPLE INTEREST. Interest which is computed only on the principal of the loan for a single period of time. (10)

SOURCE DOCUMENT. The document which is normally prepared when an accounting transaction occurs. Source documents serve as the source of information for making journal entries. (2)

SOURCE OF WORKING CAPITAL. Any transaction which results in an increase in working capital. (13)

SPECIAL JOURNAL. A journal used to record routine transactions which occur frequently. The use of special journals simplifies the posting procedure. (5)

STANDARD COST. The cost which should be incurred when producing a product or performing an operation efficiently. (14)

STATEMENT OF CASH FLOWS. The financial statement that shows the operating, investing, and financing cash flows of a company. (3)

STATEMENT OF CHANGES IN CAPITAL. The financial statement that explains the changes in the capital (owners' equity account for the period. (3)

STATEMENT OF RETAINED EARNINGS. The financial statement that shows the changes in retained earnings from one period to the next. (3)

STOCK DIVIDEND. A dividend distributed in the form of additional shares of stock. (6)

STOCKHOLDERS' EQUITY. The term used for the owners' equity of a corporation. (2)

STRAIGHT-LINE DEPRECIATION. A depreciation method which assigns an equal amount of depreciation expense to each period of the asset's useful life. (8)

SUBSIDIARY ACCOUNT. A detailed account which provides supporting information about an individual balance. (5)

SUBSIDIARY COMPANY. A company that is controlled by a parent company. (6)

SUM-OF-THE-YEARS' DIGITS DEPRECIATION (SYD). An accelerated depreciation method which uses a decreasing fraction as the depreciation rate which is used to allocate the cost less salvage value of an asset over its useful life. (8)

SURETY BOND. A contract under which one party agrees to make good the debt or default of another party. (9)

T-ACCOUNT. A representation of an account which is used for instructional or problem-solving purposes. (2)

TEMPORARY ACCOUNTS. Revenue, expense, and drawing accounts; temporary accounts are reduced to zero at the end of the accounting period through the closing process. (2)

TEMPORARY INVESTMENTS. Investments in marketable securities which are expected to be held for a short period of time; may also be referred to as marketable securities. (3)

TERM BONDS. Bonds which have a single fixed maturity date. (10)

TERM NOTES PAYABLE. A note payable repaid in one lump sum on a specific maturity date. (10)

TRADE DISCOUNT. A reduction from the list price of goods which is offered by manufacturers or wholesalers to their dealers; a method of determining the sales price. (5)

TREASURY STOCK. The shares of a corporation's own capital stock reacquired by the corporation. (11)

TRIAL BALANCE. A listing of all the account balances in the general ledger which is used to verify that the total dollar amount of debits is equal to the total dollar amount of credits. (4)

UNAPPROPRIATED RETAINED EARNINGS. The portion of the retained earnings of a corporation which have not been appropriated for a specific purpose. (11)

UNITS-OF-PRODUCTION METHOD. A depreciation method which computes depreciation expense based on the total estimated productive output of the asset. (8)

UNLIMITED LIABILITY. The liability of sole proprietors and partners for business debts not only from business assets but also from personal assets. (11)

USE OF WORKING CAPITAL. Any transaction which results in a decrease in working capital. (13)

VARIABLE COST. A cost which varies in total in direct proportion to changes in the level of activity. (14)

VARIANCE. The difference between the amount budgeted for an item and the amount which actually results for that item at the end of the period. (14)

VOUCHER. A business paper used in summarizing a transaction and approving it for recording and payment. (5)

VOUCHER SYSTEM. A system of internal control over cash disbursements which requires that a voucher be prepared and verified before any payments may be made. (5)

WEIGHTED-AVERAGE METHOD. The method that uses a weighted-average unit cost to value ending inventory and cost of goods sold. (7)

WORKING CAPITAL. Current assets minus current liabilities. (13)

WORKSHEET. An accounting tool used to make the end-of-period accounting procedures easier. (4)